Joyce and Lacan

> Daniel Bristow's book is a fresh and most inspiring engagement with Jacques Lacan's late theory, particularly with his reading of Joyce, and of several concepts resulting from this reading. Bristow takes us through this famously difficult material with great lucidity and erudition, as well as – perhaps most importantly – a very clear idea of where he wants to lead us, conceptually, as well as politically.
>
> – Alenka Zupančič

What happens when the intellectual giant of twentieth-century literature, James Joyce, is made an object of consideration and cause of desire by the intellectual giant of modern psychoanalysis, Jacques Lacan?

This is what *Joyce and Lacan* explores, in the three closely interrelated areas of reading, writing, and psychoanalysis, by delving into Joyce's own relationship with psychoanalysis in his lifetime. The book concentrates primarily on his last text, *Finnegans Wake*, the notorious difficulty of which arises from its challenging the intellect itself, and our own processes of reading. As well as the centrality of the Wake, concepts of Joycean ontology, sanity, singularity, and sexuality are excavated from sustained analysis of his earliest writings onward.

To be 'post-Joycean', as Lacan describes it, means then to be in the wake not only of Joyce, but also of Lacan's interventions on the Irish writer made in the mid-70s. It was this encounter that gave rise to concepts that have gained currency in today's psychoanalytic theory and practice, and importance in wider critical contexts. The notions of the *sinthome, lalangue*, and Lacan's use of topology and knot theory are explored within, as well as new theories being launched.

The book will be of interest to psychoanalysts, literary theorists, and students and teachers of literature, theory, or the works of Joyce and Lacan.

Daniel Bristow received his doctorate from the University of Manchester in 2014. His writing is widely published and covers a range of topics in literature, theory, and psychoanalysis, and he is co-founder of the Everyday Analysis Collective.

Joyce and Lacan

Reading, writing, and psychoanalysis

Daniel Bristow

Routledge
Taylor & Francis Group
LONDON AND NEW YORK

First published 2017 by Routledge

2 Park Square, Milton Park, Abingdon, Oxfordshire OX14 4RN
711 Third Avenue, New York, NY 10017

Routledge is an imprint of the Taylor & Francis Group, an informa business

First issued in paperback 2018

British Library Cataloguing in Publication Data
A catalogue record for this book is available from the British Library

Library of Congress Cataloging-in-Publication Data
A catalog record for this book has been requested

ISBN: 978-1-138-93806-9 (hbk)
ISBN: 978-1-138-58722-9 (pbk)

Typeset in Times New Roman
by Apex CoVantage, LLC

Contents

Figures

Key: < indicates that which position A in the unificatory/separatory principle splits its contents into.

Acknowledgements

This book is for Fiona, without whom it would not have come to be. It is dedicated to Jeremy Tambling, Ian Parker, and Liam Harte, for coaxing it into shape during its becoming. My thanks are owed, too, to so many: my father and stepmother, Ian and Zoë Bristow, and mother and stepfather, Nicola and Rob Pithouse; Tim Fernandez, for friendship and producing figure 13; Sally Nall, for redoing the knot diagrams; Alfie Bown, Isabel Palmer, Tristan Burke, James Smith, David Alderson, Daniela Caselli, Véronique Voruz, Frances Balmer, Ellen McWilliams, Fiona Peters, Richard Stamp, Ashley Beaven, Mike and Cina Minney, Alex Bristow, Kunal Modi, Lindsey Miller, Gwion Jones, and Brendan Duddy, who all contributed in so many ways; Adrian Price, for the invaluable correspondence concerning Seminar XXIII; Cormac Gallagher, Richard Klein in New York, and the staff at Karnac Books; and Fritz Senn and Sam Slote, for correspondence concerning Joyce, and to the latter for making the *Finnegans Wake* fonts available to me. Last to Kate Hawes at Routledge, and Kirsten Buchanan, Aiyana Curtis, Susan Wickenden, and Chris Mathews, whose editorial assistance has been above and beyond anything I could have expected.

Prefatory Remark

The aim of this work is to investigate some of the concepts in the late thinking and psychoanalytic theory of Jacques Lacan in relation to James Joyce. Concepts covered include firstly the '*envers*' – or the 'other side' in English – which is dealt with at length within chapters 1 and 2, and which leads to the construction of a theory of '*enverity*', the aim of which is to demonstrate other sides' combinatory roles in processes of truth, and how a two-sided structure inevitably involves a third element which unites and separates the two sides. Secondly, the *sinthome* – Lacan's successor concept to the symptom, which takes up a more fundamental and irreducible position in the subject's psychic and somatic makeup – is referred to consistently throughout in chapter 3, as are the types of knot in which this concept finds its place, in chapter 4. Thirdly, a theory of writing, as a 'discourse without speech', is introduced in relation to Joyce's *Finnegans Wake* and Lacan's concept of *lalangue*, in chapter 5. Finally, a theory of reading and writing, in relation to the interplay between meaning and *jouissance* in the Lacanian theory of sublimation, makes up chapter 6, the final chapter of this work, which aims to stress the centrality of the Lacanian notion of *dignity* in processes and events of creation (or in 'living, laughing, loving and leaving', as it is in Joyce's quadrivium).

The conjunction 'with' tends to be used most commonly in Lacanian parlance when putting two names critically together, but it is 'and' that has been selected for the title of this work, as between Joyce and Lacan – between Joyce and psychoanalysis – there is a friction such as seems to demand this particular unificatory/separatory connective. Chapter 1 of this work begins by establishing the tripartite structure of the *envers*, and by bringing it into relation to the functioning of Lacanian discourse – so as to give something of a grounding in the ever-shifting mode of articulation of the key theorist here under discussion – before going on to situate Joyce in relation to psychoanalysis, in his own day, during which his ambivalence towards the practice was made clear to all, and up to the present, in which he finds himself occupying a vital position, subsequent to Lacan's interventions on the author in the mid-1970s. It then moves into a discussion of the role of the father, and Names-of-the-Father, in relation to Joyce's notion of the artificer in *A Portrait of the Artist as a Young Man*, in its links to the *sinthome* (the concept for which of the *empty signified* is introduced here, to be taken up in more detail in the chapter 3) and the language of the *envers*. The first three chapters, especially, form something of a conceptual and theoretical framework, and may make as much reference to biographical detail as to Joyce's texts; despite the necessity of a certain distance and detachment with regard to any literary biography – in terms of its scholarly reliability – Richard Ellmann's of Joyce is so central to Joyce Studies that not to be 'duped', to whatever extent, by its fiction might in fact constitute something of an error. Close readings and literary analyses of Joyce's writings themselves are commenced more thoroughly in the latter part of the work.

NB: Throughout, in my own reference and in most quotations from primary and secondary sources (except in titles of essays), I have elected to retain the words '*envers*', '*objet petit a*', '*sinthome*', '*jouissance*', and '*lalangue*' in italics, for the purpose of consistency and uniformity, but also so as to ensure that these words' resonances are seen primarily to derive from the original French, even as they spread over into English. It is due to this consideration of and concentration on resonance, which is of course not unique to this work, that the rendering as 'object *a*' and the deitalicisations of '*sinthome*' and '*jouissance*' (a word which in fact originates from English) – that are becoming the standard in Lacanian reference – are not adopted here. Subsequent to this note, I will therefore not indicate where I have modified a quotation or translation in this manner.

for which of the *empty signified* is introduced here, to be taken up in more detail in the chapter 3) and the language of the *envers*. The first three chapters, especially, form something of a conceptual and theoretical framework, and may make as much reference to biographical detail as to Joyce's texts; despite the necessity of a certain distance and detachment with regard to any literary biography – in terms of its scholarly reliability – Richard Ellmann's of Joyce is so central to Joyce Studies that not to be 'duped', to whatever extent, by its fiction might in fact constitute something of an error. Close readings and literary analyses of Joyce's writings themselves are commenced more thoroughly in the latter part of the work.

NB: Throughout, in my own reference and in most quotations from primary and secondary sources (except in titles of essays), I have elected to retain the words '*envers*', '*objet petit a*', '*sinthome*', '*jouissance*', and '*lalangue*' in italics, for the purpose of consistency and uniformity, but also so as to ensure that these words' resonances are seen primarily to derive from the original French, even as they spread over into English. It is due to this consideration of and concentration on resonance, which is of course not unique to this work, that the rendering as 'object *a*' and the deitalicisations of '*sinthome*' and '*jouissance*' (a word which in fact originates from English) – that are becoming the standard in Lacanian reference – are not adopted here. Subsequent to this note, I will therefore not indicate where I have modified a quotation or translation in this manner.

Prefatory Remark

The aim of this work is to investigate some of the concepts in the late thinking and psychoanalytic theory of Jacques Lacan in relation to James Joyce. Concepts covered include firstly the '*envers*' – or the 'other side' in English – which is dealt with at length within chapters 1 and 2, and which leads to the construction of a theory of '*enverity*', the aim of which is to demonstrate other sides' combinatory roles in processes of truth, and how a two-sided structure inevitably involves a third element which unites and separates the two sides. Secondly, the *sinthome* – Lacan's successor concept to the symptom, which takes up a more fundamental and irreducible position in the subject's psychic and somatic makeup – is referred to consistently throughout in chapter 3, as are the types of knot in which this concept finds its place, in chapter 4. Thirdly, a theory of writing, as a 'discourse without speech', is introduced in relation to Joyce's *Finnegans Wake* and Lacan's concept of *lalangue,* in chapter 5. Finally, a theory of reading and writing, in relation to the interplay between meaning and *jouissance* in the Lacanian theory of sublimation, makes up chapter 6, the final chapter of this work, which aims to stress the centrality of the Lacanian notion of *dignity* in processes and events of creation (or in 'living, laughing, loving and leaving', as it is in Joyce's quadrivium).

The conjunction 'with' tends to be used most commonly in Lacanian parlance when putting two names critically together, but it is 'and' that has been selected for the title of this work, as between Joyce and Lacan – between Joyce and psychoanalysis – there is a friction such as seems to demand this particular unificatory/separatory connective. Chapter 1 of this work begins by establishing the tripartite structure of the *envers*, and by bringing it into relation to the functioning of Lacanian discourse – so as to give something of a grounding in the ever-shifting mode of articulation of the key theorist here under discussion – before going on to situate Joyce in relation to psychoanalysis, in his own day, during which his ambivalence towards the practice was made clear to all, and up to the present, in which he finds himself occupying a vital position, subsequent to Lacan's interventions on the author in the mid-1970s. It then moves into a discussion of the role of the father, and Names-of-the-Father, in relation to Joyce's notion of the artificer in *A Portrait of the Artist as a Young Man*, in its links to the *sinthome* (the concept

Chapter 1

James Joyce, in and out of analysis

Audi partem alteram.

– Saint Augustine

Le monde est à l'envers.

– William Shakespeare

EN vers / droit

This formulation from Maurice Roche's *Codex* will operate throughout this work as a guiding thread.[1]

On all sides, sheeting[2]

On 20 June 1975 – the last day of the fifth International James Joyce Symposium – Jacques Lacan delivered his second lecture on the topic 'Joyce the Symptom' to the audience congregated at the Sorbonne in Paris. His first speech had inaugurated the event on Bloomsday four days before, but it is in his second that he comes to a definition of what it means to be 'post-Joycean'.[3] In effect it means realising what *the other side* – or, in French, *l'envers* – of the *symptom* is.

In 1995 Roberto Harari published his seminal work, *How James Joyce Made His Name*; it centred on the Seminar that Lacan dedicated to Joyce under the title *Le sinthome*, delivered in the academic year following the Symposium, 1975–1976. At its end he concludes that the 'pathway' that that Seminar opens up 'allows us to give psychoanalysis a new name: to call it, now that Lacan has swept the way clear, a *post–Joycean* psychoanalysis'.[4] This chapter will thus explore what it may mean to be 'post-Joycean', and this in the three integrated areas of reading, writing, and psychoanalysis, and it will concentrate on what the other side of the symptom – the '*sinthome*', as Lacan latterly designated it – is.

Thus, to begin with psychoanalysis: its most important discovery – that of the unconscious – was made by Sigmund Freud at the tail end of the nineteenth century. To refamiliarise ourselves with its concept we will look to the very first paragraphs of Freud's introduction to his 1915 monograph on the subject, 'The Unconscious':

> We have learnt from psycho-analysis that the essence of the process of repression lies, not in putting an end to, in annihilating, the idea which represents an instinct, but in preventing it from becoming conscious. When this happens we say of the idea that it is in a state of being 'unconscious', and we can produce good evidence to show that even when it is unconscious it can produce effects, even including some which finally reach consciousness. Everything that is repressed must remain unconscious; but let us state at the very outset that the repressed does not cover everything that is unconscious. The unconscious has the wider compass: the repressed is a part of the unconscious.
>
> How are we to arrive at a knowledge of the unconscious? It is of course only as something conscious that we know it, after it has undergone transformation or translation into something conscious. Psycho-analytic work shows us every day that translation of this kind is possible. In order that this should come about, the person under analysis must overcome certain resistances – the same resistances as those which, earlier, made the material concerned into something repressed by rejecting it from the conscious.[5]

Freud, in his paper on repression, also of 1915, had discussed how repression's functioning is primarily detectable in the '*return of the repressed*'. The 'translation' back into the conscious from the unconscious that Freud talks of earlier is then not only the first indicator of repression, but of the unconscious also, of which repression is a constituent part. Something of the 'recirculation' that commences Joyce's last major work, *Finnegans Wake*, is therefore locatable here; it is almost as if Freud's 'Unconscious' should begin with the non-capitalised 'r' of the *Wake*'s first sentence; though with the 'r' of 'repression' rather than of 'riverrun'. Indeed, we are here returned to repression and the unconscious – as we are in Joyce to 'Howth Castle and Environs' – without actually having left off from them.[6]

This theme of the *return of the repressed* is later concentrated on and developed by Lacan: 'Repression', he states, 'cannot be distinguished from the return of the repressed in which the subject cries out from every pore of his being what he cannot talk about.'[7] It is thus that the unconscious forces the articulation of its repressed content through symptomal *returns*, such as in slips of the tongue, dreams, tics, bungled actions, and other such parapraxes. It is in these very articulations that we find proof that 'the unconscious itself obeys its own grammar and logic: the unconscious talks and thinks', as Slavoj Žižek puts it, apropos of Lacan.[8]

As we know, Lacan himself famously stated that '*the unconscious is structured like a language*', and in the *Écrits* – in 'The Instance of the Letter in the Unconscious' – he describes the processes of its interpretation in psychoanalysis as akin to the reading of hieroglyphics, citing the French Egyptologist Jean-François Champollion as the discoverer that Freud should be most likened to, over Christopher Columbus, for example.[9] These reflections find further elaboration in a contemporaneous interview, conducted by Madeleine Chapsal for *L'Express* in May 1957, in which Lacan suggests more explicitly the similarity between the interpretation of the unconscious and the reading, or deciphering, of hieroglyphics. 'A psychoanalyst is not an explorer of an unknown continent, or of great depths', he states; 'he is a linguist. He learns to decipher the writing which is under his eyes, present to the sight of all; however, that writing remains indecipherable if we lack its laws, its key.'[10] Thus the structuralism of psychoanalysis: in its practice, interpretation bears resemblance to the deciphering (the reading) of 'Egyptian hieroglyphics' (a form of writing), based on their overall structure:

> As long as we look for the direct meaning of vultures, chickens, the standing, sitting, or moving men, the writing remains indecipherable. When taken by itself, the sign "vulture" means nothing; it only finds its signifying value when taken within the context of the set of the system to which it belongs. Well, analysis deals with this order of phenomena. They belong to the order of language.[11]

Lacan again evokes this metaphor in 1964, in his eleventh Seminar, *The Four Fundamental Concepts of Psychoanalysis*, the structure of which was designed to be introductory to the new audience he was addressing after relocating the Seminar, and the instance of which will become important to this chapter. Although Lacan's methodology in the previously cited passage clearly combines classical psychoanalytic technique with the methods of linguistics – those of Ferdinand de Saussure, for example – it is still precisely Freudian, and this can be seen in its contradistinction to the technique of Carl Gustav Jung. Jung's method, in this regard, relies on the exact opposite of the linguistic model, matching symptomal phenomena not against the system or order of its language – not against the subject's personal history or backstory, for example – but proposing a catalogue of 'archetypes' into which the unconscious articulation must fit; i.e., proposing that the sign 'vulture' has a constant direct meaning in itself, even when isolated from other signs around it.

However, it is in this Freudo-Lacanian systematicity which is like a language, and by which the unconscious operates, that we are beginning to perceive the relation of the unconscious – and thus of psychoanalysis – to the processes of both writing and reading. In Jacques Derrida's *Resistances of Psychoanalysis* he discusses a footnote of Freud's, in *The Interpretation of Dreams*, which 'calls upon the reader as a witness in the way one might address oneself to a confessor or to some transferential addressee, some would say to an analyst, assuming that a reader is not always an analyst'.[12] For us, this passage at once succinctly delineates how the processes through which a reader interacts with a text are similar to those through which an analyst commences interpretation, and demonstrates the relation that exists between the unconscious, and writing (Freud's footnote in this case) and reading. Derrida's actual referent here, however, is the '*navel*', that part of a dream – its structuring principle – that can never be unravelled, psychoanalytically. Derrida frames the navel as always already in *excess* of interpretation, but *not* as a *resistance* to it, and thus this excess can – and has to – extend to the unconscious itself (as an element of the Real, and in its real element). The unconscious's structurality has to evade interpretation so as to maintain its very structure as unconscious; i.e., that which structures the unconscious must not, and cannot, come to consciousness. The extraction of the navel, of the unconscious's *excess*, must thus always remain a structural impossibility: in Lacan's terms, this impossibility is, then, the Real of the unconscious. (The order of the Real for Lacan designates the *impossible* or *unsymbolisable*; one way to think of the Real, in relation to the Symbolic – discounting for a moment Lacan's third order, the Imaginary – is to see it in terms of trauma: trauma is an encounter with the Real, the first symbolic impressions of which we repress; the Real is thus of necessity always foreclosed to, and from, us.)

To begin to explain the earlier summations concerning reading, writing, and the unconscious, we will introduce certain modes in which their tripartite system can be, and has been, represented. First, we will do so with recourse to a *two-sided* structure – encompassing the idea of '*l'envers*' – which we will come to term the *unificatory/separatory principle.*

To give a further inflection to the notion of '*l'envers*' – and the uses to which we will put it – we will here turn to the chapter entitled 'Front and Back' in Pierre Macherey's *A Theory of Literary Production*, in which the words '*endroit*' and '*envers*' are translated variously as 'front', 'outside', and 'back', 'inside', etc. He forewarns us here that 'the 'front' (*endroit*) and the 'back' (*envers*) can legitimately be regarded as no more than suggestive metaphors. As 'ideas' they are contaminated by the normative fallacy from which they have been only artificially separated.'[13] This 'normative fallacy' which Macherey identifies involves the first position ('A' in Figure 1.1) of the unificatory/separatory principle, which will be explored in further detail within this chapter and especially in the coming chapters; however, we will argue that this position in the principle is not in all cases normalising, and thus nor always fallacious, but is sometimes the only adequate model for demonstrating the structurality of a concept.

(The formulation from Roche referred to earlier, if turned 90° clockwise, can now be seen to show 'EN' in position A, 'droit' in position 1, and 'vers' in position

Position A

/ \

Position 1 Position 2

Figure 1.1[14] Unificatory/separatory principle (A: *Position A* < 1: *Position 1*, 2: *Position 2*)

2.) Later, Macherey identifies his own 'principle of coherence', which unites the front and back – or outside and inside – in a work, and from which principle such concepts as these binary oppositions are 'provisionally distinguished'. This principle – which Macherey is drawing out here – we will argue is not of necessity always one of 'coherence', but it is one which always does *both unite* and *separate* any two 'versions', 'aspects', or *constituents* of certain structures; a theory which is beginning to be uncovered in the following cited passage:

> However you trace the inside (*envers*) and the outside (*endroit*), the work remains unchanged; having been constructed it is stable and continuous. Whether it be actively elaborated or passively followed it offers the same kind of unity, which can be indifferently considered in alternative ways ('in front' and 'behind', to vary our spatial metaphor). Casual appearance or rigorous deduction: these are two versions or aspects of the same reality. The ending unifies them both, and to perceive this unity we relate the work to its necessary conditions. Inside and outside have been only provisionally distinguished in order to demonstrate the principle of coherence in the discourse.[15]

Thus, to locate a first instance of this unificatory/separatory principle – which Macherey begins to uncover, but not elaborate on – and to relate it to this study's set of topics – reading, writing, and psychoanalysis – a first clue will be found in a key passage from Saussure's *Course in General Linguistics*, in which the linguist delineates how we might compare a language

> to a sheet of paper. Thought is one side of the sheet and sound the reverse side. Just as it is impossible to take a pair of scissors and cut one side without at the same time cutting the other, so it is impossible in a language to isolate sound from thought, or thought from sound. To separate the two takes us into either pure psychology or pure phonetics, not linguistics.[16]

Language for Saussure is represented by a piece of paper (position A) on one side of which is thought (position 1), and on the other sound (position 2); and by extension here we can perceive linguistics also as a sheet sided by psychology and phonetics. This draws our attention again to *l'envers*; the 'other side', or the 'reverse', but also – importantly – to another necessary element in this topology: the sheet. Here unnamed specifically by Saussure, it is that which at the same time *separates* and *unites* these two sides: this founds our principle of *enverity*, or the *unificatory/separatory principle*.

In many ways, Saussure's analogy provides a formulation for the unconscious, as it can, too, for structuralism itself: the sheet, Saussure's piece of paper, is, then, the structuring principle *without which* we would have neither of its sides, but only *through which* we can have either of them; and yet it is not ontologisable in itself (i.e., without its content it cannot be thought, and with it it cannot be extricated; that is, it cannot be thought *alone*). In other words, that which *unites* psychology and phonetics in linguistics – and sound and thought in language – is at the same time that which *separates* them from each other; and this sheet that both unites *and* separates can only be thought *abstractly* if without the properties of its sides, i.e., it can only be thought purely as *form*, without *content*. It is therefore this very unificatory/separatory principle which such structuralisms as Saussure's linguistics set out to study, and yet at the same time this principle is taken as their point of departure. As Saussure puts it at the outset of the *Course*: '*The linguist must take the study of linguistic structure as his primary concern*'; setting out from linguistic structure (as a *linguist*) to study linguistic structure (the science of *linguistics*) (this is the 'forward' and 'reverse' implied in Macherey's principle, a pair of contraries that occur at one and the same time).[17]

The unificatory/separatory principle appears remarkably regularly in many thinkers' works – associated with the structuralist movement, and movements spawned by it, and even prior to it – if not ubiquitously; indeed, as Sheldon R. Brivic puts it in his *Joyce Between Freud and Jung*:

> The idea of union through separation is psychologically and culturally profound. It is stressed in some of Joyce's favorite writers: Ibsen's *Enemy of the People* concludes "the strongest man in the world is he who stands most alone," and Blake says "Opposition is true friendship." And it was and [*sic*] old idea when it serves as basis for the *Odyssey*. Reconciliation through sundering or death and rebirth is perhaps the most basic mythic pattern, as the Jungian Joseph Campbell demonstrates in *The Hero with a Thousand Faces* (Princeton: Bollingen, 1949), and it underlies the fall and redemption of Christian eschatology.[18]

In this context, the principle will be made use of to delineate certain ways in which important pairs of concepts become thinkable to structuralism. However, just as thought and sound are of course not the only constituent parts of a language – as, among others, Derrida has amply proven in his *Of Grammatology* – nor, of course, are we suggesting that reading and writing are *the only two* parts of the unconscious.[19] As Freud insists, the unconscious always 'has the wider compass'. It should be noted, too, that nor are we willingly regressing to a reliance on simple binary oppositions – via the use of this uniting/dividing principle – but rather, with it, we will seek to demarcate certain possible co-dependent originations, hypostases, and inextricabilities that go to make up such structures as the unconscious, in the first instance, and others that will become important as we go along.

Indeed, contrary to such binarism, we aim to investigate through this *pairing* also the *remainder* that gets produced by it; i.e., the very sheet which is necessarily present in Saussure's analogy, though it goes unnamed. Thus, to propose a notion of the unconscious along these lines – which move away from the idea of 'pure' form – we can claim that the unconscious is a sheet sided, for example, by writing and by reading, and that it is its sides' *indivisible remainder*.

As François Regnault precisely puts it, apropos the subject: 'All you need are two signifiers side by side in order to produce the effect of the subject: it is in the interstice of the two, but also disappears there, such that they miss or lack it.'[20] As is well known, in Lacanian theory a 'signifier is what represents a subject to another signifier'.[21] In Seminar XI, 'in order to illustrate this axiom', Lacan returns to the hieroglyphics analogy:

> Suppose that in the desert you find a stone covered with hieroglyphics. You do not doubt for a moment that, behind them, there was a subject who wrote them. But it is an error to believe that each signifier is addressed to you – this is proved by the fact that you cannot understand any of it. On the other hand you define them as signifiers, by the fact that you are sure that each of these signifiers is related to each of the others.[22]

As Regnault puts it, it is in the interstice between signifiers that 'the effect of the subject' is produced; the hieroglyphics on the stone, in Lacan's analogy, of course can only relate one to another via the middle-term of the subject, but *they are addressed one to another*. Co-dependently the subject can only commence decipherment, or interpretation, in its very interstice; the interstice of representation between signifiers. And thus – through a slight modification that does not transgress this formula's reciprocality – we can even suggest that the subject becomes a *representative*, in something of the ambassadorial sense, for these signifiers.

However, Lacan is, too, precisely indicating here that our very status as *subject* – our very *subjectivity* – is the result of *signification*: of one signifier representing us to another. With recourse to the three Lacanian orders, Lacan's formula can be explicated thus: 'We', as *subjects*, are the *remainder* in the Real of our *unity* in the Symbolic and *disunity* in the Imaginary; in other words, the *subject*, the *unconscious*, is the (real) *effect* of a signifier's (symbolic) representation to another signifier, and that this effect (the *Real* itself) is overlooked is *effected* by the imaginary, the order which registers disconnection, such as from the subject's reflection in the mirror, but connects to said mirror-image through this very registration. The emerging complexity of this Lacanian formula resides in its *play of effectivity*, and from it the question naturally arises: which order is the effect of which other two (at any one time)? But it is to work with and within this complexity, rather than to postulate it as a deadlock to resolve, that this work will aspire in the creation of its post-Joycean psychoanalytic methodology.

Thus we have so far tracked quite quickly from the concept of an inextricable *two* (the two sides of a sheet) to a Lacanian *three*, which recognises the *third* (the sheet itself) as an effect of the *two* in its own (*real*) right, but also as an effect which then gets involved in oscillatory *effective play*; i.e., the sheet is no longer strictly only the unificatory/separatory principle, but all three elements, or orders, in the tripartite system, could come to assume this position, ambassadorially. Later, we will go even further, in dealing with a *fourth* term – the *sinthome* – which might turn out to be employable in combatting this oscillatory play in its utilisability as knot or suture.[23]

Indeed, in Seminar VII, *The Ethics of Psychoanalysis*, Lacan suggests:

> There cannot be a two without a three, and that, I think must certainly include a four, the quadripartite[.] The whole psychology of the psychotic develops insofar as a term may be refused, a term that maintains the basic system of words at a certain distance or relational dimension. Something is missing and his real effort at substitution and "significization" is directed in desperation at that.[24]

In relation to Joyce and psychosis these notions will be explored at further length in chapter 2, and with this awareness of how the *two* necessarily implies the *three*, and of the coming (Joycean) *fourth* term, the '*sinthome*' (Lacan's first name for which was 'Joyce the Symptom'), we will now return to the initial concept, of the *two*, in its relation to *the other side*, and to the unificatory/separatory principle – or principle of '*enverity*' – in the remainder of this chapter, to return in the next to a rigorous formulisation of the triplicity involved in its structure.

Hear the other side, see the other side

'*Audi partem alteram*'. 'Hear the other part' Saint Augustine advises in *De Duabus Animabus*, a work that purports to refute the theological thesis, put forward by the Manichæans, that there are two distinct and separate types of human soul (those of Supreme Good and Evil).[25] In a late episode of *Twin Peaks*, this maxim is remembered and extended – in a conversation between FBI Special Agent Dale Cooper and Annie Blackburn – as: 'Hear the other side, see the other side'.[26] This, therefore, will to an extent be the aim of the remainder of this chapter: to hear, to see, *the other side. The other side*, that is, of psychoanalysis – specifically the psychoanalytic theory of Jacques Lacan – and of James Joyce; as well as of writing, and of reading.

This phrase itself, 'the other side', is employed by Russell Grigg to translate Lacan's use of the French word '*l'envers*' in the title of his seventeenth yearly Seminar, *L'envers de la Psychanalyse* (*The Other Side of Psychoanalysis*).[27] However, a decidedly different flavour is offered to the word by Jules Derocquigny's translation into French of the line 'the time is out of joint' from William Shakespeare's *Hamlet*; the phrase which forms this chapter's second epigraph: '*Le monde est à l'envers*'.[28] It is Jacques Derrida who takes special note of the translation in *Specters of Marx* – placing it amidst a score of other renderings in French – the English phrase forming the mantra on which the work's theses on temporality and (un)timeliness are based. At this point in the text a transliteration back into English – 'the world is upside down' – is offered, and Derrida comments that this '"*à l'envers*" is very close to a "*de travers*," *askew*, that seems to be closer to [Shakespeare's] original', and which also hints at *parallax*; a key concept for Žižek, and one which will, of necessity, become important throughout this work.[29] Žižek offers 'the standard definition of parallax [a]s: the apparent displacement of an object (the shift of its position against a background), caused by a change in observational position that provides a new line of sight', and then adds the further dialectical philosophical '*twist*' that this is not merely a phenomenon that *only* affects a subjective view of objective reality, but rather that the '"epistemological" shift in the subject's point of view always reflects an "ontological" shift in the object itself'; that is, that 'the subject's gaze is always-already inscribed in the perceived object'.[30] This of course has repercussions when setting out, as we are here, to *observe the obverse*, in that – as Alenka Zupančič puts it – 'the line that goes from a problem to its (more or less distorted) representation is necessarily fractured or 'out of joint,' and this is part *of the problem*, not simply *of its representation*'; that is, there is an inseparability of parts, of sides, that parallax goes to reinforce, in the fact that it itself cannot be separated (from what it views), and becomes *part of the problem* (as *gaze*), which occurs because of what we have called '*enverity*' earlier.[31]

For Derocquigny's '*le monde est à l'envers*' there may be other possible transliterations back into English, such as 'the world is turned on its side' and 'the world is in reverse'. As he states in its introductory session Lacan had also toyed with the idea of calling his Seminar *La Psychanalyse à l'envers* (literally, '*Psychoanalysis Upside Down*'), and he draws on a precursor for this from an introductory article to his *Écrits*, 'On My Antecedents', in which he rephrases his project of a 'return to Freud' as 'a revival of the Freudian project upside down'; '*a revival from the other direction* [*reprise par l'envers*]', which Bruce Fink translates in the English *Écrits* as: 'The reversed reprisal of the Freudian project'.[32] Furthermore, psychoanalysis *in the other direction* perhaps implies psychoanalysis *from psychosis*, as opposed to from neurosis, which is the psychical state Freud started out with. Psychosis – which Freud was unable to properly situate in psychoanalysis – is a phenomenon that Lacan interacted with to a great extent, bringing it in especially in his dealings with Joyce (instances of which will be explored in the coming chapter).

Thus, we have here scanned through several linked meanings for *l'envers* – 'the other side', 'upside down', 'in reverse', 'from the other direction', and, earlier, 'back' and 'inside', from Macherey – and through uncovering such multifarious possibilities and associations wrapped up with it we are beginning to become aware of this word's important and enigmatic status. As Grigg further explains in his translator's note to Seminar XVII, the word 'also carries the meaning of [. . .] "verso," "lining," "underside," "flipside," "underneath," "bad side" – connotations of the unseen, even the obscene, which "the other side" in English only barely suggests'.[33]

Nonetheless, there is strongly implied in the '*envers*', as '*the other side*', a certain disorganisation, and this is as much suggested by its opposite, the '*endroit*', as by anything else. The French '*droit*' translates to 'right' in English and is as suggestive of that which is correct, which is lawful – in the sense of *human rights*, or the gendered '*droits de l'homme*' ('rights of man') in French, for example – and of directionality and political allegiance, as the English equivalent. Furthermore, in the translation of *envers* as *verso*, it is put in implicit contrast to *recto*. Respectively, these are the words for the left- and the right-sided pages in bound books, although this is only the case in books in languages that read from left to right, for the terms are reversed for languages that read contrariwise. On the side of the '*envers*', as Lacan and Grigg have exampled, there thus can be found associations with the *seamy* – relating to the underside of a garment, for example: the seamed side on which its stitches are visible – in contrast to the *seemliness* of the '*endroit*'. Of course this is only an ostensible seemliness – it can only be *supposed* or *imagined* – as it is (literally) underpinned by a hidden-from-view seaminess, just as inherent in any form of organisation must be an irreducible kernel of disorganisation, for the former could not exist without the latter, as *droit* could not exist without *vers*, and (quite literally) vice versa. As Jonathan Pollock says of Joyce's *Finnegans Wake*, in relation to the operation of the *envers*: 'Like the universe of [Giordano] Bruno and Lucretius, it embodies an order, or cosmos, never fully disengaged from an underlying disorder, or chaos'; unable to become disengaged because of the unificatory/separatory principle.[34]

Lacan implies that in psychoanalysis 'to be post-Joycean means knowing [a form of] this'; specifically, that there is '*jouissance* inherent in the symptom, an opaque *jouissance*', he states, 'since it excludes sense'.[35] Classically, *jouissance* – a treacherous form of 'pleasure' (which is the term we find in the English editions of Freud) or 'enjoyment', that encompasses the orgasm (and its '*petit mort*') – is locatable somewhere 'beyond the pleasure principle', and therefore beyond the symptom (although it encompasses 'the paradoxical satisfaction that the subject derives from his symptom', as Dylan Evans puts it), and thus even beyond *sense*, as the symptom always makes the attempt to *render its sense*, or to *render itself sensible*, through some form of articulation; in language – in slips of the tongue or pen, in jokes, and in the language of dreams and their associations – or bodilily – in 'bungled actions', illnesses, and in other psychosomatic manifestations.[36] Alain Grosrichard brings out this dualism further in deliberating on 'a pure sensation, which is to say the other side [*l'envers*] of a simple idea'.[37] Thus, here, two linked but separate sides of sense are perceivable: that of 'sense' as *meaning* ('idea'), which articulates itself through language, and that of the 'sensible' (or 'sensation'), as relating to the *bodily senses*, which articulates itself somatically. In relinking these, through *jouissance* – and through *Joyce* – in his late work, Lacan arrives at a form of '*enjoy-meant*' ('*jouis-sens*': 'enjoy-meaning'), locatable in key psychical faculties of certain kinds of personality (of whom Joyce is Lacan's exemplar), and at an irreducible point in every type of subject; at the point of the *sinthome*.

Thus, in terms of the work and thought of Lacan, the opening chapters of this book will take as its main entrance points the two of his yearlong Seminars that deal the most directly with the other side of psychoanalysis: Seminar XVII, already extensively mentioned, and Seminar XXIII, which focuses especially on Joyce, entitled *Le sinthome*. For Lacan, the very fact that Joyce throughout his life went unanalysed, and managed to remain sane in doing so, becomes a question that receives special consideration throughout this late Seminar. For this reason I incline to group it with XVII – as well as with III, on the psychoses – as one in which Lacan thinks specifically about the other side of psychoanalysis; that is, in terms not merely of alternatives (to the practice), but also of a theorising of the *pre-analytical* condition, of the unconscious in its raw aspect – as constituted by the three Lacanian orders; the Imaginary, the Symbolic, and the Real – and the coping mechanisms that arise, successfully or otherwise, within the subject in relation to it. Again we will here defer to Zupančič for a precise introduction to this formational aspect of the unconscious, in relation to its 'forced choice' of *enjoy-meant*:

> The subject (of the unconscious) is what emerges when, in choosing between being and meaning, he can only choose meaning. This is the necessary other side of the fact that we take what is going on in our interaction with others to constitute an 'enigmatic message.'
>
> This is to say that to understand this difficulty in our interaction with others in terms of an enigmatic message already presupposes the unconscious (and cannot be its cause). The constitution of the unconscious coincides with the *presupposition* of meaning, with the forced choice of meaning (which only makes the interpretation possible), and not simply with the repression of the first representation that eludes this interpretation.[38]

Here we are brought to the realisation of the double-bind of intersubjectivity; of *being* (precisely insofar as its *means*) and *meaning*. Zupančič demonstrates that interaction – in the realm of 'enigmatic messages'; those that circulate in everyday life – is not only facilitated, but *necessitated*, by meaning. The unconscious can be formed only through the '*presupposition*', or by the *forced choice*, of meaning; a process which locates both this *presupposition* and *the unconscious* itself in positions of simultaneity. The choice – of meaning – is '*forced*' insofar as, on a subjective level at least, *to be* is *to mean*. It is by this token that the unconscious, *qua unconscious* – that is, as 'the knowledge that doesn't know itself' – gets created and finds its position in the psyche.[39] In Lacan's words:

> If we choose being, the subject disappears, it eludes us, it falls into non-meaning. If we choose meaning, the meaning survives only deprived of that part of non-meaning that is, strictly speaking, that which constitutes the realization of the subject, the unconscious.[40]

That the unconscious is structured like a language is thus demonstrated by its coming into being through meaning, and to register this being can only be done so subjectively; all of which is to say that as subjects *we cannot have* – or, rather, *we cannot know that we have* – being *sans sense*. In Seminar VII Lacan rearticulates his dictum that the unconscious is structured like a language in precisely these terms, locating the unconscious in the category of the 'unknown': 'It is because that which is known can only be known in words that that which is unknown offers itself as having a linguistic structure.'[41]

It is in this also that the integral distinction between science and subjectivity, and by extension, psychoanalysis, comes to the fore, as the psychoanalytic theorist Jean-Pierre Klotz expands on:

> The subject is what has to be foreclosed, ejected, rejected to establish science, because the results of science have to be established universally, for everyone – they must be valid for every case. If they are scientific they are universal, whereas subjectivity, with its singularity, is a protestation of an individual against universality. And to take an account of the subject of the unconscious at the beginning – the subject which is the stake of psychoanalysis – one has to take an account of the singular, not only of the universal. There is no universal truth of the subject. There is only, for every subject, the possibility of separating the singular and the universal, and of working with one's singularity as discovered by oneself through the analytical experience. That is the main reason it is necessary to do an analysis to become a psychoanalyst – to elect, to choose the singularity in one's subjectivity. It is not a criticism of science, nor does it put aside or go against science, but is *alongside* science. It is *with* science and has a link – what I call a link of separation – with it.[42]

This last notion of Klotz's, the 'link of separation', seems to be that of the 'unificatory/separatory principle', or the principle of *enverity*, which we have begun to lay out earlier, and which we will conceptualise further in chapter 2. These highlighted reciprocal processes involved in the *formation* – or constitution – and positioning of the unconscious are thus *pre-analytical* phenomena, albeit ones only realisable *through* analysis, and therefore topographically situable *on the other side* of psychoanalysis. Yet, whilst it is appropriate to stress this pre-analytical aspect hinted at by the *envers*, it must be kept in mind that there is also in this phrase, 'the other side of psychoanalysis', the integral connotation of going through a psychoanalysis; that is, of a 'coming out' *on the other side of psychoanalysis*.

It is at the beginning of Jacques-Alain Miller's article 'Suture (Elements of the Logic of the Signifier)' that this very question of the other side of psychoanalysis resurfaces. Here he evokes Freud's ruling in the *New Introductory Lectures* that, as Miller puts it, 'no one without those precise conceptions of analysis which only a personal analysis can provide has any right to concern himself (or herself) with it'.[43] In presenting 'Suture' to Lacan's Seminar group before he had himself been analysed he justified his intervention on the grounds – and through the elucidation – of the very concept on which his paper was based, *suture*:

> If not being situated on the inside does not relegate you to the outside, it is because at a certain point, excluded from a two-dimensional topology, the two surfaces join up and the periphery or outer edge crosses over the circumscription.[44]

It is from this point of joining up, of overlapping – a point which at once both brings together and separates the inside and the outside (position A in Figure 1.1) – that Miller launches his discourse, that he makes his pronouncements.

For Miller, at this time, analysis was defined as 'the theory that deals with concepts of element and combination [*combinatoire*] as such'.[45] In Lacan's schema of the 'four discourses' – set out in Seminar XVII – he would come to situate Miller's as that of the University, as opposed to those of the Master, the Hysteric, and the Analyst. Indeed, it is throughout this Seminar that Lacan takes Miller – and other founders and contributors to the short-lived but immensely important journal the *Cahiers pour l'Analyse*, in which the pronouncements on Lacan's teaching were being made – to task over this university discourse, alluding to them as 'the students at the École Normale, the Normalien elements, the little princes of the university who know quite well that you don't have to know something to teach it'.[46] Such comment might seem a mordant snub, but what Lacan is perhaps getting at here goes a step beyond the Socratic pedagogical diagnosis that Ezra Pound makes in his *ABC of Reading*; that 'the inexperienced teacher, fearing his own ignorance, is afraid to admit it. Perhaps that courage only comes when one knows to what extent ignorance is almost universal'.[47]

At the time of giving his seventeenth Seminar, 1969–1970, the *Cahiers* had just come to an abrupt end, having been terminably interrupted by the events of the student revolts of May 1968. The first issue of the *Cahiers*' topic was 'Truth', and Lacan had leant to it its lead-in article, 'Science and Truth'. It is to questions of science and truth that he is returning when he talks of his Normalien students at this point in the Seminar: for one, he claims of science – in a rebuttal of Miller's thesis – that 'the progress of mathematical logic had enabled the subject to be completely reduced – not sutured but vaporized'.[48] In other words, the *mathemes* that Lacan was using in his teaching – the sigla which demarcate psychoanalytic topographies and topologies, and which are, to an extent, 'little bits of the real' – were beginning to demonstrate that *there is no subject* in the order of the Real. The consequence of the Real – as the realm of the impossible and 'unsymbolisable' – is that no such notion can be sustained in it alone; i.e., without any recourse to the subjectively fortifying orders of the imaginary and symbolic.

More important for our purposes, Lacan here talks of truth as '*half-saying*', as only ever being able to be half-said. 'What presents itself as an enigma', he states, is something in which 'a double disposition is incarnated, by virtue of being made, like the half-saying, from two half-bodies'.[49] The exploration of this notion will be conducted throughout this work, via the concept of the 'unificatory/separatory principle', a term we will deploy in attempts to uncover the near-paradoxical and parallactic processes involved in the combination of 'half-body' *elements* (to use the language of Miller under critique), and to lead to the further elucidation of the idea of '*enverity*'. Thus, it is here, too – in this thesis on truth as only fractionally available through *half-saying* – that we can see how it is not ignorance, in contrast to truth, that is almost universal, as Pound asserts, but rather that there is a fundamental impossibility of knowledge being able to be universal, because of the inability for truth itself to be wholly said. To return to Lacan's statement concerning the Normalien students – that they 'know quite well that you don't have to know something to teach it' – we are now able to see this as rather a statement on the parallactic *enigma* of *truth*. If needed is knowledge of non-knowledge to teach, this is precisely due to the *half-sayableness* of truth itself.

It is therefore not a point about *initiation* that Lacan is making when he challenges Miller and the *Cahiers* over their pronouncements, which come out of a discourse, the university's, which is 'without those precise conceptions of analysis which only a personal analysis can provide', but something more fundamental, concerning discourses, and the differences between them, themselves. Indeed, Lacan was extremely sceptical about notions of initiation, and was taken aback to learn from the noted Joycean, James Atherton, that Joyce had 'delighted in Madame Blavatsky's *Isis Unveiled*', a work of initiatory mysticism linked with the movement of theosophy, prevalent in Ireland whilst Joyce was there.[50] Lacan met any notion of initiation – such as into theosophy in this case, which, of course, Joyce was no convert to – with extreme derision, construing it as a defection to 'mental debility'.[51] Indeed, Lacan would later in the Joyce Seminar suggest that 'analysis is, in short, the reduction of initiation to its reality, namely, to the fact that properly speaking there is no initiation'.[52]

Rather than recourse to any mystical notions of a psychoanalytic initiation then, Lacan is drawing attention to modes of discourse here, and the types of articulation that separate them. For example, in Klotz's dichotomy of science and subjectivity, half-saying comes in in the fact that these fields cannot be articulated *in full* simultaneously. The full universality of science is available only with a removal of subjectivity, and the same goes for the full singularity of subjectivity in relation to science, but in the very attempt to articulate either of these fullnesses *half-saying* must necessarily intervene (i.e., science cannot be *said* without a subject). As Lacan puts it in Seminar XVII:

> If we say something in a certain way in this field there will be another part of it which, by virtue of this saying itself, will become absolutely irreducible, completely obscure. In such a way that, in sum, there is a degree of arbitrariness, there is a choice that can be made about what is in need of clarification.[53]

This is thus both the reason for and the result of *half-saying*: there will always be an other side, an irreducible kernel, unable to be simultaneously accessed because of the inherent elisions of speech; elisions demonstrated by Octavius Caesar's statement in *Antony and Cleopatra*: 'Mine own tongue/Splits what it speaks.'[54] Thus, 'full speech', so important to the early Lacan – that which 'aim[ed] at, which form[ed], the truth such as it bec[ame] established in the recognition of one person by another' – must now be conceptualised, in light of these further ruminations, as only ever 'half-full'; its effect, full or half-full however, remains unaltered: a subject still 'finds himself, afterwards [after speaking], other than he was before'.[55]

It should be obvious that it is of course not the aim of these reflections to denigrate or take away from what can be transferred in an analysis, but rather to suggest that approaching psychoanalysis from the other side – the side that James Joyce firmly remained on in his opposition to it – might lend to this study a parallax perspective beneficial to it, as observation from a point of *obversation.* There is perhaps then the risk of constraint in my own writing critically about Lacan, due to the lack of having had a training analysis, at this point.[56] However, Miller, in the foreword to the first issue of the *Cahiers*, claims that 'for us it is only a matter of training ourselves [*de nous former*], following our teachers, in line with the rigour of the concept'.[57] In the carrying out of this work, however, it will not only be a matter of this, but a matter also of a necessitous *approach from the other direction*, with all respect to its antecedents.

'Translate your name into German': Joyce and the Tweedledee and Tweedledum of Freud and Jung

In his preface to the English edition of Seminar XI, *The Four Fundamental Concepts of Psychoanalysis*, composed in 1976, the second year of his Joyce Seminar, Lacan elucidates the preoccupation he had with Joyce's having remained out of analysis: 'I shall speak of Joyce, who has preoccupied me much this year, only to say that he is the simplest consequence of a refusal – such mental refusal! – of a psycho-analysis, which, as a result, his work illustrates.'[58] If this is so, we must nonetheless first of all situate this work within the context of Joyce's actual relations to and experiences of psychoanalysis in his own lifetime.

Thus, whilst this will entail an emphasis on Joyce's *biography* – an emphasis which will continue into the latter chapters of this work – this biography itself must be seen as inextricably linked to the body of Joyce's artistic output (indeed, there is a consensus amongst certain commentators that Joyce in fact led his life *as a work of art*); that is, as a biography not just of *an* artist but of *the* artist, as is implied in the title of his second novel (discounting *Stephen Hero*), *A Portrait of the Artist as a Young Man.* Indeed, if we were to put 'Joyce (the artist)' into position A of the unificatory/separatory principle, then into positions 1 and 2 would go his writing and (auto)biography; or, as Derrida puts it succinctly: 'Now with the event signed Joyce, a *double-bind* has at least become explicit'.[59]

The influence of psychoanalysis on Joyce and his writings has long been noted, as has his ambivalence towards its theory and practice.[60] As Richard Ellmann, Joyce's meticulous biographer, confirms, Joyce had obtained several works of psychoanalysis not long after their publication dates, including Carl Jung's *The Significance of the Father in the Destiny of the Individual* (1909), Sigmund Freud's *A Childhood Memory of Leonardo da Vinci* (1910) and *The Psychopathology of Everyday Life* (1901, although Joyce had the 1917 edition), and Ernest Jones's *The Problem of* Hamlet *and the Oedipus Complex* (1910).[61]

As the originator of psychoanalysis, Sigmund Freud brought the practice to public prominence at the turn of the twentieth century, through his discovery – or, as Lacan would put it, '*invention in the sense of a discovery*' – and examination of the unconscious, results of which were first pioneered in the 1895 text co-authored with Josef Breuer, *Studies on Hysteria*, and further expanded in Freud's landmark work, *The Interpretations of Dreams* (1900).[62] Ellmann argues that Joyce likely came to know of psychoanalysis through his friend and pupil Ettore Schmitz – later the writer of the novel *Confessions of Zeno* (1923) under his adopted pseudonym Italo Svevo – 'whose nephew, Dr. Edoardo Weiss, introduced psychoanalysis into Italy in 1910', whilst the Joyce family were living in Trieste.[63] After this introduction Joyce would remain acutely aware of Freud's career throughout his own, although the same cannot be said to be true of the other way round, as there appears no mention of Joyce by Freud.

Joyce had incorporated elements of Freud's method of the 'free association' of words into the preparatory notes for his play *Exiles* (1918), and in 1916 he had kept a dream diary in which he had recorded his wife, Nora Barnacle's, dreams and his own interpretations, which, according to Ellmann, 'showed the influence of Freud'.[64] Whilst Joyce's first major work *Dubliners* (1914) is psychologically penetrating, it was likely composed too early to have borne marks of psychoanalytic influence; nonetheless, one of its characters, Mr Duffy in the story 'A Painful Case', is philosophically informed by one of Freud's greatest theoretical forebears, Friedrich Nietzsche, a thinker who also remained an important touchstone throughout Joyce's later work.[65] Much in the way of psychoanalytic theory has been applied to the plot developments of *A Portrait of the Artist as a Young Man* (1916) and *Ulysses* (1922) by scholars, as is touched upon later, but it is perhaps in his last major work, *Finnegans Wake* (1939), that the influence of Freud and psychoanalysis is most apparent, in Joyce's compositional techniques.[66] As Jim LeBlanc argues:

> It is difficult to believe that Freud's ideas did not play a part in Joyce's creation of his "book of the night." John Bishop argues this point convincingly in *Joyce's Book of the Dark*, stating that "It seems . . . impossible for any reader seriously interested in coming to terms with *Finnegans Wake* to ignore *The Interpretation of Dreams*" (16) – or the "intrepidation of our dreams," as Taff evokes it in II.3 (*FW* 338.29–30). It is no surprise, then, that Freud's notions of nodal points and navels, and especially the language he uses to describe these dream phenomena, might be particularly useful in dealing with the night language of the *Wake*.[67]

Towards the end of the composition of 'Work in Progress' – as *Finnegans Wake* was known before its publication, because of Joyce jealously guarding its title – Joyce responded to an inquiry about what the book was going to be like that it would have the structure of 'a nocturnal state, lunar. That is what I want to convey: what goes on in a dream, during a dream.'[68] However psychoanalytic this sounds, Joyce was at pains, as he always seemed to be in regard to psychoanalysis, to distance himself from Freud's theory and practice: the *Wake* would *not* be dream-interpretation, as it would not concern itself with 'what is left over afterward, in the memory. Afterward, nothing is left', Joyce maintained, 'afterward, nothing will be left.'[69] Nonetheless, he later qualifies this in responding to charges made by others against the 'arbitrariness' of the allusions in 'Work in Progress', replying: 'It is I who could draw up the best indictment against my work. Isn't it arbitrary to pretend to express the nocturnal life by means of conscious work[?]'[70] Thus, despite previously wondering, 'why all this fuss about the unconscious[;] what about the mystery of the conscious? What do [psychoanalysts] know about that?' Joyce seems nonetheless to have been forced to make a necessary concession to the unconscious, in the methodological procedures involved in the composition of *Finnegans Wake*.[71]

Indeed, amongst scholarly studies of *Finnegans Wake* itself, and the great quantity of notebooks which Joyce worked from to construct it, references abound to psychoanalysis; the canon of its theories and works, and the roster of its proponents. To give one example, Daniel Ferrer, in his study 'The Freudful Couchmare of Λd', claims that 'one of Joyce's holograph notebooks gives us at last some irrefutable evidence of a direct (and close) contact with Freud's text in the English translation'.[72] In the following excerpt, Ferrer puts in a left-hand column certain of Joyce's notes and in the right the moments in Freud's famous case studies to which these refer, as in the example of the imaginary girlfriend 'Lodi' whom the young patient known as 'Little Hans' – whose analysis conducted by his father Freud oversaw – had conjured and told the surrogate analyst of. Freud writes about this case in 'Analysis of a Phobia in a Five-Year-Old Boy' (1909), reprinted in English in the third volume of Freud's *Collected Papers*, which Ferrer refers to as '*CP*'. In the addendum of his own comments Ferrer highlights Joyce's application of psychoanalytic technique to this case of 'Little Hans', which interestingly goes further than Freud's, or the boy's father's, own:

Lodi (idol) (crossed out)	"How did you hit upon the name Lodi? I don't know; but it's a beautiful name, all the same." *CP* p.257

> (Hans is unable to give an explanation for the name he invented for his imaginary favorite girl friend. Joyce suggests one: it might be an inversion of "idol." Next to these words we find written in the margin at right angles to the main text of the notebook: "Bruno Ornub/Nolan Nalon." The same treatment is applied to the name of the philosopher of the coincidence of contraries.)[73]

Joyce takes up Freudian technique here, in a creative capacity, in making of parapraxis a methodology to apply to the name of the philosopher Giordano Bruno (whom Joyce often referred to as 'the Nolan') – a philosopher whose thought is premised on the conception of *an other side* – and who, alongside Giambattista Vico, held tremendous sway over Joyce's work, especially *Finnegans Wake*. This creative exploration and assimilation of Freud's psychoanalytic methodology is indicative of many similar utilisations that take place throughout the composition of the *Wake*. Indeed, Ferrer gives about sixty more examples of Joyce's parsing from the case studies in his essay alone, and I have also argued that even *Finnegans Wake*'s first word, 'riverrun', could possibly involve a derivation, however unconscious, from a footnote in *The Psychopathology of Everyday Life* (to contain a combination of the German words '*urinieren*' – 'urinate' – and '*ruinieren*' – 'ruin' – between which a slip of the tongue is consistently made by one of Freud's patients).[74]

In light of the suggestive evidence that Joyce did glean material from Freud, the claim he made in 1936, that 'my imagination grows when I read Vico as it doesn't when I read Freud and Jung', should perhaps be taken with a pinch of salt, although to have admitted the contrary would have left a bitter taste in Joyce's mouth.[75] Indeed, because of the 'psychological style' that Joyce was seen to have regularly deployed in his texts he was often yoked with psychoanalysis, and it is perhaps for this reason that he strove most earnestly to dissociate himself from it, but, as Freud well knew, any such attempts at dissociation always run the risk of something's 'representation by its opposite'.[76] The association with psychoanalysis, in both positive and negative lights, is one that has not left Joyce since the beginnings of criticism of his work, and seems only to have intensified over time. An example of this intensification is found in the traduction – a conveyance from one to another place – of a bastardisation of an article, written by Ford Madox Ford on *Ulysses* in 1922, made by Christopher Butler.

Lee Spinks, in his *James Joyce: A Critical Guide*, quotes Butler's discussion of *Ulysses*, amongst others':

> P.B. Mais in the *Daily Express* sounded the cautionary note that *Ulysses* displayed 'all our most secret and most unsavoury private thoughts' (Deming 1970a: 191). In this context, as Christopher Butler points out, 'the judgement of Holbrook Jackson, that "every action and reaction of his [Bloom's] psychology is laid bare with Freudian nastiness", and of Ford Madox Ford that [*Ulysses*] was "a volume of dream-interpretations by a writer called Freud" might have struck the contemporary literate reader as authoritative.'
>
> (Butler 1990: 272)[77]

To clarify the quotation from Butler, Spinks inserts the word '*Ulysses*' in brackets. However, he also shortens, and expands, the text at various points, without indicating it diacritically. Butler's original in fact reads: 'Perhaps the judgement of Holbrook Jackson, that 'every action and reaction of his [Bloom's] psychology is laid bare with Freudian nastiness', and that 'much of the action of *Ulysses* is subconscious' (*CH I* 199), and of Ford Madox Ford that it was 'a volume of dream interpretations by a writer called Freud' (*CH I* 277), might have struck the contemporary literate reader as authoritative.'[78] Whilst this textual practice of Spinks's is striking enough in itself, what is even more extraordinary is that Ford Madox Ford – Joyce's friend, editor, and fellow modernist – has been made by Butler to claim that *Ulysses* is 'a volume of dream-interpretations *by Freud*'. What Ford had actually written in the article '*Ulysses* and the Handling of Indecencies' was this:

> Before the war, when I was less of a hermit but much more ingenuous, I used to be shocked by the fact that a great many ladies whom I respected and liked possessed copies of, and gloated as it appeared over, a volume of dream-interpretations by a writer called Freud – a volume that seemed to me to be infinitely more objectionable, in the fullest sense of the term, than *Ulysses* at its coarsest now seems to me.[79]

Thus it would seem that elements of Butler's misquotation have been corrected between his essay and Spinks's guide (the reinsertion of a hyphen in 'dream-interpretations' and of the words 'a writer called' before the word 'Freud'), but the howling misattribution to Ford of the opinion that *Ulysses* was by Freud has gone overlooked in this transmission. The apparent ease with which such an error could be maintained, despite evidence that both Butler and Spinks were working from the same source material of Ford's article excerpted in the first volume of the *James Joyce Critical Heritage*, can only suggest how easily equatable Joyce and his work are with psychoanalysis, and how transliterable his name is with Freud's. Whilst, as Ford notes in his article, in 1922 it was imperative for Joyce to distance himself from Freud's work to avoid the contagion of its charges of indecency, from which *Ulysses* was already suffering enough on its own, subsequently, the cross-contamination of Joyce studies and psychoanalysis would become so symptomatic in itself to allow of this remarkable traduction taking place among Ford's, Butler's, and Spinks's texts.

In Joyce's works, and their reception, then, there remain elements of both influence taken from and ambivalence held towards psychoanalysis. A speech that Joyce addressed to an audience at the café Les Deux Magots, in Paris, shortly before the publication of *Ulysses* – which Ellmann recounts – bolsters the fact that both of these standpoints were present in the writer himself:

> 'In *Ulysses* I have recorded, simultaneously, what a man says, sees, thinks, and what such seeing, thinking, saying does to what you Freudians call the subconscious [*sic*] – but as for psychoanalysis,' he broke off, consistent in his prejudice, 'it's neither more nor less than blackmail.'[80]

The possible reason behind this point of view will be explored in what is to follow, in conjunction with Joyce's suspicion of Carl Jung meddling with his personal finances.

In a letter dated 24 June 1921 to his friend and benefactress, Harriet Shaw Weaver, Joyce writes of his time in Switzerland:

> A batch of people in Zurich persuaded themselves that I was going mad and actually endeavoured to induce me to enter a sanatorium where a certain Doctor Jung (the Swiss Tweedledum who is not to be confused with the

> Viennese Tweedledee, Dr Freud) amuses himself at the expense (in every sense of the word) of ladies and gentlemen who are troubled with bees in their bonnets.[81]

Carl Gustav Jung was at one time Freud's greatest disciple and pupil, and indeed, protégé. He became the first President of the International Psychoanalytical Association (IPA) at its inauguration in March 1910. After this, however, the relationship between Freud and Jung became quickly strained because of major divergences in their respective theoretical approaches. Freud broke with Jung, which resulted in the latter resigning his IPA presidency in May 1913; he thereafter went on to develop the school of analytical psychology, which redirected psychological emphasis away from sexuality, towards mythology and religion, and the notion of the collective unconscious. Jung was also the psychotherapist with whom Joyce would have the most empirical experience.

On 1 October 1919 Joyce called in at his bank in Zurich to receive his monthly stipend from one of his patrons, Edith Rockefeller McCormick; he was curtly informed '*der Kredit ist erschöpft*' ('your credit is cut off').[82] Not long previously Mrs McCormick had recommended to Joyce to seek psychoanalytic treatment from Jung, with all costs to be covered at her expense. Joyce found the idea 'unthinkable'.[83] Afterwards, he sought to transfer the blame for the withdrawal of his funding onto an appropriate party. Eventually he settled on Jung himself as the most likely cause of the sanction, suspecting he had advised McCormick to pull her subsidy, as he had done in relation to another of McCormick's financial recipients, for whose dissipation he believed himself to have effected a cure through this attrition.[84] Joyce's further mistrust of Jung, and of psychoanalysis itself, would only blossom after this first suspicious encounter.

In 1932 Jung published an essay in the *Europäische Revue* entitled '"Ulysses": A Monologue'. An earlier version of this article, which Jung had composed in 1930, had been planned to appear elsewhere, initially in the first issue of a new literary review which Daniel Brody was planning to bring out through his Zurich-based printing press, the Rhein-Verlag. These aspirations were soon quashed because of the tightening of political tensions in Germany. The article was then destined to appear as the introduction to the German edition of *Ulysses*, or as a preface to the German translation of Stuart Gilbert's *James Joyce's* Ulysses: *A Study*, as *Das Rätsel Ulysses*, but both of these projects fell through also.[85] When the article – which was disparaging of *Ulysses*, to say the least – was forwarded to Joyce, he replied to Brody with 'a curt wire, '*Niedrigerhängen*,'' it said, 'meaning 'Ridicule it by making it public.''[86] The literal meaning of this phrase, as R.F.C. Hull explains, is '"Hang it lower" or, figuratively, "Show it up by printing it." (Joyce [wa]s quoting Frederick the Great, who upon seeing a placard attacking him directed that it be hung lower for all to behold.)'[87]

Later, Joyce enquired of Brody: 'Why is Jung so rude to me? People want to put me out of the church to which I don't belong. I have nothing to do with psychoanalysis.' Brody promptly responded: 'There can only be one explanation. Translate your name into German.'[88] 'Freud' is the rough translation of Joyce's name into German – 'joy' being '*Freude*' – a particularly Joycean coincidence the consonance of which Lacan would take further in his introductory lecture on 'Joyce le Symptôme' in 1975, extending the pun to the concept of *jouissance*, which he always kept central to his reflections on Joyce. 'If the reader is fascinated with a name that echoes Freud's own, it is because Joyce has a relation to joy, to *jouissance*, if he is written in the English language', as Lacan states.[89]

Jung's article, which he claimed to be 'not literary but professional', is rather a personal reflection written with a literary affectation and in a style of pastiche that unfortunately falls short of either homage to or mockery of *Ulysses*.[90] As he claimed in his 1932 letter to Joyce, accompanying the revised article, after 'brooding over [*Ulysses*] for about three years', and coming to view 'the 40 pages of non stop run in the end [a]s a string of veritable psychological peaches', 'I couldn't help telling the world how much I was bored, how I grumbled, how I cursed and how I admired' the work.[91] He did so in '"Ulysses": A Monologue', claiming there that he was baffled by the 'many-sidedness' of the text, and suggesting that 'the book can be just as well read backwards'.[92] As well as providing influence for certain rejoinders, or 'backwords', in *Finnegans Wake* – such as the advice that 'the words which follow may be taken in any order desired', and 'writing thithaways end to end and turning, turning and end to end hithaways writing' – Jung's article nonetheless displays certain interesting insights, amidst its general air of 'professional' disdain and moral 'lamentation' for Joyce, and the 'schizophrenia' he attributes to him on the basis of his reading.[93] In the article, he claims that in the 'community of moderns' that forms Joyce's readership, *Ulysses* must 'reveal something that they did not know or feel before. They are not infernally bored by it, but are helped, refreshed, instructed, converted, "restratified"', and he suggests that Joyce, whom he deems a 'prophet of negation' like Freud, is 'needed to reveal to them the other side of reality'.[94]

In these statements, and most likely despite them, Jung seems to propose similarly to Declan Kiberd that '*Ulysses* was designed to produce readers capable of reading *Ulysses* – a sentence which is not the tautology it seems – with the very diffi?culty [*sic*] intended by Joyce as an intrinsic part of the experience'.[95] More presciently, and perhaps less purposefully, Jung is seemingly also anticipating further strains of analytic penetration, such as into the interaction between works of literature and the psyche in the rhizomatic theories put forward by Gilles Deleuze and Félix Guattari in their collaborative works on schizoanalysis. In terms of *restratification*, and in parallel to theories of approaching schizophrenia, they suggest that to combat a cell that 'becomes cancerous, mad, proliferates and loses its configuration, takes over everything; the organism must resubmit it to its rule or restratify it, not only for its own survival, but also to make possible an escape from the organism', in effect, then, to reinscribe it in the Freudian death drive, which, in the short-circuiting of its propulsion towards death, maintains life.[96] Finally, Jung's reflections, despite their personal awkwardness in this essay, also anticipate something of Lacan's realisations of Joyce's presentation of an other side of psychoanalysis, and of an other side of *the symptom*.

Joyce, however, saw Jung's letter, enclosed with the article, as 'imbecile', despite proudly accepting its well-known compliment that he had penetrated the depths of 'the real psychology of a woman' in the final, Penelope, episode of *Ulysses*; a boast to which his wife, Nora, rejoindered that he knew 'nothing at all about women'.[97]

Regarding '"Ulysses": A Monologue', Joyce commented that Jung seemed 'to have read *Ulysses* from first to last without one smile' and recommended that 'the only thing to do in such a case is to change one's drink'.[98] But Freud had already had his work cut out for him in persuading the clinically teetotal psychiatrist to drink at all. Ernest Jones, in his biography of Freud, recounts that

> Jung had been brought up in the fanatical anti-alcoholic tradition of [the] Burghölzli [psychiatric hospital in Zurich] and Freud did his best to laugh him out of it. He succeeded in changing Jung's previous attitude toward alcohol – but then fell to the ground in a faint

after precipitating his conversion.[99] Jung's disparagement of drink – a vice regularly indulged in by the Irish writer – became a weapon to be used against Joyce, whom he denounced as 'a latent schizoid who used drinking to control his schizoidal tendencies'.[100] Such animosities between these two figures stood fast, colouring their opinions of each other's respective literary and psychological practices; that is, until they were forced into a temporary truce caused by the plight of Joyce's daughter, Lucia.

Because of Lucia's suffering from mental and behavioural disturbances that became too much for the Joyces to handle privately they were forced to submit their daughter to the treatment of healthcare professionals; at this time Lucia Joyce was 27 years of age. She was put into the hands first of Wolfgang Maier at Burghölzli, and then eventually entrusted to the care of Jung in 1934 – who was then at the Küsnacht clinic – after much resistance on the part of her father. Jung's treatment of her, however, met with little success.

As Carol Loeb Shloss recounts in her biography of Joyce's daughter, Lucia is said to have 'bridled at Jung's insistence on remembering dreams', and responded to such psychical penetrations that she believed her 'trouble' was rather located 'somewhere in the body'.[101] The end result of this period of turmoil was that she was diagnosed as schizophrenic (which Jung saw as a holdover from her father's apparently 'latent' form of the illness). 'Neither Maier, who examined her again, nor Jung was able to establish a therapeutic relationship with her', Shloss states; 'in the absence of such rapport, Maier now called her "catatonic," and Jung conceded that he could think of nothing to lessen her suffering.'[102]

This seems to be because Jung was only able to work, in conjunction with Lucia, from the conviction that she suffered because of her father's transference of his symptoms onto her. As he wrote to Patricia Hutchins, the author of *James Joyce's World*:

> If you know anything of my Anima theory, Joyce and his daughter are a classical example of it. She was definitely his 'femme inspiratrice,' which explains his obstinate reluctance to have her certified. His own Anima, i.e., unconscious psyche, was so solidly identified with her, that to have her certified would have been as much as an admission that he himself had a latent psychosis. It is therefore understandable that he could not give in. His 'psychological' style is definitely schizophrenic, with the difference, however, that the ordinary patient cannot help himself talking and thinking in such a way, while Joyce willed it and moreover developed it with all his creative forces, which incidentally explains why he himself did not go over the border. But his daughter did, because she was no genius like her father, but merely a victim of her disease. In any other time of the past Joyce's works would never have reached the printer, but in our blessed XXth century it is a message, though not yet understood.[103]

This case could also have been a contributory factor to the qualification of the discussion of the overdevelopment of the 'Eros' in a daughter – which, Jung maintains, produces 'an unconscious incestuous relationship with the father' – made in a footnote to Jung's *Four Archetypes*, published in 1934, contemporaneous with his consultations over Lucia.[104] 'In other cases', he states there, 'the father's psychology is responsible; his projection of the anima arouses an incestuous fixation in the daughter.'[105]

It is due to Jung's reliance on the masculine/feminine binary that he brings in this notion of the 'femme inspiratrice', and locates the archetypes of the anima and animus in the 'collective unconscious', the former as the fundamentally feminine 'inner personality' that is found (repressed) in all males, and the latter the fundamentally masculine 'inner personality' in females. Although these ideas may have taken their lead from Freud's notion of the bisexuality inherent in the human species, Jung would come to postulate them as natural dualistic facts of the unconscious. In contrast, Lacan would base his formulae of sexuation on the fact that such a gender binary is historically and culturally maintained (not that it is the inherent truth of a natural order). In a method similar to, and no doubt influenced by, Michel Foucault's archaeologies of epistemological shifts, Lacan understands the discourse of the masculine/feminine divide as a system which has symbolically arisen in our species, and – whilst it is due to this that its register must nonetheless be drawn on, as well as critiqued – it is not that masculinity and femininity have always ontologically and empirically existed *as such*. That is, whilst biological sexual difference is a fact in the real, it is the symbolic and imaginary orders that have made of this the binaristic dichotomy propounded through the ages in cultural and anthropological classifications, and produced all the discriminatory affects that go along with them.[106] Furthermore, the real of sexual difference encompasses more than just a two-way split, but sexual difference's resultant symbolic binarism comes about because of the exclusion of any third (hermaphroditism, for example), in the manner of the rule of the 'exception that proves the rule', and also, somewhat, of the unificatory/separatory principle.

However, one of the returns of this third, of the real, in the symbolic, is transgenderism, for which Lacan's theories (and Joyce's methodologies, in the creation of an androgyny in the character of Leopold Bloom, for example) are thus much more accommodating than Jung's.[107]

Lucia's resistances to Jung are well documented. Jung had recounted to Ellmann that she had at one point exclaimed: 'To think that such a big fat materialistic Swiss man should try to get a hold of my soul!'[108] However, the earlier reflections on Jung's essentialist theories, and their bases, are important in relation to Lucia because of the possibility that what she presented to Jung fell outside of his go-to categories, which would have entailed that *his resistances*, as well as hers, would have contributed to the failure of the treatment. In hindsight, Jung is recorded as saying, much later: 'We know far too little about the contents and the meaning of pathological mental products, and the little we do know is prejudiced by theoretical assumptions. This is particularly true of the psychology of schizophrenia.'[109] Thus, when Joyce uses the term 'the law of the jungerl' in *Finnegans Wake*, we should perhaps therefore read it as Joyce perceiving that in the jungle of Lucia's illness, and its treatment, both the laws of *Jung* and of the *young girl* herself were competing for establishment, with their equal weighting and respective stubbornness over concessions contributing to the cancelling-out of one another.[110]

The old father and the novel artificer

It would appear that – most likely because of the amount of time he spent on Joyce's *Ulysses* and on his own ' "Ulysses": A Monologue' – Jung had gotten stuck analysing Lucia's father's psychology more than her own. As he states in the letter to Hutchins, in Joyce's work he perceived a message, though one 'not yet understood', yet these would be the very words Joyce would use to describe Lucia's own writings and messages, which Jung dismissed as a displaying of 'schizoid elements': he 'granted that some of her portmanteau words and neologisms were remarkable, but said they were random'.[111] Whether any better results could have been achieved via a classical Freudian analysis can of course not be known.

Nevertheless, there arise in Jung's reflections certain elements anticipatory of how Lacan would take them further, namely in his reflections on Joyce's relation to the *father* – and the Names-of-the-Father – and in his conceptualisation of the *sinthome*, both of which elements function in combination. The father, and the Name-of-the-Father – what Lacan calls the 'pivot of discourse' in Seminar XVI – have of course always been vital aspects in Lacan's thought, and in psychoanalysis itself, and Lacan stresses this again in his first 'Joyce le Symptôme' report, in relation to the author himself and his creations of the characters Stephen Dedalus and Leopold Bloom in *Ulysses*, the former – like Telemachus in Homer's *Odyssey* – popularly read as in search of a father, whom the latter – corresponding to Odysseus (otherwise known as Ulysses, when Latinised) – is seen to represent.[112] Lacan claims: 'Joyce already points out, and so indicates, that all psychic reality – that is, the symptom itself – depends in the end on a structure in which the

Name-of-the-Father is an unconditional element.'[113] Lacan's definition of reality here (its equation with the symptom) demonstrates how integral the symptom has become, at this stage in his thinking, to the very structuration of (and structuration produced by) the psyche. This definition also recalls something of Jung's conviction that Joyce presented an 'other side of reality' to readers of *Ulysses*, a novel which the psychotherapist saw as definitive of symptomatic embodiment.

Later in the Joyce Seminar Lacan also traces this father-seeking trajectory of Stephen Dedalus to the end of *A Portrait of the Artist as a Young Man*, Joyce's novel which preceded *Ulysses*, by quoting its last line – Dedalus's diary entry of 27 April (1903): 'Old father, old artificer, stand me now and ever in good stead'.[114] He concludes:

> It is to his father that he addresses this prayer – his father whose precise characteristic is to be an unworthy, lacking father, and who Stephen is to search for throughout *Ulysses*, in settings where he has no chance of finding him.[115]

At the start of Seminar XXIII, Lacan had said of Joyce that he 'could not have had a worse start [than] to be born in Dublin, with a drunken and more or less Fenian father, namely, a fanatic, from two families'.[116] Lacan read that for Joyce the paternal function of his father, John Joyce, was severely lacking; that instead of the Father of the Law Joyce experienced from the off the *obscene father*, permissive to the extent that his own enjoyment was given free rein. The 'two families' Lacan refers to thus signify Joyce's father's 'marriage to the drink' and his political allegiance as a 'Fenian', a word which in French – as Jacques Aubert points out in his notes to the text – bears a resemblance to '*feignant*' – 'feigning' – a character trait which, along with Simon Dedalus, 'Captain' Jack Boyle in Sean O'Casey's *Juno and the Paycock* epitomises.[117] It is from this type of father that Joyce would have to attempt to derive the least paternal vestige.

Indeed, if Joyce's alter-ego is Stephen Dedalus, then something of this realisation of the paucity of his father's *fatherliness* comes through in Stephen's dissatisfaction with Simon Dedalus, brought out in *A Portrait*, in the enumeration of 'his father's attributes':

> – A medical student, an oarsman, a tenor, an amateur actor, a shouting politician, a small landlord, a small investor, a drinker, a good fellow, a story-teller, somebody's secretary, something in a distillery, a tax-gatherer, a bankrupt and at present a praiser of his own past.[118]

Whilst Lacan's summation of John Joyce's character might be overly one-sided, its extrapolations nonetheless find resonance in Joyce's own character, and the filial characters he created. Lacan argued that Joyce was able to supplement the deficiency of his 'phallic equipment' – left in the wake of the father's failure to fortify this in the son – by his art.[119] This gets at the notion of the *sinthome*, utilisable as an artistic supplement for the lacking father, and which for Joyce would be the *artifice* by which he could *make a name for himself* in order to replace that lacking essential signifier of the Name-of-the-Father. This was the discovery that Jung had also begun to note in perceiving Joyce's ability to will a 'schizophrenic' mind-set and to harness it with his 'creative forces' in order not to 'go over the border' of sanity; but Jung was unable to think a concept like the *sinthome*, instead relying on the damnatory judgement that Joyce was simply a genius, which Lucia was not. Thus, this mode of analysis – through which an attempt could have been made to determine whether such a coping mechanism as the *sinthome* may have been deployable by Lucia – was unopen to Jung, as are what results its application may have yielded, to us.

For Lacan, the *sinthome* would become an other side of the Name-of-the-Father, that *fourth term* which ties together the orders of the Real, the Symbolic, and the Imaginary. That is, it replaces the father with the *artificer*, functioning on its own '*as a name*', as opposed to the functioning of the father as '*he who names*'.[120] The *sinthome* – already *the other side of the symptom*, in that, as opposed to its being an impediment to the conjoining of the Real, Symbolic, and Imaginary orders of the psyche, it is rather this conjoining's facilitator – fulfils the same role that the function of the father, or the Name-of-the-Father, would in a subject from a more typical familial background. As Lacan argues in 'Joyce le Symptôme I':

> The father is that fourth element[,] that fourth element without which nothing is possible in the knot of the symbolic, imaginary and real. But there is another way to name it, and that is where I will stop today, in order to show you what all this has to do with the Name-of-the-Father to which Joyce testifies, what we call the *sinthome*. It is insofar as the unconscious knots itself into a *sinthome*, which is what there is singularly in each individual, that one can say that Joyce, as it is written somewhere, identifies with the individual. He has made himself privileged enough to have, an extreme point, incarnated in himself the symptom.[121]

Joyce seems here to have flipped the symptom, in its role as an inhibitor, through the realisation in it of his own *sinthome* – that irreducible and unanalysable point of singularity uniquely inherent in all individuals. Thus, rather than an *empty signifier*, which is what the symptom begins as – in that its referent is enigmatic and undirected specifically, prior to its interpretation – the *sinthome* perhaps should be read as an *empty signified*, a 'little bit of the real' in the individual (and in the symptom) into which a signification, an instance of subjective singularity, gets stuck, and repeats, forming around itself one's subjectivity and idiosyncrasy, and its chain of signifiers which can allow of its almost endless punning possibilities. Indeed, as Lacan claims of the Real in Seminar XXIII: 'We can only reach bits of Real[;] the Real is always a bit, a stump. A stump certainly around which thinking embroiders'.[122]

Regarding the Real's relation to the *sinthome* as *empty signified* Eric Laurent summates in 'The Purloined Letter and the Tao of the Psychoanalyst' that 'Lacan's idea is that it would be wonderful for psychoanalysis to propose that a certain function of the signified, not of the signifier, gives us a real'.[123] Miller clarifies this in suggesting that in Lacanian notation

> we can also write the subject with the small *s* of the signified. Lacan used this letter in this way and not just at the beginning of his teaching. He started out by writing the subject as an effect of signification produced by the signifier. Then he wrote it as a missing signifier, $, but not without continuing to write it, all the same, from time to time, when the need arose, as small *s*, especially when writing it as subject supposed to know ['*sujet suppose savoir*' in French, which can be condensed to '*sss*'].[124]

To present the subject this way is thus 'to write it as an empty set', which – 'however empty it may be', as Miller puts it – 'is under the domination of the signifier'.[125] Thus, this subject, 'as the subject *of* the signifier, as a signifying void, immediately introduces the necessity for a signifier to come to fill the lack, namely this initial mark', which we are construing here as the *sinthome* as *empty signified*.[126] Of course, Lacan clarifies in 'The Signification of the Phallus' that first and foremost 'it is Freud's discovery that gives the signifier/signified opposition its full scope' in this respect: 'For the signifier plays an active role in determining the effects by which the signifiable appears to succumb to its mark, becoming, through that passion, the signified'; that is, in *becoming* the signified the signifier *comes into* the signified.[127] These initial reflections on the signified in relation to the subject – and to processes of subjectivation – will be extended in the sustained analysis of the *sinthome* to follow in chapter 3.

Ellie Ragland expands on the earlier notions concerning the Real – in their relation to the letter (that 'initial mark'), and thus to the *sinthome* – in her essay 'The Practice of the Letter and Topological Structure', by advancing the hypothesis that

> that which is central to spoken (or written) language and at the same time external to it, even *organizatory* of it, is the partial drives – the oral, the anal, the scopic, the invocatory – that Lacan first noted in his formula for drive ($◇D). Miller points out in 'Extimité' that the drives bring a piece of the real into play, a *Stück* (piece) left over from early experience of the loss of objects that first *cause* desire (Miller 1985–86). In other words, language cannot entirely cover remnants of the real that first place discontinuity or disturbance in language, indeed, as the cause round which it is organized. In this context, the Lacanian real is not that of his first period of teaching, that which was full and impossible to symbolize. It is, rather, the *re*-pressed part of *jouissance* that returns as the real to disrupt the would-be consistencies that language expresses. And the real returns most particularly round the objects-*cause*-of-desire and the partial drives to which they give rise.[128]

It is in these reintroductions of inconsistencies and disturbances that Joyce's language in *Finnegans Wake* – exemplary of what Lacan calls *lalangue* – finds its importance in the late topological structures of Lacan's thinking: the permeation of all language with its *other side* or *other sides*. This can be seen in language's very ontological basis (as 'discourse without speech'), as well as in its wordplay, an example of which has entered earlier in relation to the *empty signified* coincidently, in the overlap of the 'little bit of the Real', the *Stück*, that gets *stuck* in the *sinthome*, which, in itself, is a little bit of the Real too, and thus this chain of signifiers that arises becomes creative of a *mise en abyme*.

Whereas – in Lacan's division of the word 'symptom' in 'Joyce le Symptôme I' – the first part of the word, 'sym', might connote the synthesis utilised in the symptom's fissiparous signification (what Freud would call its mode of 'condensation'), we can see, too, the use to which Lacan envisages the nonsensical and irreducible other half of the word being put; that is, in '*ptom*[*ing*] the coincident bits' of the Real.[129] It is in this light that in Seminar XX (1972–1973) Lacan prepares the groundwork for the claim he makes in the 1976 English preface to Seminar XI – that 'Joyce's work illustrates his mental refusal of psychoanalysis' – by asking the question: 'What happens in Joyce's work?' He answers: 'The signifier stuffs *(vient truffer)* the signified.'[130] Although he here states that Joyce's work is 'not readable', at this point in his career he still claims that it is analysable. However, it is in Seminar XX that he is seen to be on the way to uncovering that 'opaque *jouissance*' that is inherent in the symptom, that unanalysable *enjoy–meant* of the *sinthome*.

By assuming his *sinthome*, through – as Harari puts it – 'working on his own *jouissance*', and by 'incarnating himself in the symptom', Joyce – from the other side of psychoanalysis – seems to awaken in Lacan the realisation of what such a process means for psychoanalysis, and how a 'post-Joycean' psychoanalysis could come to be situated.[131] For Lacan, Joyce was working with 'little bits of Real' in dealing with his own *jouissance*, and in putting the (written) *letter* in *Finnegans Wake* in direct contact with its other side: *litter*; trash, excreta, nonsense, inconsistencies, disturbances, discarded fragments, coincidents of contraries.[132] As Miller puts it in his 'Joyce with Lacan':

> The insignia of Joyce [comes about through his] handling the letter outside of signified effects, for the purpose of pure *jouissance*. Evoking psychosis was in no way applied psychoanalysis; on the contrary, it was *with* the Joyce-symptom held to be unanalyzable, calling the analyst's discourse into question, in so far as a subject who is identified with his or her symptom is closed off to the artifice of analysis. And perhaps an analysis has no better end . . .[133]

In 1935 Theodor Adorno wrote to Walter Benjamin, about his *Arcades Project* – which aimed to document the Paris of the 1800s – 'you will be able to unearth incomparably more conclusive evidence from your material and define the specific shape of the world of things in the 19th century, perhaps viewing it from its seamy side – its refuse, remnants, debris.'[134] This, it seems, is how Joyce set out to view things, and to represent them in the *Wake*, and, following in his wake, it is how Lacan would interact with the order of the Real and commence his at once clinically precise topological and punningly pleochroic late psychoanalytic investigations of the 1970s, in his spoken Seminars and written '*poubellications*'.[135]

However, as Geoff Boucher warns in his essay 'Joyce: Lacan's Sphinx', 'we should be careful [. . .] before we ascribe to this interplay of misreadings and reversals [that is Seminar XXIII] the status of a wholly new psychoanalytic theory'; he maintains that in Seminar XXIII 'Joyce become[s] Lacan's symptom'.[136] Boucher is undoubtedly right to be cautious, but it is with such reversals and misreadings – elements of the *envers* and elements affected by the Real – that both Joyce and Lacan are predominantly concerned in their respective late works. Nonetheless, for both, such concerns were important from the beginning, and were fostered over time, as Louis Althusser stressed – in the case of Lacan – as early as 1964, in his essay 'Freud et Lacan':

> Since he has to teach the theory of the unconscious to doctors, analysts or analysands, in the rhetoric of his speech Lacan provides them with a dumbshow equivalent of the language of the unconscious (which, as is well known, is in its ultimate essence '*Witz*', successful or unsuccessful pun and metaphor).[137]

To extend Althusser here, it could even be suggested that Lacan's theory, which he delivered in his Seminars year in year out, is *the other side* of (his) psychoanalysis – i.e., of (his) psychoanalytic practice – in its wide-ranging free association of topics and themes which represent the inverse of the clinical position of analyst, in all its interpretative precision, penetrative silence, and even situative *lack* (*qua* position of *objet petit a*).[138] As Lacan's biographer Elisabeth Roudinesco puts it: 'It was in his own Seminar, said Lacan, that he felt he was really analyzed.'[139]

To repeat the quotation from the Comte de Buffon that Lacan privileges as the first words of the *Écrits*, then, in relation to this linguistic 'dumbshow' of Lacan's: 'the style is the man himself'.[140] In particular, Lacan's notorious style operates always with an awareness of its *enverity* – the necessity of its *half-saying* in its delivery – splitting between theoretically veritable precision and variable '*connerie*' (a term regularly deployed by Lacan that Cormac Gallagher, at his most Hiberno-Joycean, translates as 'feckology').[141] In Seminar XXIV – *L'insu que sait de l'une-bévue s'aile à mourre* – Lacan begins to use the neologism '*varité*', or 'varity' (condensing 'verity' [*vérité*] and 'variety' [*variété*]), as he begins to demonstrate that – as Harari puts it – 'there are varieties of truth, to be expressed through condensation as "varity" ', and that 'the *sinthome* blocks' specific truths.[142] Unlike Harari here, however, who suggests that varity 'goes beyond the aphorism about truth being half-said, and thus not-all', we will suggest that *sinthomic* varity is in fact the very reason for the *enverity* of the half-said. Thus, to put Lacan's *sinthomic* style into *Wake*an words: 'In an effort towards autosotorisation, [he] effaces himself in favour of the idiology' that says: 'Fix on the little fellow in my eye, Minucius Mandrake, and follow my little psychosinology'; that is, that which combines the *work* of (his, i.e., Lacan's) psychological practice and the *play* of (his) *sinthomic* discourse.[143]

Althusser's depiction of Lacan's methodical discourse is notable too for its similarity to descriptions of Joyce's working methods, such as in Declan Kiberd's thesis that the reading of *Ulysses* creates readers capable of reading *Ulysses*. Here, Lacan's 'half-saying' becomes yet more didactically resonant. Indeed, as he suggests in Seminar XXIII, 'it is not for nothing that what one says lies'.[144] As we have seen in the unificatory/separatory formulations thus far enumerated, it is through the fact that the lie occupies an irreducible place in the subject's speech that truth can be approached, in its rivening position; that is, the *lie* inherent in the half-said is necessary to the possibility of the reception of its articulation. 'There' – as Lacan says much earlier – 'you have both sides of the structure, foundational speech and lying speech'; without which sides we would not have the structure itself.[145]

The *sinthome*, however, does pose a threat to this, in that it is irreducible in and of itself, and completely inscribed in play, in its multi-possibilitous punning effects; it can eradicate the possibility of equivocation – the other side of varity – *through* its ultimately limitless varity. As Lacan stresses: 'The only weapon we have against the *sinthome* [is] equivocation[,] because it is uniquely by equivocation that interpretation works. There must be something in the signifier that resonates.'[146] This very resonance is what Lacan came to ponder extensively in his dealings with Joyce in the twenty-third Seminar, and is what will be returned to over and again in this work. It is thus that out of the interplay of Lacan's and Joyce's late works, in which both take these symptomal and *sinthomic* strands much further – in some cases, to their extremes – certain schemata arise for an other side of psychoanalysis, its 'post-Joycean side', which, whether integrable or not, will nonetheless inform the theory and practice of forthcoming psychoanalysis, and its *revivals from the other direction.*

Notes

1 Maurice Roche, *Codex* (Paris: Seuil, 1974) p.157. Quoted in David Hayman, 'Some Writers in the Wake of the *Wake*', in Samuel Beckett and others, *In the Wake of the Wake*, ed. by David Hayman and Elliott Anderson (Madison: University of Wisconsin Press, 1978) p.31.

2 This is a truncation of a question taken from *Ulysses*: 'Do you see the tide flowing quickly in on all sides, sheeting the lows of sands quickly, shellcocoacoloured?' See James Joyce, *Ulysses* [1922], ed. by Hans Walter Gabler and others (New York: Vintage Books, 1986) 3.326–327, p.38; James Joyce, *Ulysses: The 1922 Text*, ed. by Jeri Johnson (Oxford: Oxford World's Classics, 1998) p.45. All subsequent references to *Ulysses* will follow this format by citing first the Gabler edition, with episode number followed after a dot by line number, followed by page – as previously shown, and as is standard in Joycean reference – then with reference to the original 1922 text as reissued in Johnson's Oxford edition.

3 Jacques Lacan, 'Joyce le symptôme II' [1975], in *Joyce avec Lacan*, ed. by Jacques Aubert (Paris: Navarin, 1987) p.36. This is from the second lecture Lacan gave at the James Joyce Symposium, 1975. There are currently only unofficial translations of this talk available; Dominique Hecq's is relied on here. Bloomsday is the name given to June 16, in honour of it being the day on which Joyce's *Ulysses* is set: 16 June 1904.

4 Roberto Harari, *How James Joyce Made His Name: A Reading of the Final Lacan* [1995], trans. by Luke Thurston (New York: Other Press, 2002) p.359.
5 Sigmund Freud, 'The Unconscious' [1915], trans. by C.M. Baines and others, in Sigmund Freud, *The Standard Edition of the Complete Psychological Works of Sigmund Freud, Volume XIV (1914–1916): On the History of the Psychoanalytic Movement, Papers on Metapsychology and Other Works*, ed. by James Strachey, with Anna Freud, assisted by Alix Strachey and Alan Tyson, 24 vols (London: Vintage, 2001) XIV, p.166. Hereafter the standard edition will be referred to as *SE*, followed by volume and then page number.
6 See James Joyce, *Finnegans Wake* [1939], ed. by Robbert-Jan Henkes and others (Oxford: Oxford World's Classics, 2012) p.3, 1–3. As is customary, as well as page reference, I will also give the line numbers in the standard edition of *Finnegans Wake*.
7 Jacques Lacan, 'Response to Jean Hyppolite's Commentary on Freud's "Verneinung"' [1954], in Lacan, *Écrits: The First Complete Edition in English* [1966], trans. by Bruce Fink, in collaboration with Hélöise Fink and Russell Grigg (New York: W. W. Norton, 2006) p.322.
8 Slavoj Žižek, *How to Read Lacan* (London: Granta Books, 2006) p.3. For a more detailed study of how Žižek tracks the unconscious – from G.W.F. Hegel, through Freud, to Lacan – see my entry on the 'Unconscious', in *The Žižek Dictionary*, ed. by Rex Butler (Durham: Acumen Press, 2014) pp.254–258.
9 Jacques Lacan, *The Seminar of Jacques Lacan, Book XI: The Four Fundamental Concepts of Psychoanalysis* [1964], ed. by Jacques-Alain Miller, trans. by Alan Sheridan (New York: W. W. Norton, 1981) p.20, for example; and Jacques Lacan, 'The Instance of the Letter in the Unconscious, or Reason Since Freud' [1957], in *Écrits*, p.425. He had also drawn allusion to Freud's 'Champollion-like decipherment of Schreber' in his third Seminar, two years prior. See Jacques Lacan, *The Seminar of Jacques Lacan, Book III: The Psychoses, 1955–1956*, ed. by Jacques-Alain Miller, trans. by Russell Grigg (New York: W. W. Norton, 1993) p.10.
10 See Madeleine Chapsal, 'Clefs pour la psychanalyse' [Keys to Psychoanalysis: Interview with Jacques Lacan], *L'Express*, 31 May 1957. Uncredited English translation Available from: <http://blog.sina.com.cn/s/blog_49c058ef0100p84z.html> [accessed 7 January 2012] (paragraph under heading 'Articulated and Decipherable').
11 Ibid.
12 Jacques Derrida, 'Resistances', in *Resistances of Psychoanalysis* [1996], trans. by Peggy Kamuf, Pascale-Anne Brault, and Michael Naas (Stanford: Stanford University Press, 1998) pp.3–4.
13 Pierre Macherey, *A Theory of Literary Production* [1966], trans. by Geoffrey Wall (Abingdon: Routledge Classics, 2006) p.23.
14 This may be compared with Joseph Campbell and Henry Morton Robinson's rendering of Joyce's 'B-C climactogram' mentioned in *Finnegans Wake* (p.165, 23):

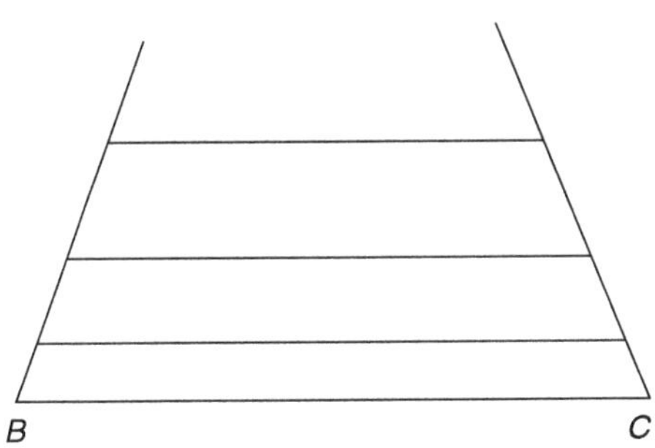

Figure 1.2 B-C climactogram

Although position A is perhaps implicit here – in the showing of its possible derivatives '*B*' and '*C*' – its primariness is not explicitly demonstrated, as in the unificatory/separatory principle. See Joseph Campbell and Henry Morton Robinson, *A Skeleton Key to Finnegans Wake* (London: Faber and Faber, 1944) p.106, footnote 5.

15 Macherey, *A Theory of Literary Production*, p.27.

16 Ferdinand de Saussure, *Course in General Linguistics* [1906–1911], ed. by Charles Bally and others, trans. by Roy Harris (Chicago and La Salle: Open Court, 1986) p.111.

17 Ibid. p.9.

18 Sheldon R. Brivic, *Joyce Between Freud and Jung* (Port Washington: Kennikat Press, 1980) p.8.

19 See the treatment of the neglected yet fundamental role of writing in Jacques Derrida, *Of Grammatology* [1967], trans. by Gayatri Chakravorty Spivak (Baltimore: John Hopkins University Press, 1997) Corrected ed., particularly pp.1–87.

20 François Regnault, 'Structure and Subject' [2009], trans. by Cécile Malaspina, rev. by Peter Hallward, in *Concept and Form: Volume 2, Interviews and Essays on the* Cahiers pour l'Analyse, ed. by Peter Hallward and Knox Peden, 2 vols (London: Verso, 2012) II, p.21.

21 Jacques Lacan, 'The Subversion of the Subject and the Dialectic of Desire in the Freudian Unconscious' [1960], in *Écrits*, p.695.

22 Lacan, *Seminar XI: The Four Fundamental Concepts of Psychoanalysis*, p.199.

23 In its numerical place, Lacan's concept of the *sinthome* bears some resemblance to James Clerk Maxwell's conceptualisation of the fourth dimension as that which can provide a key to life, which Rosemary Jann cites in her introduction to Edwin Abbott Abbott's *Flatland*: 'Physicist James Clerk Maxwell imagined his soul as a trefoil knot that (according to the theorizing of German mathematician Felix Klein) could be untied only in the fourth dimension.' See Rosemary Jann, 'Introduction', in *Flatland: A Romance of Many Dimensions* [1884], ed. by Edwin A. Abbott (Oxford: Oxford World's Classics, 2006) p.xxv. Lacan makes much reference to the Klein bottle – described by Felix Klein in 1882, the year of Joyce's birth – throughout his work.

24 Jacques Lacan, *The Seminar of Jacques Lacan, Book VII: The Ethics of Psychoanalysis, 1959–1960*, ed. by Jacques-Alain Miller, trans. by Dennis Porter (London: Routledge Classics, 2008) p.80.

25 See Saint Augustine, 'On Two Souls, Against the Manichæans [De Duabus Animabus contra Manichæos]' [391], trans. by Albert H. Newman, in *Nicene and Post-Nicene Fathers, Volume IV: The Anti-Manichæan Writings, the Anti-Donatist Writings*, ed. by Philip Schaff and others, 14 vols (Grand Rapids, MI: T. & T. Clark, 1886–1900) IV, p.107. 'Does Freud's discovery represent the confirmation, at the level of psychological experience, of Manichaeism?' Lacan rhetorically asks in 'The Instance of the Letter in the Unconscious', answering unequivocally that 'there can, in fact, be no confusion on this point: what Freud's research introduced us to was not some more or less curious cases of dual personality.' He emphasises in a note to the question: 'One of my colleagues went as far as this thought in wondering if the id (*Es*) of Freud's last doctrine wasn't in fact the "bad ego." (Added in 1966) You see the kind of people I had to work with.' See Lacan, 'The Instance of the Letter in the Unconscious', in *Écrits*, p.435 and p.441, note 24.

26 *Twin Peaks*, season 2, episode 19, 'Variations on Relations', writ. by Mark Frost and Harley Peyton, dir. by Jonathan Sanger, 1991.

27 Jacques Lacan, *The Seminar of Jacques Lacan, Book XVII: The Other Side of Psychoanalysis* [1969–1970], ed. by Jacques-Alain Miller, trans. by Russell Grigg (New York: W. W. Norton, 2007).

28 See William Shakespeare, *Hamlet*, in *Complete Works of Shakespeare, Volume III: Tragedies*, ed. by Peter Alexander, 4 vols (London: William Collins and Sons, 1958)

III, Act I, Scene V, 189, p.461, and the translation in William Shakespeare, *La tragédie de Hamlet, prince de Danemark*, trans. by Jules Derocquigny (Paris: Les Belles-Lettres, 1936) p.69.
29 Jacques Derrida, *Specters of Marx: The State of Debt, the Work of Mourning and the New International* [1993], trans. by Peggy Kamuf (Abingdon: Routledge Classics, 2006) p.22 [my italics added].
30 Slavoj Žižek, *The Parallax View* (Cambridge, MA: MIT Press, 2006) p.17.
31 Alenka Zupančič, *Why Psychoanalysis?* (Uppsala: NSU Press, 2008) p.29 [my emphases].
32 Lacan, *Seminar XVII: The Other Side of Psychoanalysis*, p.12, Jacques Lacan, 'On My Antecedents', in *Écrits*, p.53.
33 Grigg, 'Translator's Note', in Lacan, *Seminar XVII: The Other Side of Psychoanalysis*, p.9.
34 Jonathan Pollock, 'Textual Atomism in *Finnegans Wake*', in *Renascent Joyce*, ed. by Daniel Ferrer, Sam Slote, and André Topia (Gainesville: University Press of Florida, 2013) p.19.
35 Lacan, 'Joyce le symptôme II', in *Joyce avec Lacan*, p.36 [trans. by Hecq]. See note 3 in this chapter.
36 Dylan Evans, 'Jouissance', in *An Introductory Dictionary of Lacanian Psychoanalysis* (London: Routledge, 1996) p.93.
37 Alain Grosrichard, 'An Eighteenth-Century Psychological Experiment' [1966], trans. by Knox Peden and Peter Hallward, in *Concept and Form: Volume 1, Key Texts from the* Cahiers pour l'Analyse, ed. by Peter Hallward and Knox Peden, 2 vols (London: Verso, 2012) I, p.214.
38 Zupančič, *Why Psychoanalysis?* p.42.
39 Žižek locates the unconscious in a category of 'unknown knowns'; that is, of 'things we don't know that we know, [or] the "knowledge that doesn't know itself," as Lacan used to say.' See Slavoj Žižek, *Organs Without Bodies: On Deleuze and Consequences* [2004] (Abingdon: Routledge Classics, 2012) p.85.
40 Lacan, *Seminar XI: The Four Fundamental Concepts of Psychoanalysis*, p.211.
41 Lacan, *Seminar VII: The Ethics of Psychoanalysis*, p.39.
42 Jean-Pierre Klotz, 'The Littoral Condition of the Letter', in *The Literary Lacan: From Literature to Lituraterre and Beyond*, ed. by Santanu Biswas (Calcutta: Seagull Books, 2012) p.200.
43 Jacques-Alain Miller, 'Suture (Elements of the Logic of the Signifier)' [1966], trans. by Jacqueline Rose, in *Concept and Form, Vol. 1*, p.91.
44 Ibid. p.92.
45 Jacques-Alain Miller, 'Foreword, Volume 1: Truth' [1966], trans. by Cécile Malaspina and Peter Hallward, in ibid. p.57.
46 Lacan, *Seminar XVII: The Other Side of Psychoanalysis*, p.26.
47 Ezra Pound, *ABC of Reading* [1934] (New York: New Directions, 1960) p.85.
48 Lacan, *Seminar XVII: The Other Side of Psychoanalysis*, p.105.
49 Ibid. p.120.
50 See Jacques Lacan, 'Joyce le Symptôme' [1975], in *Le seminaire, Livre XXIII: Le sinthome* [1975–1976], texte établi par Jacques-Alain Miller (Paris: Éditions du Seuil, 2005) p.168. This is a reprinting, in the book's appendix, of the first lecture Lacan gave at the 1975 Joyce Symposium; again there are only unofficial translations of this, and I here rely on Daniel Collins's.
51 Ibid.
52 Lacan, *Le seminaire XXIII: Le sinthome*, p.30. See, in English, Jacques Lacan, *The Seminar of Jacques Lacan, Book XXIII: Joyce and the Sinthome, 1975–1976*, trans. by Cormac Gallagher (London: Karnac, unofficial translation, n.d.) session II, p.3, from which this translation is taken. Gallagher's page numbers begin from the number one for each session of Lacan's Seminars.

53 Lacan, *Seminar XVII: The Other Side of Psychoanalysis*, p.109.
54 William Shakespeare, *Antony and Cleopatra*, in *Complete Works of Shakespeare, Volume V: Tragedies and Poems*, Act II, Scene VII, 121–122, p.195.
55 Jacques Lacan, *The Seminar of Jacques Lacan, Book I: Freud's Papers on Technique, 1953–1954*, ed. by Jacques-Alain Miller, trans. by John Forrester (New York: W. W. Norton, 1988) p.107.
56 As Lacan himself wrote in his case study of 'Aimée' in his thesis: 'The omission [of a psychoanalysis], which was not made voluntarily on my part, circumscribes both the scope and value of my work.' See Jacques Lacan, *De la psychose paranoïaque dans ses rapports avec la personnalité* [1932] (Paris: Seuil, 1975) p.303. Quoted in Elisabeth Roudinesco, *Jacques Lacan: An Outline of a Life and a History of a System of Thought*, trans. by Barbara Bray (Cambridge: Polity Press, 1999) p.50.
57 Miller, 'Foreword, Volume 1: Truth', in *Concept and Form, Vol. 1*, p.57.
58 Jacques Lacan, 'Preface to the English-Language Edition' [1976], in *Seminar XI: The Four Fundamental Concepts of Psychoanalysis*, p.ix.
59 Jacques Derrida, 'Ulysses Gramophone: Hear Say Yes in Joyce' [1984], trans. by François Raffoul, in *Derrida and Joyce: Texts and Contexts*, ed. by Andrew J. Mitchell and Sam Slote (Albany: State University of New York Press, 2013) p.61.
60 For illuminating book-length studies of Joyce's, and his works', relation to psychoanalysis, see Brivic, *Joyce Between Freud and Jung* and Jean Kimball, *Joyce and the Early Freudians: A Synchronic Dialogue of Texts* (Gainesville: University Press of Florida, 2003).
61 See Richard Ellmann, *James Joyce: New and Revised Edition* (Oxford: Oxford University Press, 1983) p.340, note 2; Richard Ellmann, *The Consciousness of Joyce* (Oxford: Oxford University Press, 1977) p.54; and also Jean Kimball, *Odyssey of the Psyche: Jungian Patterns in Joyce's* Ulysses (Carbondale: Southern Illinois University Press, 1997) p.155, note 16, for a useful list of articles on Joyce's use of and allusions to psychoanalytic texts.
62 Jacques Lacan, 'Geneva Lecture on the Symptom' [1975], trans. by Russell Grigg, *Analysis*, 1 (1989) 7–26 (p.15) [my emphasis]. See Josef Breuer and Sigmund Freud, *Studies on Hysteria* [1895], trans. by James and Alix Strachey, in Freud, *SE*, II, and Sigmund Freud, *The Interpretation of Dreams* [1900], trans. by James Strachey, in Freud, *SE*, IV–V.
63 Ellmann, *James Joyce*, p.340.
64 See ibid. p.358 and pp.436–438. In the *Exiles* notes Joyce lists the verbal association: 'blister-amber-silver-oranges-apples-sugarstick-hair-spongecake-ivy-roses-ribbon'. See James Joyce, 'Entries in a Notebook, Now at Buffalo', in *Poems and* Exiles, ed. by J.C.C. Mays (Harmondsworth: Penguin Twentieth-Century Classics, 1992) pp.347–348.
65 See James Joyce, 'A Painful Case', in *Dubliners* [1914] (London: Penguin Modern Classics, 1973) p.110. See the chapter '"James Overman": Joyce Reading Nietzsche', in Sam Slote, *Joyce's Nietzschean Ethics* (New York: Palgrave Macmillan, 2013) pp.1–18.
66 See, for example, amongst much other work, the Jungian studies of *A Portrait* and *Ulysses* in full: Hiromi Yoshida, *Joyce and Jung: The "Four Stages of Eroticism" in* A Portrait of the Artist as a Young Man (New York: Peter Lang, 2007) and Kimball, *Odyssey of the Psyche*.
67 Jim LeBlanc, 'The Ass Dreams of Shaun's Bottomless Heart: Shakespeare and the Dream-Work in *Finnegans Wake* 403–407', in *Renascent Joyce*, p.86.
68 James Joyce, quoted in Jacques Mercanton, 'The Hours of James Joyce' [1963], trans. by Lloyd C. Parks, in *Portraits of the Artist in Exile: Recollections of James Joyce by Europeans*, ed. by Willard Potts (San Diego: Harcourt Brace Jovanovich, 1986) p.207.
69 Ibid.

70 Ibid. p.213.
71 Ellmann, *James Joyce*, p.436.
72 Daniel Ferrer, 'The Freudful Couchmare of Λd: Joyce's Notes on Freud and the Composition of Chapter XVI of *Finnegans Wake*', *James Joyce Quarterly*, 22nd ser., 4 (1985) 367–382 (p.367).
73 Ibid. p.371.
74 See D.C. Bristow, 'Following the riverrun: *Finnegans Wake*'s First Word', *Notes & Queries*, 60th ser., 2 (2013) 291–292.
75 Ellmann, *James Joyce*, p.693.
76 For a review of how this process is found at work in dreams, see Freud, *The Interpretation of Dreams*, in *SE*, V, p.471.
77 Lee Spinks, *James Joyce: A Critical Guide* (Edinburgh: Edinburgh University Press, 2009) p.197.
78 Christopher Butler, 'Joyce the Modernist', in *The Cambridge Companion to James Joyce*, ed. by Derek Attridge (Cambridge: Cambridge University Press, 1990) p.272.
79 Ford Madox Ford, 'Extract from "*Ulysses* and the Handling of Indecencies" [1922], *English Review*, xxxv (December 1922) 538–48', in *The Critical Heritage: James Joyce, Volume 1, 1907–27*, ed. by Robert H. Deming, 2 vols (London: Routledge, 2002) I, p.277.
80 Ellmann, *James Joyce*, p.524.
81 James Joyce, *Selected Letters of James Joyce*, ed. by Richard Ellmann (London: Faber and Faber, 1975) p.282.
82 Ellmann, *James Joyce*, p.467.
83 Ibid. p.466.
84 See ibid. pp.467–469.
85 For details of the article's publication history, see R.F.C. Hull, '"Ulysses": A Monologue: *Appendix*', in Carl Gustav Jung, *The Spirit in Man, Art and Literature*, trans. by R.F.C. Hull (Abingdon: Routledge Classics, 2003) pp.155–158.
86 Ellmann, *James Joyce*, p.628.
87 Hull, '"Ulysses": A Monologue: *Appendix*', p.155.
88 Ellmann, *James Joyce*, p.628.
89 See Lacan, 'Joyce le Symptôme', in *Le seminaire XXIII: Le sinthome*, p.167. I rely on Aaron Benanav's translation here.
90 Jung, quoted in Hull, '"Ulysses": A Monologue: *Appendix*', p.156.
91 Jung, quoted in Ellmann, *James Joyce*, p.629.
92 Carl Gustav Jung, '"Ulysses": A Monologue', in *The Spirit in Man, Art and Literature*, p.133, p.130.
93 See Joyce, *Finnegans Wake* p.100, 28; p.121, 12–13; p.114, 16–17.
94 Jung, '"Ulysses": A Monologue: *Appendix*', p.141.
95 Declan Kiberd, *Ulysses and Us: The Art of Everyday Living* (London: Faber and Faber, 2009) p.17.
96 Gilles Deleuze and Félix Guattari, *A Thousand Plateaus: Capitalism and Schizophrenia, Vol. 2* [1980], trans. by Brian Massumi (London: Continuum, 2004) p.180. Freud, in *Beyond the Pleasure Principle*, claims that '*the aim of all life is death*', but from this 'arises the paradoxical situation that the living organism struggles most energetically against events (dangers, in fact) which might help it to attain its life's aim rapidly – by a kind of short-circuit'. See Sigmund Freud, 'Beyond the Pleasure Principle' [1920], trans. by James Strachey, in Freud, *SE*, XVIII, pp.38–39.
97 Ellmann, *James Joyce*, p.629.
98 Ibid. p.628.
99 Ernest Jones, *The Life and Work of Sigmund Freud* [1953–1957], ed. and abridged by Lionel Trilling and Stephen Marcus (London: Pelican Books, 1964) pp.410–411.
100 Ellmann, *James Joyce*, p.680.

101 Carol Loeb Shloss, *Lucia Joyce: To Dance in the Wake* (London: Bloomsbury, 2004) p.275.
102 Ibid. p.274.
103 Carl Gustav Jung, quoted in Patricia Hutchins, *James Joyce's World* (London: Methuen, 1957) pp.184–185, footnote 1.
104 Carl Gustav Jung, *Four Archetypes: Mother, Rebirth, Spirit, Trickster* [1934, rev. ed. 1954], trans. by R.F.C. Hull (London: Routledge Classics, 2003) p.23.
105 Ibid. p.23, footnote 6.
106 As Marie-Hélène Brousse indeed puts it:

> Psychoanalysis implies a definition of sexuality as sexuation. The point is not so much to stress the dimension of chronological development of this process as to take note of a disparity between the biological real of sex – defined in the human species by the difference between male and female, and so by a duality – and its symbolic determinations, namely the different solutions imposed on the subject by the structure of language and the defiles of the signifier. Sexuation is a process of complex identifications and so analysis, which is a movement of the fall of identifications, has for objective to reach the point of separation between the *jouissance* that sustains the subject and the identifications with which the subject covers it.

See Marie-Hélène Brousse, 'Sexual Position and the End of Analysis', in *The Later Lacan: An Introduction*, ed. by Véronique Voruz and Bogdan Wolf, trans. by Heather Chamberlain and others (Albany: State University of New York Press, 2007) p.251.
107 Patricia Gherovici expands on this in her essay on transgenderism in relation to Lacanian psychoanalysis, 'The Transsexual Body Written: Writing as *Sinthome*':

> The transsexual struggle illustrates what psychoanalysis has shown: that the phallus, which has no relation to anatomy, is a signifier used by both men and women to signify their sex and help them embody their sexuality. At times, the signifier and the organ are confused with one another. The phallus is 'no signifier of sexual difference' but of 'sex unity' (there is only one signifier to signify two diverging positions). In psychoanalysis, as well as in the unconscious, man knows nothing of woman, and woman nothing of man. The phallus epitomizes the point in the myth where the sexual becomes the passion of the signifier.
>
> (Lacan 1970: 64; my translation)

See Patricia Gherovici, 'The Transsexual Body Written: Writing as *Sinthome*', in *The Literary Lacan*, p.269.
108 Ellmann, *James Joyce*, p.679.
109 Carl Gustav Jung, 'Recent Thoughts on Schizophrenia', in *The Psychogenesis of Mental Disease* [1956], trans. by R.F.C. Hull (Princeton: Bollingen Series, 1960) p.250, quoted in Shloss, *Lucia Joyce*, p.5.
110 Joyce, *Finnegans Wake*, p.268, footnote 3. This phrase is differently discussed in relation to Jung in Luke Thurston, *James Joyce and the Problem of Psychoanalysis* (Cambridge: Cambridge University Press, 2004) pp.128–139. It is also perhaps here that we can see an instance of something like *signification in reverse* (inherent in our conceptualisation of the *sinthome* as *empty signified*) in that the signified ('jungerl') – stuffed with its signifiers ('jungle', 'Jung', 'young girl', etc.) – feeds back to and modulates these signifiers. To coin another example: although we may ourselves already question whether the unconscious homogeneously exists between Freud and Jung a conjugation such as 'the jungconscious' would force that question upon us; it would force the question of the psychoanalysts' different conceptualisations of the unconscious to open up in the very signifiers that stuff the portmanteau's signified.
111 Ellmann, *James Joyce*, p.679.

112 Jacques Lacan, *The Seminar of Jacques Lacan, Book XVI: From an Other to the other, 1968–1969*, trans. by Cormac Gallagher (London: Karnac, unofficial translation, n.d.) session IX, p.14.
113 Lacan, 'Joyce le Symptôme', in *Le seminaire XXIII: Le sinthome*, p.167 (trans. by Benanav).
114 James Joyce, *A Portrait of the Artist as a Young Man* [1916], ed. by Jeri Johnson (Oxford: Oxford World's Classics, 2000) p.213.
115 Lacan, *Le seminaire XXIII: Le sinthome*, p.69. I here rely on Luke Thurston's unofficial translation from the Seminar's appearance in the French Lacanian journal *Ornicar?* See Jacques Lacan, 'Le Sinthome: Jacques Lacan's Seminar XXIII, 1975–6', ed. by Jacques-Alain Miller, *Ornicar?* 6–11 (1975–1976), trans. by Luke Thurston, p.20. I will hereafter refer first to the French, and then in shorthand to Gallagher's translation as *Seminar XXIII: Joyce and the Sinthome* or to Thurston's as 'Le Sinthome'.
116 Lacan, *Le seminaire XXIII: Le sinthome*, p.15; Lacan, *Seminar XXIII: Joyce and the Sinthome*, session I, p.7.
117 See Jacques Aubert, 'Notes de Lecture', in *Le seminaire XXIII: Le sinthome*, p.190, and Sean O'Casey, 'Juno and the Paycock' [1924], in *Sean O'Casey: Plays One:* Juno and the Paycock, Within the Gates, Red Roses for Me *and* Cock-A-Doodle Dandy, 2 vols (London: Faber and Faber, 1998) I.
118 Joyce, *A Portrait of the Artist as a Young Man*, p.203.
119 Lacan, *Le seminaire XXIII: Le sinthome*, p.15; Lacan, *Le Sinthome*, p.3.
120 Lacan, 'Joyce le Symptôme', in *Le seminaire XXIII: Le sinthome*, p.167 (trans. by Benanav) [my emphases].
121 Ibid. pp.167–168.
122 Lacan, *Le seminaire XXIII: Le sinthome*, p.123; Lacan, *Seminar XXIII: Joyce and the Sinthome*, session IX, p.7.
123 Eric Laurent, 'The Purloined Letter and the Tao of the Psychoanalyst', in *The Later Lacan*, p.35.
124 Jacques-Alain Miller, 'The Sinthome, a Mixture of Symptom and Fantasy', in ibid. p.57.
125 Ibid. pp.57–58.
126 Ibid. p.58. I have here emphasised the word '*of*' because *as empty signified* the *sinthome* must be conceptualised as giving rise to the subject *of* the signifier that comes to fill it; a process which will be elaborated in chapter 3.
127 Lacan, 'The Signification of the Phallus' [1958], in *Écrits*, p.578.
128 Ellie Ragland, 'The Practice of the Letter and Topological Structure', in *The Literary Lacan*, p.224.
129 Lacan, 'Joyce le Symptôme', in *Le seminaire XXIII: Le sinthome*, p.161 (trans. by Benanav) [my emphasis].
130 Jacques Lacan, *The Seminar of Jacques Lacan, Book XX: Encore: On Feminine Sexuality, the Limits of Love and Knowledge, 1972–1973*, ed. by Jacques-Alain Miller, trans. by Bruce Fink (New York: W. W. Norton, 1998) p.37. As Bruce Fink glosses, '*truffer* literally means to garnish with truffles; figuratively it means to stuff, lard, fill, or pepper' (see ibid. footnote 34). Thus it is that Lacan possibly purposefully stuffs – or 'riddles', as is a further meaning of '*truffer*' – even this *signified* with another enigmatic signifier; a reference to Joyce's only meeting with Marcel Proust, in which – according to Arthur Power's famous anecdote of the event – Joyce claimed that 'all [Proust] said to me was 'Do you like truffles? 'Yes,' I replied, I am very fond of truffles.' And that was the only conversation that took place between the two most famous writers of their time.' See Arthur Power, *Conversations with James Joyce*, ed. by Clive Hart (Chicago: University of Chicago Press, 1974) p.79. Joyce also stuffs his own and Proust's names with *each other*, making: 'Marcelle Proyce and James Joust'. See James Joyce, 'Letter to Sylvia Beach, October 1922', in *James Joyce*, p.508, footnote (for more on the play with names see note 2 in chapter 3 of the present work).

131 Harari, *How James Joyce Made His Name*, p.82.

132 This, Lacan suggests – as early as 1955 – is also what the psychoanalyst deals with in their clinical practice: 'The comparison that can be made between the analyst and a rubbish dump is justified'. See Lacan, *Seminar III: The Psychoses*, p.29. Here, however, it is precisely the 'rubbish' of invaluable utterances in the analysand's speech that needs only to be 'endured' by the analyst, rather than worked on, or with.

133 Jacques-Alain Miller, 'Joyce with Lacan', trans. by Russell Grigg, in *The Literary Lacan*, pp.4–5. For an alternative translation, see Jacques-Alain Miller, 'Joyce avec Lacan – Préface', trans. by Josefina Ayerza and Cory Reynolds, *Lacanian Ink*, 11 (1995) 7–11 (p.11).

134 Theodor W. Adorno, 'Letter to Walter Benjamin, 2 August, 1935', trans. by Harry Zohn, in Theodor W. Adorno and others, *Aesthetics and Politics* [1977], ed. by Rodney Livingstone, Perry Anderson, and Francis Mulhern (London: Verso Radical Thinkers, 2007) p.118.

135 See Lacan, *Seminar XX: Encore*, p.26. This neologism, which in French connotes both 'publication' and 'dustbin' (*poubelle*), as well as something of 'beauty' (*belle*), was used by Lacan to describe his *Écrits*.

136 Geoff Boucher, 'Joyce: Lacan's Sphinx', in *The Literary Lacan*, p.164, p.142.

137 Louis Althusser, 'Freud and Lacan' [1969, in English], trans. by Ben Brewster, in *On Ideology* (London: Verso Radical Thinkers, 2008) p.156.

138 To use Derrida's phrase, the *listening* position of analyst can be construed as 'the ear of the other', which 'says me to me' in the process of analysis. See Jacques Derrida, 'Roundtable on Autobiography', in *The Ear of the Other: Otobiography, Transference, Translation* [1982], ed. by Christie McDonald, trans. by Peggy Kamuf (Lincoln: University of Nebraska Press, 1988) p.51.

139 Roudinesco, *Jacques Lacan*, p.75.

140 Jacques Lacan, 'Overture to this Collection', in *Écrits*, p.3.

141 See, for example, Jacques Lacan, *The Seminar of Jacques Lacan, Book XIX . . . Ou pire/ . . . Or worse, 1971–1972*, trans. by Cormac Gallagher (London: Karnac, unofficial translation, n.d.) session II, p.4, for this translation of '*connerie*'. In Seminar XXIII, Gallagher also uses the translation 'stupidity', and Thurston 'bullshit', whereas in Seminar XX, Fink translates Lacan's playing with the word's syllables as 'cunt-torsions'; see Lacan, *Seminar XX: Encore*, p.75.

142 Harari, *How James Joyce Made His Name*, p.122. See Jacques Lacan, *The Seminar of Jacques Lacan, Book XXIV: L'insu que sait de l'une-bévue s'aile à mourre, 1976–1977*, trans. by Cormac Gallagher (London: Karnac, unofficial translation, n.d.) session 10, pp.111–113. The title of this Seminar can be very roughly translated – in one version of many, at least – as 'One knew that it was a mistaken moon on wings of love', which is how Malcolm Bowie has it in his chronology of Lacan's works. See Malcolm Bowie, *Lacan* (Cambridge, MA: Harvard University Press, 1993) p.213.

143 Joyce, *Finnegans Wake*, p.352, 18–19 [italicised in original], p.486, 12–14. Whilst fixation on 'the little fellow in my eye' is a technique utilised in hypnosis, it has also the connotation here of the *objet petit a*; indeed, of 'the gaze, *qua objet a*', as Lacan puts it. See Lacan, *Seminar XI: The Four Fundamental Concepts of Psychoanalysis*, p.77. 'Psychosinology' – which combines 'psychology' and 'sinology', the study of China – indeed hints also at the '*sin*' of *sinthome*, and the plethora of puns that can be made from it.

144 Lacan, *Le seminaire XXIII: Le sinthome*, p.17; Lacan, *Seminar XXIII: Joyce and the Sinthome*, session I, p.9. In French, this odd formulation works as a homophonic pun: '*Ce qu'on dit ment*', pronounced like 'condiment'. Whilst this has its own context in the Seminar, it no doubt also relates to the concept of '*truffer*', as discussed in note 130 in this chapter.

145 Lacan, *Seminar III: The Psychoses*, p.37.

146 Lacan, *Le seminaire XXIII: Le sinthome*, p.17; Lacan, *Seminar XXIII: Joyce and the Sinthome*, session I, p.10.

Chapter 2

Was Joyce mad? *not by a transparent sheet . . .*

Joycean ontology

The second epigraph to Derrida's essay 'Cogito and the History of Madness' is taken from a recollection of Joyce discussing his modernist masterpiece *Ulysses* in Jacques Mercanton's 'The Hours of James Joyce'. Joyce here says of the work: 'In any event this book was terribly daring. A transparent sheet separates it from madness.'[1] Thus we return to the 'sheet' that was discussed at the beginning of chapter 1. It is this specific 'sheet' – Joyce's, with its peculiar and particular property of 'transparency' – that we will now attempt to theorise in relation to the centrality we have found it to hold for Saussure, and then by combining it with Lacan's polar reference to the symptom and the '*sinthome*' in the next chapter. It will be by invoking the unificatory/separatory principle outlined at the outset of this work that we shall attempt to commence this theorisation.

First, however, we should confront a criticism that this principle may be open to receiving, which is that it is, in effect, a readymade, a model into which can be put any three contents or criteria interchangeably; into the positions of A, 1, and 2 in the diagram shown in the previous chapter, Figure 1.1. In what we have looked at so far we would have to put – from Macherey, for example – 'coherence' in position A, '*endroit*' in 1, and '*envers*' in 2. By replacing Macherey's 'principle of coherence' with our less value-oriented unificatory/separatory principle, we could – from our other examples – position in A, from Roche, 'EN', in 1 'droit', and in 2 'vers', or in A Saussure's sheet, and in 1 thought, and in 2 sound. Similarly we could place linguistics in A, psychology in 1, and phonetics in 2; the unconscious in A, reading in 1, and writing in 2; or the 'transparent sheet' in A, *Ulysses* (and Joyce, vicariously) in 1, and madness in 2.

As a model it is not, however, any the less valid for the aforementioned criticism; it still works to clarify certain relations between certain things, and in especial cases it may prove to be the only valid means of such demonstration. In *The Four Fundamental Concepts of Psychoanalysis* Lacan makes a distinction between the terms '*model*' and '*Grundbegriff*', or '*fundamental concept*', suggesting that a 'model is never a *Grundbegriff*, for, in a certain field several models may function correlatively'; however, 'this is not the case for a *Grundbegriff*, for a fundamental concept', which must by definition be the *only* functor in its field.[2] Thus we will set out to demonstrate that in the case of the unconscious the unificatory/separatory principle may be the only functor by which it can be represented; that is, that its position must always be A, that it is in no circumstance placeable in positions 1 or 2.

Irreducible antagonism

Now to draw a short genealogy: having evoked this principle's utilisation in the linguistic and literary theories of Saussure and Macherey, as well as briefly in others, it will be demonstratively worthwhile tracing it through some works of other thinkers linked with our analysis, working towards examples findable in the working and literary methods and tropes of James Joyce.

We begin with Marx and Freud. It is identified early in *Capital* that 'the sale and the purchase [of a commodity] constitute one identical act, an exchange between a commodity-owner and an owner of money, between two persons as opposed to each other as the two poles of a magnet'.[3] Initially, we can see how we are actually met with two derivable models here, the first being that of a commodity and the second of its sale-purchase: so, in the first instance, into position A goes the commodity, and into 1 sale, and into 2 purchase; and in the second, into A goes sale-purchase (as 'one identical act'), and into 1 the commodity-owner, and into 2 the money-owner. However, it is the fact that this pronouncement of Marx's draws our attention to the very structurality of 'antagonism' in his system that is of interest here. In the second instance, Marx stresses that the two owners that are involved in the act of a sale-purchase are as opposed as the poles of a magnet. The magnet here holds the place of *antagonism*, in that as well as separating these adversarial poles, it also binds them. This concept of antagonism, which will become essential to this work, has already had its importance elaborated by Althusser and his students in their reading of Marx, as is demonstrated by Étienne Balibar's definition in *Reading Capital*:

> 'Antagonism', 'not in the sense of individual antagonism' (*nicht im individuellen Sinn*), i.e., not a struggle between men but an antagonistic structure; it is *inside the economic base*, typical of a determinate mode of production, and its terms are called 'the level of the productive forces' and 'the relations of production'.[4]

It is an antagonistic structure, *inside the base of things*, that constitutes such an 'identical' – though non-self-identical – act as a commodity's sale/purchase. Thus, the identical act is itself radically antagonistic *in itself*; i.e., its structure (or form) is an antagonism which, when sided by its contents – in this case, the buyer (money-owner) and seller (commodity-owner) – becomes apparent; the poles which constitute it are united and separated at once, repellent to one another, but bound, like the poles of a magnet; and a magnet is always structured by its poles: a magnetic monopole is a physical impossibility.

In Freud similar instances abound – we will concentrate on those in his article on the 'Mystic Writing-Pad' later – and we will here take an interesting example from his 1905 work, *Jokes and Their Relation to the Unconscious*, in which he early on makes this observation about the technique of jokes:

> Technique alone is insufficient to characterize the nature of jokes. Something further is needed which we have not yet discovered. But on the other hand it remains an uncontradicted fact that if we undo the technique of a joke it disappears. For the time being we may find difficulty in thinking how these two fixed points that we have arrived at in explaining jokes can be reconciled.[5]

The two points which have here already been arrived at in explaining the joke-work are the techniques of 'displacement' and 'representation by the opposite', and the third necessary connector, which is hinted at by Freud, is of course the unconscious, to which these points relate, and *in which* jokes and their effects are formed. That the unconscious can occupy only the position of the unificatory/separatory principle (position A in Figure 1.1) is here demonstrable in the fact that Freud points out; if the technique of a joke is undone it will disappear; its technique must remain unconscious, and in remaining so it at once unites *and* separates the constituent parts of the joke-work; i.e., in terms of displacement it unites and separates the original idea to and from what it is displaced by, and in representation by the opposite it unites and separates the original idea and its opposed stand-in in the joke. We will return to these theories of Freud's in due course, especially in relation to Joyce's jocular – or, rather, *jocoserious* – constructions in *Finnegans Wake*.[6]

We even find the principle itself still at work in such fields as quantum physics, in the theory of 'agential realism', for example, for which – as Žižek explains, through Karen Barad – the 'basic ontological unit is the *phenomenon* in which both sides are irreducibly and inextricably entangled: phenomena display "the ontological inseparability of objects and apparatuses" '; i.e., when taking a measurement in quantum mechanics the very act of measuring affects the results; this is due to the apparatus being one side of the '*phenomenon*', and that which is measured the other, or to put it in our principle's terms, position A is the *phenomenon*, 1 the measurable, and 2 the measuring apparatus.[7]

Joyce himself was aware of the underpinnings of this principle and made use of them even in some of his earliest writings, as we can see from his 1912 essay – written originally in Italian – 'The Universal Literary Influence of the Renaissance', in which he finds the principle in the work of his favourite philosopher: 'Giordano Bruno himself says that all power, whether in nature or the spirit, must create an opposing power without which man cannot fulfil himself, and he adds that in every such separation there is a tendency towards a reunion.'[8] Although couched in the more metaphysical, and even magical, language that Bruno employs, the unificatory/separatory principle is nonetheless at the very core of the Nolan thinker's system, in which 'contraries coincide both in principle and reality', as he puts it (coincidents of contraries, for example, such as in the '*endroit*' and the '*envers*').[9] Rather than merely referring to a somewhat mystical notion of yin and yang forces (which, as we have seen, for example, Jung based his ideas of the masculine and feminine on), here in Bruno, and certainly in Joyce's reading of him, there is an emphasis on 'separation' *and* 'reunion', on the tendency towards reunion that is inherent in separation, which much resembles the structurality of a magnet, as well as that of the *fort/da* scene, in which a child separates himself or herself to and from a toy, for example, to learn to cope with separation from and reunion with loved ones: according to this principle, then, without a zero-level opposition of some kind (an 'opposing power') there would not be able to come into being anything at all (any 'power' in itself); there would be no ontology.

Joyce perceives these workings too in Christianity – the religion which had been so pivotal in shaping his outlook on life and the world – and especially in relation to the Christianity that had torn his country, Ireland, in two. In the lecture 'Ireland: Island of Saints and Sages' he pithily describes the 'coherent absurdity' of Catholicism as the other side of 'the incoherent absurdity that is Protestantism'; and it is this religion – riven by these two prominent sides – that had of course held much sway over the literary scene in early twentieth-century Ireland.[10] Indeed, Willard Potts in his *Joyce and the Two Irelands* shows how this unificatory/separatory principle had taken its full effect in relation to religion and the divisions it had instantiated that in some ways served to unite the ambitions of the Irish Literary Revival, which aspired to W. B. Yeats's goal of arriving at a 'unity of culture', in response to the separations caused by religious and political rifts.[11] In *Ulysses* too Joyce brings out a deep dualism at the heart of his country, in Stephen Dedalus's conversation with the Englishman, Haines:

> – I am a servant of two masters, Stephen said, an English and an Italian.
> – Italian? Haines said.
> A crazy queen, old and jealous. Kneel down before me.
> – And a third, Stephen said, there is who wants me for odd jobs.
> – Italian? Haines said again. What do you mean?
> – The imperial British state, Stephen answered, his colour rising, and the holy Roman catholic and apostolic church.[12]

Of course, it is again identifiable here that an antagonism is at the centre of things: in the religious instance, Christianity's core can be seen as inherently antagonistic, spawning – from position A – Catholicism, 1, and Protestantism, 2, in Ireland. The two Irelands that Potts identifies similarly can be seen to spring from this antagonism at the heart of the country, and this extends to Joyce's deployment of the concept of Stephen's being a servant to two masters, an English and an Italian. Marian Eide, in her *Ethical Joyce*, claims that 'the authority that sometimes calls on Stephen for odd jobs is Erin, the errant island nation', and suggests that 'Stephen hears the nation *Eire* (the Irish word for Ireland) as err or error'.[13] Errancy and error are certainly tied up with the political history of the country – as will be explored in relation to the (mis)spelling of the word 'hesitancy', and its role in *Finnegans Wake*, subsequently – but it is perhaps here also readable in Joyce's words that what calls on Stephen for odd jobs is his subjectivity itself, at an irreducible and necessitous point, to put it in structuralist terms; as *indivisible remainder*. Irish subjectivity, for Joyce in 1904, is thus necessarily sided by British State imperialism – and its Protestantism – and the Roman Catholic Church; as the *signifiers which represent the subject one to another*.

These points, from the early Joyce – which hint at something of his ontological bearing, in relation to the previously identified principle and the centrality of antagonism – remained all-important factors for him, through *Ulysses*, as we have seen, right into the composition of *Finnegans Wake*, the technique of which Jacques Mercanton draws out and makes comment on in his interviews with and discussion of Joyce in his article. In recopying pages for Joyce, Mercanton received the writer's guidance on how to read the *Wake*, through the explanations of his compositional techniques. 'As we read' – Mercanton comments, about he and Joyce reading over the pre-published work's pages together –

> he showed me the constant factors which, according to him, were intended to guide the reader. Thus, a Japanese word would always be followed by a Chinese word – an image for the antagonism that is the permanent background to the history of all men.[14]

In this image we can find a match for the very unificatory/separatory principle we have been discussing throughout, and in relation to its structural link with antagonism. In effect – and he does so explicitly later on – Joyce names antagonism itself as that which resides (always already) in position A; that is, antagonism will thus always be inherent in whatever we place in position A, and will be the very structurality of position A itself, which is to be sided by other, ingeminous criteria; a Japanese word and a Chinese word in this example. This placing of words from multiple languages in the singular language of a sentence in *Finnegans Wake* – as well, of course, as throughout the work as a whole – is strongly evocative of the story of Babel, and places it in a position of ontological originariness; a position which we will return to in relation to Derrida's essay 'Two Words for Joyce' – and his discursions on Babel in *The Post Card* – in chapter 5, suffice it to point out, here, that (in one version of the story at least) it is the *fall* of the tower of Babel that begins things.[15]

Situating antagonism as the 'background to the history of all things' – as Mercanton infers that Joyce does – gives us the indication of antagonism as the point of irreducibility for Joyce, as the base structurality of things; the ontological unity of the 'phenomenon', in Barad's sense. Also, this position for antagonism in Joyce's logic accords with its position as belonging to the Real in Lacan's terms, and with its links to the Freudian *navel*, as well as of course to its centrality in Marx. Indeed, Joyce says as much when questioned by Mercanton about the dream-structurality of *Finnegans Wake*, and we return here to his response to those who had criticised his 'Work in Progress' with charges of its arbitrariness, as mentioned in the previous chapter:

> It is I who could draw up the best indictment against my work. Isn't it arbitrary to pretend to express the nocturnal life by means of conscious work, or through children's games?" [. . .]
>
> "Isn't it arbitrary of me to make use of forty tongues I don't know in order to express the dream state? Isn't it contradictory to make two men speak Chinese and Japanese in a pub in Phoenix Park, Dublin? Nevertheless, that is a logical and objective method of expressing a deep conflict, an irreducible antagonism."[16]

As Joseph Campbell and Henry Morton Robinson put it in their *A Skeleton Key to* Finnegans Wake (1944): 'In short, the antagonists [here, the Chinese and Japanese words] are the two sides of a one-same power of nature. [. . .] They are 'polarised for reunion by the symphysis of their antipathies'', as Joyce has it in the *Wake* itself.[17] Nevertheless, Joyce seemed to have been be aiming at something which Freud was conscious of being an impossibility in the interpretation of dreams – that is, a representation of the navel itself – despite being aware that its expression by means of any conscious work was an impossibility, or, at best, arbitrary guesswork, which had to be pretended, this being a certain disavowal in Joyce in the Mannonian formula of: 'I know well, but all the same . . .', to which we will return later. But 'that is what Joyce *want*[*ed*] to convey: what goes on in a dream, during a dream. Not what is left over afterward, in the memory.'[18] As Joyce thereafter put it, as if precisely addressing the navel of the dream: 'Afterward, nothing is left." He shrugged his shoulders. "Afterward, nothing will be left."'[19] Afterward – as Patrice Maniglier aptly summates – what we have left is nothing of the dream, but only 'the endless process of associations, that is, in the substitution of signs which constitute the interpretation'.[20]

The fall

This irreducibility that Joyce attributes to antagonism thus places it, as we have said, at a point of origin, though of course not at a singular, unified, organic, or prelapsarian point, with which origin is often conflated, but at, or in, a more fuzzy and shifting, aggravated field of difference and deferral, at a place of non-fixity such as is findable in Derrida's concept of *différance*, which precisely takes in both these notions of difference and deferral at once.[21] Thus, in this place, as Žižek puts it in his essay 'A Plea for a Return to *Différance*', the 'logic of 'the 'minimal difference', of the constitutive non-coincidence of a thing with itself' is in operation; this is the logic of the antagonism that is necessitous to position A in Figure 1.1., which is the originary split that then allows of Bruno's coincidence of contraries, which, as the central antagonism's sides, go on to occupy positions 1 and 2.[22] Antagonism being *central* to the unificatory/separatory principle thus makes of it *decenterment* itself, and it is in that this split is the principle's *truth* that we arrive also at calling it the principle of '*enverity*'; encompassing the truth, *verity*, of the always-implied (but inarticulable, because of truth's *half-sayableness*) other side, the *envers*. As Lacan himself precisely puts it in 'Responses to Students of Philosophy Concerning the Object of Psychoanalysis' in the *Cahiers pour l'Analyse*:

> It is, on the contrary, at that moment of coincidence itself, insofar as it is grasped by reflection, that I intend to mark the site through which psychoanalytic experience makes its entrance. At simply being sustained within time, the subject of 'I think' reveals what it is: the being of a fall. I am that which thinks: 'Therefore I am', as I have commented on elsewhere, noting that the 'therefore', the causal stroke, divides inaugurally the 'I am' of existence from the 'I am' of meaning.[23]

Here we see the *fall* as a 'causal stroke', an 'inaugural divider', a 'unifier/separator' the non-coincidence of which is at the heart of subjectivity, a subjectivity which then – in the *coincidence*, the '*forced choice*' of being, or existence, and meaning – thus wears the 'armor of an alienating identity', as Lacan calls it in 'The Mirror Stage', as this coincidence comes in at the point of *registration* – of connection and disconnection at once – that is lynchpin of the imaginary order.[24]

In terms of the Fall, and its originariness; in its historical contextualisation, we see that common to Western tradition – founded on the theological model of the Judeo-Christian belief system – is the placement of our origin in a prelapsarian moment (at the point of the creation of the world of Adam and Eve and the Garden of Eden at the beginning of the Bible); a thinking which has seeped over into so many discourses outside of its religiosity; i.e., into – in terms of ecology – the belief that nature is a unified whole from which we have fallen and thus retrospectively corrupted. A certain postmodern, or existentialist, counterargument to this would be that the prelapsarian moment never existed, and we have always found ourselves in the postlapsarian world; a certain dystopia in which disunity and corruption is always already present (however, in this, there is still some implication of prelapsarianism, albeit disavowed, as we will soon see). In contradistinction to these, 'Joycean ontology' seems placeable in a third originary structure, that of *the lapsarian moment itself*; thus, rather than there having been a pre-existing unity (pre-existing our disunity) to which we should strive to return, or a sudden entrance into a place which is always already a disunity, in which any idea of a previous unity is a lie, Joyce is perhaps taking as his springboard *the moment of the Fall itself.*

We can evoke something of this from a close reading of a sentence from another of Joyce's early works, his article on James Clarence Mangan of 1902, in which he states that 'surely life, which Novalis has called a malady of the spirit, is a heavy penance for him who has, perhaps, forgotten the sin that laid it upon him.'[25] Contrary, for example, to R.W. Maslen's assessment of Sir Philip Sidney's – and the poet in general's – (ontological) point of departure, in which 'the poet takes the fallen world merely as his starting point, his imaginative springboard to higher things', which takes the previously identified postmodern position (and thus premonitorily so), Joyce here is not suggesting that life sets off from a point already in the fallen world, from what original sin has led to.[26] Instead, Joyce identifies *sin itself* as that which lays life upon one; he doesn't hark to a pre-existing life prior to sin, but claims sin, the Fall, as the originary moment; in Adaline Glasheen's words, he 'postulates a steady state of Creation-Fall'.[27] Thus, Joyce here seems to be in accord with the precise way in which Žižek reads Hegel's ontology, for whom:

> The story he is telling in his account of a dialectical process is not the story of how an original organic unity alienates itself from itself, but the story of how this organic unity never existed in the first place, of how its status is by definition that of a retroactive fantasy – the Fall itself generates the mirage of what it is the Fall from.[28]

Thus, this postulation of Joycean ontology – which we see repeated in his work from the aforementioned moment in the Mangan essay to *Finnegans Wake*, which, it can be claimed, *always begins with a fall* – leads us to a rendering of our unificatory/separatory model which has ontological consequences in theology and philosophy alike, in which we must place in position A, *lapsarianism*, or the Fall itself, in 1, *prelapsarianism*, and in 2, *postlapsarianism*; indeed, in accord with Žižek's earlier reading of Hegel, the notions either of there having ever been a prelapsarian world, place, or moment, or of there having been an origin in an always-already-there postlapsarian world are only the consequences of lapsarianism itself, retroactively generating its own myth; or, to put it in Lacan's terms, it is the (contingent) generation in the Real of our symbolic-imaginary ontological status.

Joycean sanity

Thus, with reference to the principle of *enverity*, or the unificatory/separatory principle, we have arrived at a notion of Joycean ontology in respect to the centrality of an irreducible antagonism, which the notion of the Fall exemplifies in thus not only theological, but also philosophical, ontological terms. It will now be by working with the late topologies of Lacan that we will attempt to arrive at a psychoanalytic reading of the notion of the 'transparent sheet' that Joyce brought up in his conversation with Mercanton, and that Derrida uses as an epigraph to his essay on madness.

Transparency

The notion of the transparent sheet, of transparency in general, obviously made an impression on Mercanton, as he draws reference to it again at the end of his recollective piece, in describing Joyce: 'I noticed again in that peaceful and smiling face, under the hair turned white, the pallor, the wear, and as it were a nocturnal transparency.'[29] Mercanton's impression is of nocturnality and transparency having left their impression on Joyce. Why this may have been the case we will look at first in relation to transparency, disavowal, and opacity, and then with further elaboration in relation to Lacan's dual notions of symptom and *sinthome* in the coming chapter.

In the essay '"Je sais bien, mais quand meme . . ."' – '"I Know Well, but All the Same . . ."' in English – Octave Mannoni attempts to define and clarify Freud's term *Verleugnung*, or 'Disavowal', by making reference first to Jean Laplanche and Jean-Bertrand Pontalis's dictionary, *The Language of Psychoanalysis* – in which the term is rendered in French '*le déni de la réalité*' ('the denial of reality') – and through claiming that an experience that is disavowed is 'not effaced; [bu]t becomes permanently ineffaceable: it leaves an *indelible stigma* [and in the case of the *Wake*, an *indelible sigla*] with which the fetishist is forever marked'.[30] Disavowal is thus here linked to fetishism – as it is in Freud – in that whatever has been refuted is thereafter preserved as a fetish; the refutation itself being repudiated, or disavowed. In the earliest, infantile, example, 'when a child first becomes aware of the anatomy of the female body [the mother's], he discovers, in reality, the absence of a penis'; thereafter the fetishist 'disavow[s] the experience that proves to him that women do not have a phallus, but he does not cultivate the belief that they do have one; he cultivates a fetish because they *do not* have one'.[31]

To apply this to Joyce, if we take him at his word: if he was able to perceive that a transparent sheet separated his book from madness this is to suggest that he was able to perceive the madness itself that the sheet separated it from, through said sheet's transparency; this sheet then, with its property of transparency, appears to be one of disavowal, allowing Joyce to perceive the madness beyond, but to not fall into it: 'I know well the madness there, but all the same . . .'. However, this does not actually fit entirely neatly into the Mannonian formula for disavowal as, although there may be the secondary repudiation of madness via the transparent sheet – that which separates *Ulysses*, or Joyce, from madness – in the 'all the same . . .', there is not the primary refutation of madness itself; it could be said rather to be courted via the transparent sheet, as opposed to being defended against by it. Thus, whilst it certainly encompasses elements of fetishistic disavowal, Joyce's statement should perhaps here be read in terms of radical *decision*, embracing the inflection that Derrida gives to this notion in his 'Cogito and the History of Madness':

> The Decision, through a single act, links and separates madness, and it must be understood at once both as the original act of an order, a fiat, a decree, and as a schism, a caesura, a separation, a dissection. I would prefer *dissension*, to underline that in question is a self-dividing action, a cleavage and torment interior to meaning *in general*, interior to logos in general.[32]

Here we see again the operation of the unificatory/separatory principle, in the simultaneous occurrence of *link* and *separation*, in a *decision*, encompassing fastening and schisming. Decision itself is often typically seen as a process of link, bridging one manifest formation to another, as the latter formation would only be arrivable at through a decision being taken or made. But, in Derrida, the *undecidable* is always inherently involved in an act of decision; i.e., in its fullest realisation, if a decision could *genuinely* go either way (which can only be an idealised fantasy, in its discounting any hierarchal preferentiality), then the moment of decision itself can only be pervaded by a certain madness at its locus (in the place of antagonism in position A, with that which it can go either way to being sides 1 and 2); 'a decision worthy of its name (if there is any) must take place in the midst of the undecidable', as Simon Morgan Wortham has it.[33] To write this decision, in its fullness, as '*de-scission*' – as a replacement for Derrida's '*dissension*' – might be psychoanalytically preferable here, in that this neologism renders the *cut*, in both the prefix '*de-*', and in '*scission*'; the *link* of decision; and the *decidedness* of decision too, in that once a *de-scission* has been made, a certain fidelity to its effects must come into play, as it represents a moment of decided, irrecoverable, and irrevocable change, its happening, or having happened – an *event* itself – and one that comes about precisely through the *forced choice*, which, as we have seen, is both a choice *and* an imposition at once. Indeed, as the Lacanian philosopher Alain Badiou describes it:

> [Such] an evental fidelity is a real break (both thought and practised) in the specific order within which the event [has taken] place (be it political, loving, artistic or scientific . . .). I shall call 'truth' (*a* truth) the real process of fidelity to an event: that which this fidelity *produces* in the situation.[34]

Such a *de-scission* thus also stresses the determining impossibility of neutrality; that is, that there is antagonism – *différance* – at the base of things, rather than an innocuous neutral state.

This rendering also allows us to relink the concept with fetishistic disavowal. In Lloyd C. Parks's translation of Joyce's phrase from Mercanton's article, Joyce is made to say, 'nonetheless, that book was a terrible risk. A transparent leaf separates it from madness.'[35] The first clause of the phrase is almost exactly that of an 'I know well, but all the same . . .', but it is the transparent separatory leaf that still unsettles things here. As mentioned earlier, madness is not initially refuted for – or by – Joyce, in the manner in which the refutation of the female phallus comes about through the observation of its lack in the female anatomy, which then goes on to be repudiated by the fetishist. Madness is apparently there in full view for Joyce, unrefuted, and which he courts in *Ulysses*, but he repudiates it only through the deployment of the transparent sheet, linking him to it whilst separating him from it. In terms of the *de-scission* then, Joyce's repudiation via the transparent sheet is preserved in its link of separation, and through this he *decides* to embrace that madness, work with it, create from it. The *de-scission* can thus be seen as *the cutting out of a cut*, in something of the mode of Hegelian sublation, which cancels and yet preserves a concept at once, raising it to a new dimension; the cut is here excerpted and utilised, in part through fetishistic disavowal, which is risk-reducing, but also in part through 'terrible daring' – in courting and playing with madness (psychosis) – which is of course a tremendous risk.

When Joyce made this pronouncement concerning the transparent sheet that separated *Ulysses* from madness the work had already been in print for over a decade and he had been in the process of the composition of 'Work in Progress' for that amount of time too; it is therefore not too much of a push to see the statement as transposable also to the working methodologies involved in the creation of *Finnegans Wake*. As a working methodology, or creative tool – specifically for writing – we will now look at the two-sided transparent sheet in relation to Freud's 'A Note Upon the Mystic Writing-Pad' (1925), in which he refers to and explains the toy writing device, and from which I will quote at length:

> The Mystic Pad is a slab of dark brown resin or wax with a paper edging; over the slab is laid a thin transparent sheet, the top end of which is firmly secured to the slab while its bottom end rests on it without being fixed to it. This transparent sheet is the more interesting part of the little device. It itself consists of two layers, which can be detached from each other, except at their two ends. The upper layer is a transparent piece of celluloid; the lower layer is made of a thin translucent waxed paper. When the apparatus is not in use, the lower surface of the waxed paper adheres lightly to the upper surface of the wax slab.
>
> To make use of the Mystic Pad, one writes upon the celluloid portion of the covering-sheet which rests upon the wax slab[:] a pointed stilus scratches the surface, the depressions upon which constitute the 'writing'. [. . .] If one wishes to destroy what has been written, all that is necessary is to raise the double covering-sheet from the wax slab by a light pull, starting from the free lower end.[36]

The Mystic Writing-Pad, a toy device still familiar today, bears a remarkable relation, for Freud, to the systematicity of the psyche, but also here to the systematicity of creation and composition in Joyce, which relates to how he may have kept what many saw as the insanity that would inevitably envelop him – as it had his daughter – at bay. Jung of course was a proponent of this point of view that a latent form of the madness that afflicted Lucia was in Joyce, but the latter's 'defiant attitude was that she was no madder than her father'.[37] Ellmann, however, argues that Joyce 'was bitterly sane, and foolish fond like Lear', being linked yet separated, as he and his work were, by this transparent sheet, acting as a screen through which to see madness, whilst protecting against it.[38] Indeed, as Miller suggests in 'Lacan with Joyce', in relation to this, and in a precise rendering of the 'protective' quality of the sheet:

> Joyce was compelled to put the relation between sound and sense down black on white, for he was not totally protected from the echoes [of language] by the Name-of-the-Father, any more than he could protect his own daughter, who was schizophrenic. Writing functioned as a screen [*paravent*] to protect him from the infinite echoes of language;

whilst – we must add – of course providing him access to these, compositionally.[39]

As has already been touched upon, and as will be discussed at length in chapter 4, Joyce uses his *sinthome* – compositionally, in his writing – to knot the insufficiently tied triad of the Real, Symbolic, and Imaginary, and to supplement the (constitutively) lacking Name-of-the-Father. It is this constitutivity of the Name-of-the-Father that provides the reason for Lacan's reinforcing its absolute essentiality in the *Sinthome* Seminar, as *even in its lack* it constitutes our subjectivity, as is shown in both Joyce's and Lucia's cases. As is stressed in the title of Lacan's twenty-first Seminar, even those 'non-dupes' who have realised that there is no Name-of-the-Father – as there is no Other – err in this belief (this being due – as Lacan had earlier derived from the work of Jeremy Bentham – to the subject's necessitous reliance on the structure of fiction), and how better to phrase this than in the French which antithetically contains both of these sentiments: *Les non-dupes errant*? The non-dupes err in *les nom du père/parent* ('the name of the father/parent').[40]

Thus it is that the transparent sheet, in its psychical and compositional attributes, is all-important for both Freud and Joyce. In explaining the doubled property of the transparent sheet in the writing-pad Freud goes on to say:

> If, while the Mystic Pad has writing on it, we cautiously raise the celluloid from the waxed paper, we can see the writing just as clearly on the surface of the latter, and the question may arise of why there should be any necessity for the celluloid portion of the cover. Experiment will then show that the thin paper would be very easily crumpled or torn if one were to write directly upon it with the stilus. The layer of celluloid thus acts as a protective sheath for the paper, to keep off injurious effects from without. The celluloid is a 'protective shield against stimuli'; the layer which actually receives the stimuli is the paper. I may at this point recall that in *Beyond the Pleasure Principle* [ibid., 18, 27 ff.] I showed that the perceptual apparatus of our mind consists of two layers, of an external protective shield against stimuli whose task it is to diminish the strength of excitations coming in, and of a surface behind it which receives the stimuli, namely the system *Pcpt.–Cs*.[41]

There is again much in this that may relate to Joyce's transparent sheet, in its role as a 'protective sheath' that defends against the injurious effects of the madness it separates Joyce and his work from, and yet links it to, by providing a window to it. To put these reflections back into the terms of the principle of *enverity* we can postulate that behind the 'two layers' of the perceptual apparatus of the mind that Freud mentions lies the unconscious as their organisatory principle, that is, *as the wax slab*. Finally, Freud remarks that, after lifting the covering-sheet,

> the Mystic Pad is clear of writing and once more capable of receiving impressions. But it is easy to discover that the permanent trace of what was written is retained upon the wax slab itself and is legible in suitable lights. Thus the Pad provides not only a receptive surface that can be used over and over

> again, like a slate, but also permanent traces of what has been written, like an ordinary paper pad: it solves the problem of combining the two functions *by dividing them between two separate but interrelated component parts or systems*. But this is precisely the way in which, according to the hypothesis which I mentioned just now, our mental apparatus performs its perceptual function. The layer which receives the stimuli – the system *Pcpt.–Cs.* – forms no permanent traces; the foundations of memory come about in other, adjoining, systems.[42]

Here once again we see how a solution for a problem concerning how to combine two functions is arrived at through *dividing* them, uniting and separating them at once. In this relation, Joyce's transparent sheet, although he gives no indication of its being two-ply like the writing-pad's, is nonetheless *two-sided*, in the same sense as Saussure's example, the sheet of paper which cannot be cut with scissors side from side. Thus, to simplify Freud's analogy in combining it with Joyce's we might postulate that there is an adhesion between the underside of Joyce's single transparent sheet and the 'wax slab' it sticks to; in this case, madness. The upper side receives the impressions that Joyce may make and transfers them to this underside – which adheres more strongly to the wax slab, displaying said depressions – but in its capacity as receptor it also acts as the shield protecting Joyce from the inscriptions, whilst, of course, allowing him to see them; it is indeed enabling of both writing *and* reading.

On the other side, as Freud points out, is the permanent trace – the indelible sigla of the remaining impressions on the wax slab – which Joyce is able to remain separated from because of this remarkable transparent covering-sheet, which he designated himself in his discussions with Jacques Mercanton. Whilst these conceptualisations might seem to form a highly theoretical interaction with a singular phrase, their importance should become perceivable as we here bring them in relation with psychoanalytic reflections on the phenomenon of the psychoses.

As Clayton Crockett suggests, for Lacan 'psychosis is the refusal to enter into the symbolic order, to cling to the Real, and, since this is impossible, it results in hallucinations.'[43] In theoretical terms, concerning hallucinations, in 'On a Question Prior to Any Possible Treatment of Psychosis' Lacan maintains that 'a hallucination is a *perceptum* without an object', and that it is often dealt with in treatment by asking the *percipiens* (the subject of the perception) to solely account for it; this, however, misses the step 'of inquiring whether the *perceptum* itself bequeaths a univocal meaning to the *percipiens* who is asked here to explain it'.[44] This step, which demonstrates that a hallucination is not reducible 'to any particular *sensorium*, and especially not to any *percipiens*', initially suggests that psychoses and their hallucinations nonetheless occupy a significative place – that of a type of echo chamber – in the Real, despite their decathexis from (consensus) reality, which is the symbolic order, or, indeed, from the (individual) reality which – as Lacan labelled it in the Joyce Seminar – is the symptom.[45] As Jung said of Joyce's work, such hallucinations then perhaps 'constitute a message, though not yet understood'. Indeed, as has so often been attributed to them, the linguistic constructions in *Finnegans Wake* display this hallucinatory quality in their chameleon ability to singularly present multiple meanings at once; 'the expression of the[ir] concepts [is] achieved only through the rhythmic "hallucination of the word" ', as Eugène Jolas had put it in his 1928 manifesto 'The Revolution of the Word', drawing on a phrase of Arthur Rimbaud's.[46]

Lacan exemplifies these very reflections in his own reading of a line that he privileges from *Finnegans Wake*, and in so doing he demonstrates the necessity of the step of inquiring into whether the *perceptum* in hallucination has a univocal meaning for the *percipiens*, or even if it's reducible to a particular *sensorium* (in that his reading incorporates elements of both phonic and scopic transformation). The line is: 'Who ails tongue coddeau, aspace of dumbillsilly?', in which Lacan – citing the assistance of Jacques Aubert in locating this phrase – purportedly finds the French: '*Où est ton cadeau, espèce d'imbécile?*'.[47] This phrase roughly translates back into English as 'where is your gift, you imbecile?', the question of which we will address in the next chapter, and will become crucial to the remaining work. Lacan in fact asks in 'Joyce the Symptom': 'If I had encountered this text in writing, would I or not perceive: '*Où est ton cadeau, espèce d'imbécile?*'[48] The reason perhaps for the rhetorical tone of this question is that the transliteration in fact comes from William York Tindall's 1969 work *A Reader's Guide to* Finnegans Wake, in which it appears as a suggested bilingual rendering of the original sentence; a fact that was no doubt not lost on the congregation of Joyceans at the fifth Symposium, and is thus hinted at – but not said explicitly – by Lacan.[49] We see in the roundabout way that this hallucination of the *Wake*'s original words was arrived at Lacan's very point about univocity of meaning in relation to hallucination, in that if Lacan is the uncertain recipient of the Frenchified question – the wary *percipiens* of its hallucination – it is because its singularity has in fact not come from him but from Tindall, who by proxy stands in for a place (the symbolic) in the real; that is, for the big Other. Lacan has thus acted out here the (*psychotically-supposed*) intervention of the Real, and so it is that Tindall's *singular* reading must remain clear of being seen as a *univocal* one, as it only comes from this particular ego – Tindall's – finding its reflection in Joyce's, in the words of his original; subsequently picked up on by Lacan.

In his third Seminar, *The Psychoses*, Lacan suggests that

> the moment the hallucination appears in the real, that is, accompanied by the sense of reality, which is the elementary phenomenon's basic feature, the subject literally speaks with his ego, and it's as if a third party, his lining, were speaking and commenting on his activity.[50]

Here, *the other side*, the lining, the hallucination itself, is shown in fact to be a semblance; accompanied only by *a sense* of reality, and only *as if* it were a third party, but it is indeed the subject's *ego* that is spoken with. Lacan's later pronouncement, 'that there is no Other of the Other', meaning 'that there is no metalanguage that can be spoken', clarifies things here.[51] The hallucination is thus not the Real, or the big Other itself, speaking, breaking into the symbolic – as it might be perceived as by the *percipiens* – but rather it is the ego as it enters the Real and becomes a *perceptum* of its *objectlessness*, of its guarantorial absence, speaking into a silence that, if the echo of which is heard, is reinscribed in the symbolic; thus, the hallucination is the ego mistaking itself for occupying an impossible place in the Real, that of the Other of the Other. Therefore, a metalanguage does not speak in the Real, but its emptiness the subject may articulate to itself via the supposed reception of a hallucinatory *perceptum*. It is, then, a psychosis without this hallucination – without its *paranoiac* aspect – that risks becoming lost to *incommunicability*, a threat that Derrida suggests looms in his reflections on madness, as is touched on later.

In terms of Lacan's three orders – Real, Symbolic, and Imaginary – as we began to demonstrate in the previous chapter, if they are put into the positions of our principle of *enverity* they are liable to oscillate each between each position, because of what Lacan calls their shared and equal 'consistence', and 'continuity'.[52] In the previous examples the Real obviously does not speak, but it seems to echo: to echo the psychotic hallucination, its 'madness'; that is, at base, to echo the ego of the subject. Indeed, in Seminar III, Lacan delineates how that when the question concerning the psychoses – '*Who speaks?*' – was finally asked, 'it constituted a small revolution to observe that the source of auditory hallucination was not external.'[53] In coming from the ego, and being returned by the echo in the Real, the hallucination is then reinscribed in the symbolic, via an imaginary relation. Thus, even in such a model as this, of psychosis, the equivalence of the orders and their operations maintains the impossibility of placing any one in the rivening position of antagonism (position A). Thus, if the orders remain consistent in the psyche a certain order can be maintained; however, if they become out of kilter, a fourth term will need to be introduced, the *sinthome*, which Lacan later brings in in relation to Joyce.

In *The Psychoses* Lacan suggests that 'the dialectical changeability of actions, desires, and values' – that is taken as being characteristic of psychosis – 'is characteristic of human behavior' in general.[54] Hence, by combining the previous propositions we can see now why in the Joyce Seminar the later Lacan suggests that

> there is no relation between paranoiac psychosis and the personality. Because it's the same thing. In so far as a subject makes a triple knot of the imaginary, the symbolic, and the real, its only support is their continuity; all three have one and the same consistence. And this is what paranoiac psychosis consists of.[55]

Lacan is making this comment in relation to his doctoral thesis, *Paranoiac Psychosis and its Relation to the Personality*, and gives the fact that he now sees paranoiac psychosis and the personality as the same thing as the reason for his not having had it published.[56] This equation of the two has become central to subsequent Lacanian analysis, and is that which forms the thesis of Darian Leader's work *What is Madness?*, which he begins by asking the question: 'Are delusion and sanity to be rigidly separated or, on the contrary, could the former be not only consistent with but even a condition of the latter?'[57] The psychoses are thus welcomed into the psychoanalytic register as the psychical condition of a large percentage of subjects, formative in them of certain behavioural patterns and coping mechanisms, but this may not be so for Joyce, whose transparent sheet will maintain his distinction until we arrive at the *sinthome*.

Commenting on Foucault's *History of Madness* (1961) Derrida, in 'Cogito and the History of Madness', claims that

> the expression "to say madness itself" is self-contradictory. To say madness without expelling it into objectivity is to let it say itself. But madness is what by essence cannot be said: it is the "absence of the work," as Foucault profoundly says.[58]

Here we are perhaps returned to the indictment of arbitrariness that was levelled at Joyce's work. In *Finnegans Wake* he claimed he aimed at reconstructing the lunar dream-state itself, as opposed to what is left afterward, as opposed to dream *interpretation*; and, in terms of madness, there is in the *Wake* a certain attempt to realise the Real in a manner seemingly trying to bypass the symbolic whilst necessarily going via it; it is thus an attempt to render 'little bits of Real', and to harness something of *lalangue*, a concept of Lacan's we will discuss in depth in chapter 5. Therefore the *Wake* does not 'say madness itself', and nor is it quite 'madness saying itself'; as we know, it remains separated from madness by the transparent sheet. Neither is it 'the absence of the work', as Joyce worked constantly on it, and as we have it now in published form (the reasons for which Lacan wondered at); its structure is rather that it somehow manages to 'cling to the Real' without a full-scale refusal of the symbolic (in something of the manner in which the translucent sheet clings to the wax slab in Freud's writing-pad); the process of which is hallucinatoriness.

Thus, to conjoin these reflections of Derrida's with Lacan's interventions on the treatment of psychosis – which was often earlier seen as an illness untouchable by psychoanalysis – and by combining them through Joyce's unificatory/separatory interaction with madness, we might postulate that the silence of madness in fact *speaks* – *through* the subject: not *by* the Real, but echoing *in* it, *as* hallucination – but that it can come into the realm of reason only if it is *heard*; that is, heard as a *perceptum of objectlessness*. Thus, to elucidate these summations in relation to the subject and the unconscious, as Lacan puts it: the subject 'becom[es] this something which, from within the field in which nothing can be said, appeals to all the rest, to the field of everything that can be said', or, to reformulate Wittgenstein's dictum 'whereof one cannot speak, thereof one must be silent', we could suggest that for the subject, 'wherefrom it cannot be spoken, *it speaks*'.[59]

Such postulations on madness must be wary of risking the 'assumption' that Derrida warns of: 'That reason can have a contrary, that there can be an other of reason, that reason itself can construct or discover, and that the opposition of reason to its other is *symmetrical*.'[60] However, the principle of *enverity* resists such a symmetricality, which suggests the measurability of madness: if the transparent sheet may allow a *perceptum*, a little bit of the Real, of madness to become viewable, the magnitude of that which it may separate its utiliser from, and by what margin, yet cannot be known. In strikingly Derridean terms, Hunter S. Thompson gives an explanation of this, in relation to *the edge of reason*, at the end of his first gonzo work, *Hell's Angels*:

> The Edge . . . There is no honest way to explain it because the only people who really know where it is are the ones who have gone over. The others – the living – are those who pushed their control as far as they felt they could handle it, and then pulled back, or slowed down, or did whatever they had to when it came time to choose between Now and Later.
>
> But the edge is still Out there. Or maybe it's In.[61]

Opacity

Thus, in answering the question 'was Joyce mad?' by suggesting 'not by a transparent sheet', we can make no comment on the actual thinness or thickness of the sheet itself; by what margin it may have separated Joyce from the *incommunicable* of the other side. By providing this answer to this central question, too, it preserves something of the animating ambiguity that has grown up around it, and around Lacan's opinion on it. As we can see from sampling two instances of Lacanian interaction with the question, the verdict is split: René Rasmussen, for example – in his article 'On Joyce and Psychosis' – argues that 'one of Lacan's main theses is that Joyce was psychotic but in a stabilised way'.[62] Harari, on the other hand – based on his own analyses, and convincingly – states the exact opposite; he argues:

> There could never have been, on [Joyce']s part, a demand for analysis, or an acceptance of his daughter's treatment. Yet this is not to imply that Joyce was a "stabilized" psychotic. Lacan emphasized that in such a situation it is only in the third generation that psychosis breaks out, and Lucia Joyce belonged, precisely, to that generation.[63]

Thus, it is in Rik Loose's summation that these differences – separated only by such a hair's-breadth sheet as Joyce's transparent one – are given a precise backing with reference to the *Sinthome* Seminar, which as we shall see leaves all of their ambiguity readily available, of necessity. As he states:

> Does Lacan conclude in *Seminar XXIII: Le Sinthome*, that Joyce's *sinthome* prevented him from becoming psychotic? In this seminar Lacan wonders "was Joyce mad? What was it that inspired his writings?" He will not give a positive answer to the first question. He carefully avoids it. A little later in the same lecture he comes back to this question and says: "The question I raise at

> the end of this little chat, is about whether or not Joyce was mad. Why should he not have been? It's not a privilege."[64]

'In other words', Loose states – in terms rather more reminiscent of Wilfred Bion's thought than Lacan's – 'everyone has a kernel of madness in him or her.'[65] Nonetheless, this brings us to the postulation that the psychotic structure may in fact occupy a central place in the constitution of the subject, as was just discussed earlier in relation to Lacan's doctoral thesis; a postulation at which Lacan (re)arrived via his interaction with Joyce.

As to Joyce's transparent sheet itself, we may now look further into its functioning, in terms of its signifying properties. Lacan begins his paper, 'The Instance of the Letter in the Unconscious, or Reason Since Freud', by 'situating it between writing and speech – it will be halfway between the two'.[66] Whilst this has connotations for Lacan's later postulation of a 'discourse without speech', which we will look into in chapter 5, he hereafter goes on to discuss Saussure's concepts of signification: the signifier and the signified, and especially the bar that separates them, a bar which the translator of the *Écrits*, Bruce Fink, has already subtly inserted, in the long dash (—) that breaks up the aforementioned sentence (Lacan, or his editor, François Wahl, uses a colon (:) in the original):[67]

> To pinpoint the emergence of the discipline of linguistics, I will say that, as in the case of every science in the modern sense, it consists in the constitutive moment of an algorithm that grounds it. This algorithm is the following:
>
> $$\frac{S}{s}$$
>
> It is read as follows: signifier over signified, "over" corresponding to the bar that separates the two levels.[68]

In this algorithm, Lacan later states, the bar, —, 'denotes the irreducible nature of the resistance of signification as constituted in the relations between signifier and signified'.[69] This brings us to the impasse of what Roland Barthes calls 'the mythical signifier: its form is empty but present, its meaning absent but full', and which he describes via this analogy in which window-pane and scenery cannot be focused on simultaneously, united and separated as they are by a form of transparent sheet:

> If I am in a car and look at the scenery through the window, I can at will focus on the scenery or on the window-pane. At one moment I grasp the presence of the glass and the distance of the landscape; at another, on the contrary, the transparence of the glass and the depth of the landscape; but the result of this alternation is constant: the glass is at once present and empty to me, and the landscape unreal and full.[70]

In the first instance the awareness of the signifier bars access to the signified, whilst in the second the impasse is dissolved in that the signifier appears to disappear into the signified, its bar being crossed over. Lacan afterwards in 'The Instance of the Letter' goes to produce the notation for this in the sign +, which 'manifests here the crossing of the bar, —, and the constitutive value of this crossing for the emergence of signification. The crossing expresses the condition for the passage of the signifier into the signified'.[71] As Lacan states in Seminar XX, in Joyce's work the crossing of the signifier into the signified is found everywhere: 'The signifier stuffs the signified'.[72] This thus appears to beg the question of the necessity of the bar at all, but it is here identified by Lacan as the essential term of this tripartite structure in Saussure's linguistics. It of course occupies position A in our unificatory/separatory principle; the bar has to separate what would otherwise be the same, acting, thus, as the sheet does: it is that which allows the signifier to slip into the signified through maintaining their distinction.

In his third Seminar Lacan states that 'our starting point, the point we keep coming back to, since we shall always be at the starting point, is that every real signifier is, as such, a signifier that signifies nothing'.[73] Drawing on the earlier reflections concerning the bar, we can now begin to unpack this starting point. A 'real signifier' suggests a signifier in the Real; thus, the Real of 'signifier-signified' would discount the unifying/separating bar of signification, without which there would be nothing; therefore, what Žižek calls 'the positive/constitutive ontological function of the veil' is needed.[74] This point in Žižek comes from Jacques-Alain Miller, who, as Santanu Biswas suggests, 'captured these connotations succinctly by stating that the function of a semblance is to 'veil nothing', and to posit something in the place of nothing by *veiling* nothing' (and in this we see reappear the operation of *hallucination*).[75]

This, then, is the function of the sheet, screen, or veil; to separate *nothing*, the Real, from – whilst unifying it with – itself, so as to create 'reality'. To give this its full philosophical bearing we will quote again from Žižek's *Less Than Nothing*, throughout which unificatory/separatory screens play a major role:

> We have one and the same reality, separated from itself (or, rather, redoubled) by a screen. This inversion-into-itself by way of which reality encounters itself on a fantasmatic stage is what compels us to abandon the univocity of being: the field of (what we experience as) reality is always traversed by a cut which inscribes appearance into appearance itself. In other words, if there is a field of reality, then it is not enough to claim that reality is inherently fantasmatic, that it is always constituted by a transcendental frame; this frame has to inscribe itself into the field of reality.[76]

Žižek precedes this by suggesting that 'what is "really" beyond the limit, on the other side of the screen, is not nothing, but rather *the same reality we find in front of the screen*'.[77] We will here conflate this '*same reality*' with *nothing* so as to be in keeping with the connotations adumbrated by Miller's *veil* earlier, but also because their (re)unification may maintain as much importance as their distinction if we suggest that *reality* and *nothing* are in fact *the same* if not separated from themselves by a Hegelian 'negation of negation'; indeed, by becoming '*not nothing*', via the operation of the screen. As Žižek later states: 'By hiding nothing, the veil creates the space for something to be imagined – the veil is the original operator of creation ex nihilo.'[78] In these statements we see the role of the *fantasmatic* in its ontological function of putting into play the imagination by inscribing itself into the field. As in our earlier ruminations on Joycean ontology the role of *fantasy* thus functions correlatively to that of *the Fall*, from which a retroactive-projective positation of reality comes into subsistence.

From this inscription of the screen, or frame, itself in the picture – the originary function of which is to *veil nothing* – thus comes its deployment as a mechanism for the maintenance of fantasy in such psychical manoeuvres as screen memories, for example, which Freud describes as phenomena that combine a recorded instance from childhood and an unconscious resistance to it (its screening) at once, creating a united/divided compromise memory which hints at the powerful trace that has been omitted by this screening process, whilst appearing seemingly innocent and indifferent.[79] As well as in psychology we can see this function of the screen in the field of fiction also, such as in Oscar Wilde's novel *The Picture of Dorian Gray* (1891), where the screen is deployed, in semi-inverted form, by Gray as a device to hide his becoming-monstrous portrait behind, in the attempt to hinder its real affects infecting his miraculously maintained fantasy.

In Joyce's early life and work this concept of the screen maintains an important, if somewhat detached, relevance too. First, by biographical association, there is the quasi-mythical incident concerning the reading of his first published work – the collection of poems *Chamber Music* – to a widow whom his friend (and role model for Buck Mulligan in *Ulysses*) Oliver St. John Gogarty had taken him to see, who, halfway through the reading 'had to interrupt to withdraw behind a screen to a chamber pot', to which Gogarty exclaimed, 'there's a critic for you!', and which Joyce's brother Stanislaus called 'a favorable omen' for a book of that title.[80] In *Ulysses*, as Ellmann points out, Joyce reincorporates the scene in Bloom's thinking: 'Chamber music. Could make a kind of pun on that. It is a kind of music. I often thought when she. Acoustics that is. Tinkling'; an instance of reinscription which, in effect, operates by the very process that Freud outlined for his concept of the screen memory.[81]

As far as *Ulysses* and charges of its being indecent were concerned, however, it was the summarisation of judge John M. Woolsey at the end of the obscenity trial on 6 December 1933 that in the book 'Joyce was seeking to represent the screen of consciousness, by means of a clear foreground and a background visible but somewhat blurred and out of focus in varying degrees.'[82] As Lacan summarised himself at the end of his year on the psychoses; similarly to Joyce, he had

> greatly insisted upon the fact that what has been repressed within appears without, re-emerges in the background – and not in a simple structure, but in a position that is, as it were, internal, which makes the subject himself, [. . .] the agent of persecution, ambiguous, problematic.[83]

If Woolsey's diagnosis – coupled with Lacan's prognosis – indeed gets at Joyce's methodology, hinting at the transparent sheet in fact containing an element of opacity, then this process is extended in the portmanteau words of *Finnegans Wake*, in which foreground *and* background intermix, and which by turns appear innocent and indifferent – as is the operative mode of Freud's screen memories – and then suddenly and visibly pierced by that 'opaque *jouissance*' that Lacan talks of in his reflections on Joyce. It is due to this that the hallucinatoriness of the *Wake*'s language offers us further insight into the operation of hallucination itself; thus, not only does a hallucination echo in the Real – as in its auditory manifestation – it may also *reflect* there, in its visual, as we have seen in Lacan's reading of the 'dumbillsilly' question, which comes via Tindall's.

Joyce's sheet's transparence becoming opaque thus produces the possibility of its reflecting. As Lacan argues, Joyce-the-Symptom is reflected in it, but also our own readings are too, and these readings themselves transfer from one to another, thus effecting processes in the sheet of both transparence and transference. Thus, to combine our reflections on ontology and the Fall earlier with this concept of the '*originary*' screen, which *unites* and *separates* the same at once, we follow and apply to Joyce the precise and poetic formulation in Werner Hamacher's essay 'Lingua Amissa', in which he extends Miller's and Žižek's reflections on screens, veils, and frames, in bringing them in relation to Marxian formulae on the inextricabilities of appearance and reality. In Joyce's linguistic constructions, like in 'reality' itself, therefore, 'the screen, the cloth is the ground-figure which appears only in disappearing and in which disappearing appears, thus the abyss as ground and the figure as none.'[84] Joyce's transparent/transferent sheet, then – unificatory/separatorily inscribed in the picture that is *Ulysses*, that is *Finnegans Wake*, and that is his own psychical makeup – is now rather perceivable as translucent, like the thin waxed paper of the writing-pad's sheet, because of the catachresis of its remaining at once *figuratively* transparent, whilst providing an *abyssal* grounding, an opaque *jouissance*, through which – as its opacity increases – its *exuded* sense becomes *excluded* sense (which then enters into the cathexic cycle of excess, *surplus*, bodily, *jouis-sens*). This is thus formative in Joyce of a bittersweet sanity, which – rather than reducing its psychical activity towards zero – maximises its tension and flourishes, whilst it fatigues, in its central antagonism.

Notes

1 Quoted in Jacques Derrida, 'Cogito and the History of Madness', in *Writing and Difference* [1967], trans. by Alan Bass (London: Routledge Classics, 2001) p.36. The phrase appears in Mercanton, 'The Hours of James Joyce', in *Portraits of the Artist in Exile: Recollections of James Joyce by Europeans*, ed. by Willard Potts (San Diego: Harcourt Brace Jovanovich, 1986) p.226, as: 'Nonetheless, that book was a terrible risk. A transparent leaf separates it from madness.'

2 Jacques Lacan, *The Seminar of Jacques Lacan, Book XI: The Four Fundamental Concepts of Psychoanalysis* [1964], ed. by Jacques-Alain Miller, trans. by Alan Sheridan (New York: W.W. Norton, 1981) p.163. It should be noted here that the four

fundamental concepts of psychoanalysis – *the unconscious, repetition, the transference*, and *the drive* – that Lacan identifies, are to be taken as operational *within their own fields*.

3 Karl Marx, 'From Volume One' [1867], trans. by Samuel Moore and Edward Aveling, in *Capital: An Abridged Edition*, ed. by David McLellan (Oxford: Oxford World's Classics, 1995) p.73. I prefer this translation to Fowkes's here because it is more illustrative of the duality inherent in the central concept.

4 Étienne Balibar, 'On the Basic Concepts of Historical Materialism', in Louis Althusser and Étienne Balibar, *Reading Capital* [1968], trans. by Ben Brewster (London: Verso, 1979) p.203. We here follow Ernesto Laclau and Chantal Mouffe's definition of antagonism, as a structuring principle of discourse and the social, in justifying the use and relevance of this concept:

> Certain discursive forms, through equivalence, annul all positivity of the object and give a real existence to negativity as such. This impossibility of the real – negativity – has attained a form of presence. As the social is penetrated by negativity – that is, by antagonism – it does not attain the status of transparency, of full presence, and the objectivity of its identities is permanently subverted. From here onward, the impossible relation between objectivity and negativity has become constitutive of the social.

See Ernesto Laclau and Chantal Mouffe, *Hegemony and Socialist Strategy: Towards a Radical Democratic Politics* [1985] (London: Verso Radical Thinkers, 2014) p.115.

5 Sigmund Freud, *Jokes and Their Relation to the Unconscious* [1905], trans. by James Strachey, in *SE*, VIII, pp.73–74. Whilst this passage is fitting at this point in our work, Freud gets to the heart of the matter in one of his earliest compositions – the *Project for a Scientific Psychology*, of 1895 – in which antagonism ('excitation', and, later, pain) and *enverity* (the split between the neuronal systems φ and ψ) are presented as tripartite ontological constituents (of the human nervous system): 'From the first the nervous system had two functions: the reception of stimuli *from outside* and the discharge of excitations of *endogenous* origin[.] It was from this latter obligation, indeed, that, owing to the exigencies of life, a compulsion came about towards further biological development[.] We might then conjecture that it might actually be our systems φ and ψ each of which had assumed one of these primary obligations. The system φ would be the group of neurones which the external stimuli reach, the system ψ would contain the neurones which receive the endogenous excitations. In that case we would not have *invented* the two [classes], φ and ψ, we should have *found* them already in existence.' See Sigmund Freud, 'Project for a Scientific Psychology' [1895], trans. by Eric Mosbacher and James Strachey, in *SE*, I, p.303.

In other words, we may present the nervous system ontologically in terms of the unificatory/separatory principle thus:

Charge of excitations

/ \

φ ψ

6 Joyce uses the uncommon word 'jocoserious', meaning jocular and serious at once, in *Ulysses*. See James Joyce, *Ulysses* [1922], ed. by Hans Walter Gabler and others (New York: Vintage Books, 1986) 17.369, p.553; James Joyce, *Ulysses: The 1922 Text*, ed. by Jeri Johnson (Oxford: Oxford World's Classics, 1998) p.629.

7 See Slavoj Žižek, *Less Than Nothing: Hegel and the Shadow of Dialectical Materialism* (London: Verso, 2012) p.932, quoting Karen Barad, *Meeting the Universe*

Halfway: Quantum Physics and the Entanglement of Matter and Meaning (Durham: Duke University Press, 2007) p.128.

8 James Joyce, '*L'influenza letteraria universale del rinascimento* [The Universal Literary Influence of the Renaissance]' [1912], trans. by Conor Deane, in *Occasional, Critical, and Political Writing*, ed. by Kevin Barry (Oxford: Oxford World's Classics, 2000) p.188.

9 Giordano Bruno, *Cause, Principle and Unity* [1584], trans. by Robert de Lucca, in *Cause, Principle and Unity, and Essays on Magic*, ed. by Robert de Lucca and Richard J. Blackwell (Cambridge: Cambridge University Press, 1998) p.23.

10 Joyce, '*L'irlanda: Isola dei Santi e dei Savi* [Ireland: Island of Saints and Sages]' [1907], trans. by Conor Deane, in *Occasional, Critical, and Political Writing*, p.121. Coherency and incoherency residing side by side here goes again to destabilise Macherey's singular 'principle of coherence' discussed earlier.

11 See Willard Potts, *Joyce and the Two Irelands* (Austin: University of Texas Press, 2000) p.8, and pp.202–203, note 65.

12 Joyce, *Ulysses*, 1.638–644, p.17; Joyce, *Ulysses: 1922*, p.20.

13 Marian Eide, *Ethical Joyce* (Cambridge: Cambridge University Press, 2002) p.64.

14 Mercanton, 'The Hours of James Joyce', in *Portraits of the Artist in Exile*, p.221.

15 Of course in Genesis the tower is not felled, but it is in the pseudepigraphic *Book of Jubilees*, for example.

16 James Joyce, quoted in Mercanton, 'The Hours of James Joyce', in *Portraits of the Artist in Exile*, p.213.

17 Joseph Campbell and Henry Morton Robinson, *A Skeleton Key to Finnegans Wake* (London: Faber and Faber, 1944) p.72. See James Joyce, *Finnegans Wake* [1939], ed. by Robbert-Jan Henkes and others (Oxford: Oxford World's Classics, 2012) p.92, 10–11.

18 Mercanton, 'The Hours of James Joyce', in *Portraits of the Artist in Exile*, p.207 [my emphasis].

19 Ibid.

20 Patrice Maniglier, 'Acting Out the Structure', in *Concept and Form: Volume 2, Interviews and Essays on the* Cahiers pour l'Analyse, ed. by Peter Hallward and Knox Peden, 2 vols (London: Verso, 2012) p.28. This point is brought out consistently by Freud himself, such as in his study of Jensen's *Gradiva*, in which he asks: 'Are we to venture on an attempt at interpreting this dream too – that is, at replacing it by the latent thoughts from whose distortion it must have arisen?' See Sigmund Freud, 'Delusions and Dreams in Jensen's *Gradiva*' [1907], trans. by James Strachey, in *SE*, IX, p.73.

21 The translator of *Of Grammatology*, Gayatri Spivak, translates *différance* as 'differance', whereas other translators, such as Alan Bass, retain the French word in italics in their translations; we maintain this latter practice (unless quoting Spivak's translation) so as to be able to easily identify moments in which *différance* is operative.

22 Slavoj Žižek, 'A Plea for a Return to *Différance* (with a Minor *Pro Domo Sua*)', in *Adieu Derrida*, ed. by Costas Douzinas (Basingstoke: Palgrave Macmillan, 2007) p.119.

23 Jacques Lacan, 'Responses to Students of Philosophy Concerning the Object of Psychoanalysis' [1966], trans. by Jeffrey Mehlman, in Lacan, *Television: A Challenge to the Psychoanalytic Establishment*, ed. by Joan Copjec, trans. by Denis Hollier and others (New York: W. W. Norton, 1990) p.108.

24 Jacques Lacan, 'The Mirror Stage as Formative of the *I* Function as Revealed in Psychoanalytic Experience' [1949], in *Écrits: The First Complete Edition in English* [1966], orig. ed. by François Wahl, trans. by Bruce Fink, in collaboration with Héloïse Fink and Russell Grigg (New York: W.W. Norton, 2006) p.78. See also Lacan's definition in the 1953 lecture 'The Symbolic, the Imaginary, and the Real': 'We must absolutely define the ego's imaginary function as the unity of the subject who is alienated from himself.' See Jacques Lacan, 'The Symbolic, the Imaginary, and the Real' [1953], in *On the Names-of-the-Father* [2005], trans. by Bruce Fink (Cambridge: Polity, 2013) p.24.

25 James A. Joyce, 'James Clarence Mangan (1902)', in *Occasional, Critical, and Political Writing*, p.55.
26 R.W. Maslen, 'Introduction', in Sir Philip Sidney, *An Apology for Poetry (or The Defence of Poesy)* [1595], ed. by Geoffrey Shepherd and R. W. Maslen (Manchester: Manchester University Press, 2002) p.42.
27 Adaline Glasheen, 'Opening Paragraphs (contd.)', *A Wake Newslitter*, New ser., 2.6 (December 1965) 17–22 (p.21). This Samuel Beckett puts into a similar tripartite theological structure, postulating that Joyce's work represents a state of 'purgatory': 'In what sense, then, is Mr. Joyce's work purgatorial?' he asks. 'In the absolute absence of the Absolute. Hell is the static lifelessness of unrelieved viciousness. Heaven is the static lifelessness of unrelieved immaculation. Purgatory a flood of movement and vitality released by the conjunction of these two elements.' See Samuel Beckett, 'Dante . . . Bruno. Vico . . . Joyce', in Samuel Beckett and others, *James Joyce/Finnegans Wake, A Symposium: Our Exagmination Round His Factification for Incamination of Work in Progress* [1929] (New York: New Directions, 1962) 2nd edn. p.22.
28 Žižek, *Less Than Nothing*, p.952.
29 Mercanton, 'The Hours of James Joyce', in *Portraits of the Artist in Exile*, p.252.
30 Octave Mannoni, '"I know very well, but all the same . . ."' [1969], unofficial translation by Wendy A. Hester, in *The University of Berkeley Comparative Literature Reader*, p.86. For an official translation of this passage – over which the above is preferred in this instance – see Octave Mannoni, '"I Know Well, but All the Same . . ."' [1969], trans. by G.M. Goshgarian, in *Perversion and the Social Relation*, ed. by Molly Anne Rothenberg, Dennis A. Foster, and Slavoj Žižek (Durham: Duke University Press, 2003) p.70. For more on *Wake*an sigla, see Roland McHugh, *The Sigla of Finnegans Wake* (Austin: University of Texas Press, 1976).
31 Mannoni, '"I Know Well, but All the Same . . ."', in *Perversion and the Social Relation*, p.69, p.70.
32 Derrida, 'Cogito and the History of Madness', in *Writing and Difference*, p.46.
33 Simon Morgan Wortham, *The Derrida Dictionary* (New York: Continuum Books, 2010) p.30.
34 Alain Badiou, *Ethics: An Essay on the Understanding of Evil* [1993], trans. by Peter Hallward (London: Verso Radical Thinkers, 2012) p.42.
35 Joyce, quoted in Mercanton, 'The Hours of James Joyce', in *Portraits of the Artist in Exile*, p.226.
36 Sigmund Freud, 'A Note Upon the Mystic Writing-Pad' [1925], trans. by James Strachey, in *SE*, XIX, pp.228–229. For the importance of this short essay to Derrida, see Jacques Derrida, 'Freud and the Scene of Writing', in *Writing and Difference*, in which he is led to pronounce that 'the subject of writing is a *system* of relations between strata: the Mystic Pad, the psyche, society, the world' (p.285).
37 Ellmann, *James Joyce*, p.686.
38 Ibid.
39 Jacques-Alain Miller, 'Lacan with Joyce: The Seminar of the Clinical Section of Barcelona' [1996], *Psychoanalytical Notebooks*, 13 (May 2005) 7–32 (pp.27–28).
40 See Jacques Lacan, *The Seminar of Jacques Lacan, Book XXI: Les non-dupes errant, 1973–1974*, trans. by Cormac Gallagher (London: Karnac, unofficial translation, n.d.).
41 Freud, 'A Note Upon the Mystic Writing-Pad', in *SE*, XIX, pp.229–230.
42 Ibid. p.230.
43 Clayton Crockett, *Interstices of the Sublime: Theology and Psychoanalytic Theory* (New York: Fordham University Press, 2007) p.57.
44 Jacques Lacan, 'On a Question Prior to Any Possible Treatment of Psychosis' [1955–1956], in *Écrits*, p.446.
45 Ibid.

46 Eugène Jolas and others, 'The Revolution of the Word' [1928], in *MANIFESTO! A Century of Isms*, ed. by Mary Ann Caws (Nebraska: University of Nebraska Press, 2001) p.530.
47 Joyce, *Finnegans Wake*, p.15, 18; Jacques Lacan, 'Joyce le Symptôme', in *Le seminaire XXIII: Le sinthome* [1975–1976], texte établi par Jacques-Alain Miller (Paris: Éditions du Seuil, 2005) p.166 (see trans. by Benanav).
48 Ibid.
49 See William York Tindall, *A Reader's Guide to* Finnegans Wake [1969] (New York: Syracuse University Press, 1996) p.42. Although this point is missed by the author, for an interesting further elucidation of this particular phrase, see Pierre Thèves, '*Où est ton cadeau, espèce d'imbécile?*' trans. by Philip Dravers and Vincent Dachy, *Psychoanalytical Notebooks*, 13 (2005) 35–45.
50 Lacan, *Seminar III: The Psychoses*, p.14.
51 Jacques Lacan, 'The Subversion of the Subject and the Dialectic of Desire in the Freudian Unconscious' [1960]', in *Écrits*, p.688.
52 See Lacan, *Le seminaire XXIII: Le sinthome*, p.53; Lacan, 'Le Sinthome', p.16, as quoted more fully below.
53 Lacan, *Seminar III: The Psychoses*, p.23, p.24.
54 Ibid. p.23.
55 Lacan, *Le seminaire XXIII: Le sinthome*, p.53; Lacan, 'Le Sinthome', p.16.
56 Lacan in fact here means 'republished' as he had had the thesis published by Le François in 1932; it was largely ignored by the psychiatric community, but regarded well by the surrealists in reviews that appeared in their associated journals. It was, however, reprinted through Seuil in 1975. See Elisabeth Roudinesco, *Jacques Lacan: An Outline of a Life and a History of a System of Thought*, trans. by Barbara Bray (Cambridge: Polity Press, 1999) pp.58–60.
57 Darian Leader, *What is Madness?* (London: Penguin, 2012) p.2.
58 Derrida, 'Cogito and the History of Madness', in *Writing and Difference*, p.51.
59 Lacan, *Seminar III: The Psychoses*, p.157.
60 Derrida, 'Cogito and the History of Madness', in *Writing and Difference*, p.48.
61 Hunter S. Thompson, *Hell's Angels* (London: Penguin, 1967) p.323. In many ways Hunter Thompson (through his lifestyle) was to the over-medicated culture of the current 'bipolar times' – as Darian Leader phrases it – what Joyce was to a society becoming overly (or – to put it more cynically – fashionably) reliant on psychoanalysis; that is, *its other side*, its mental – *and bodily* – refusal.
62 René Rasmussen, 'On Joyce and Psychosis', *Psychoanalytical Notebooks*, 13(2005) 45–54 (p.45).
63 Roberto Harari, *How James Joyce Made His Name: A Reading of the Final Lacan* [1995], trans. by Luke Thurston (New York: Other Press, 2002) p.170.
64 Rik Loose, 'Joyce's Administration', *Psychoanalytical Notebooks*, 13 (2005) 83–91 (p.85). For Loose's references, see Lacan, *Le seminaire XXIII: Le sinthome*, p.77, p.87; Lacan, *Seminar XXIII: Joyce and the Sinthome*, session VI, p.2, p.12.
65 Loose, 'Joyce's Administration', p.85. Bion argues that in 'the severe neurotic [. . .] there is a psychotic personality concealed by neurosis as the neurotic personality is screened by psychosis in the psychotic'. See W.R. Bion, 'Differentiation of the Psychotic from the Non-Psychotic Personalities' [1957], in *Second Thoughts: Selected Papers on Psycho-Analysis* (London: H. Karnac, 1984) p.63.
66 Lacan, 'The Instance of the Letter in the Unconscious, or Reason Since Freud' [1957]', in *Écrits*, p.412.
67 See Roudinesco, *Jacques Lacan*, p.325, for information on Wahl's responsibility for the punctuation in the *Écrits*.
68 Lacan, 'The Instance of the Letter in the Unconscious', in *Écrits*, pp.414–415.

69 Ibid. p.428.
70 Roland Barthes, 'Myth Today', in *Mythologies* [1957], trans. by Annette Lavers (London: Vintage Classics, 2009) p.147.
71 Lacan, 'The Instance of the Letter in the Unconscious', in *Écrits*, p.429.
72 A unique instance of this process in literature is the point in B. S. Johnson's *Albert Angelo* at which we encounter two rectangular holes in consecutive leaves, allowing us to 'see through' them to a part of a sentence four numbered pages beyond. After a break in the story of five asterisks ('* * * * *') we are shown this sentence, *in medias res*: 'Struggling to take back his knife, and inflicted on him a mortal wound above his right eye (the blade penetrating to a depth of two inches) from which he died instantly.' On the next but one page the action concerns a scuffle and the word 'struggling' is preceded by the character's name 'Terry', but, if we ignore the above glimpsed ('*signifiant*') sentence (the one seen through the hole), it would read: 'Terry just stepped out in front of her, and looked down at her. She apologised!' Then, when we can read the sentence in its actual context, on the page it was excerpted from, we realise it concerns the stabbing death of the playwright Christopher Marlowe in 1593. Here we have three significations with which the signifier (that is, the placement of the rectangular hole in the preceding pages – under the asterisks, and after the word 'Terry') has stuffed the signified (the sentence concerning the stabbing) through its radical *cut* (the rectangular hole itself, occupying the place of the bar, or transparent sheet), which is thus even a de-scissive *cut-out cut*. See B. S. Johnson, *Albert Angelo* [1964], in *Omnibus: Albert Angelo, Trawl, House Mother Normal* (London: Picador, 2004) p.149, p.151, and p.153.
73 Lacan, *Seminar III: The Psychoses*, p.185.
74 Žižek, *Less Than Nothing*, p.692.
75 Santanu Biswas, 'A Literary Introduction to 'Lituraterre', in *The Literary Lacan: From Literature to Lituraterre and Beyond*, ed. by Biswas (Calcutta: Seagull Books, 2012) p.185.
76 Žižek, *Less Than Nothing*, pp.374–375.
77 Ibid. p.374.
78 Ibid. p.692.
79 Sigmund Freud, 'Screen Memories' [1899], in *SE*, III, pp.306–307.
80 Ellmann, *James Joyce*, p.154.
81 Quoted in ibid. footnote. See Joyce, *Ulysses*, 11.979–981, p.232; Joyce, *Ulysses: 1922*, p.271.
82 Ellmann, *James Joyce*, p.666.
83 Lacan, *Seminar III: The Psychoses*, p.313.
84 Werner Hamacher, 'Lingua Amissa: The Messianism of Commodity-Language and Derrida's *Specters of Marx*', trans. by Kelly Barry, in Aijaz Ahmad and others, *Ghostly Demarcations: A Symposium on Jacques Derrida's* Specters of Marx (London: Verso Radical Thinkers, 2008) p.210, note 1.

Chapter 3

From Joyce-the-symptom to the *sinthome*

As soon as the foetus
Has its brain completely articulated,
The prime mover turns to him in gladness
At such a piece of nature's handiwork,
And breathes a new spirit, filled with power,
Which draws the active element it finds there
Into its own substance, and makes itself
A single soul, living, sentient, and self-reflective.
– Dante

Joycean singularity

> This is where one falls, if I can put it this way, upon truth – the "upon" could equally well be replaced by "from." One falls upon truth, that is to say, a remarkable thing, if we envisage this reference to be absolute, it could be said that anyone who adhered to it – but, of course, it is impossible to adhere to it – would not know what he is saying.[1]

This statement of Lacan's in Seminar XVII, we could suggest, is enigmatic. As enigmatic as any of Lacan's statements, it is of course necessarily so. It at once seems to be delivered in a language all of its own, *in toto* – a 'Lacanguage' we could say, following Lacan's predilection for punningly playing with his own name, as Joyce had, in Seminar XXIII – whilst appearing extremely precise in every detail.[2] It in fact summarises each of the Lacanian points of departure we have enumerated heretofore – the terms of the principle of *enverity*, the *half-sayableness* of truth, and the ontological positioning of *the Fall* – in one expression. We first see the centrality of the fall in that it makes of the prepositions 'upon' and 'from' its two sides, two resultant actions that come about because the fall itself is not a clingable- or adherable-to constant for the subject; the subject must come down on, or from, either side of it. In so doing the truth of the fall cannot be fully said, only half-said, in that we are always only ever falling *upon* it or *from* it – and even if it could be adhered to fully, as Lacan says, it would still only be half-said, if articulated, as the subject indeed '*would not know* what he is saying'. Thus we see how truth splits and makes fall what it speaks; this is the precise operation of *enverity*. To put this into the terms of the unificatory/separatory principle we can see here clearly the refractivity of Position A; in its antagonistic core, which makes two sides of whatever fills the position, it also redirects either side's attempts at adherence, in a moment of instantaneous inversion: to *fall upon* truth means equally to *fall away* from it; to *hit upon* truth will be to be *batted away* by it.

If truth and the Fall are synonymous, in position A, they can nevertheless be separated into their nounal and verbal states (the nouns truth/the Fall, and the verb *to fall, falling*); these can then be divided between position A and its extensions – the bars indicating the sides position 1 and position 2 – as shown in Figure 3.1:

Position A

Truth/The Fall

(*Fall*) /   \ (*Fall*)

Position 1   Position 2

Upon   *From*

Figure 3.1 Unificatory/separatory principle (A: *Truth/The Fall* < 1: *Upon*, 2: *From*)

This then goes to reinforce that not only is the inherent antagonism which is in the base of things, splitting them into their sides, these sides' unificatory/separatory principle, it is also – to extend Ragland's term – their organisatory/disorganisatory principle, through its non-adherence and refractivity; i.e., with the addition of the verb *to fall* to the diagram – in the place of the indicatory slanted bars – we can see that in terms of *truth*, either *approaching* or *retreating* is *falling*, synonymising the *upon* with the *from*, whilst simultaneously maintaining it as its other side, the result of which is a topology similar to that of the Möbius strip:

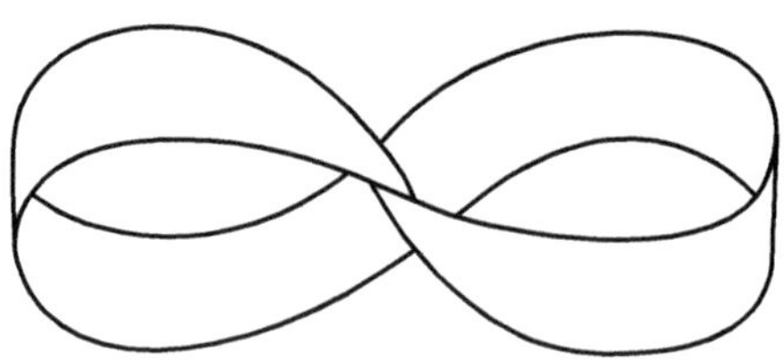

Figure 3.2 Möbius strip

The Möbius strip, pictured in Figure 3.2, is a topological structure in which a sheet is half-twisted and attached end to end so as to form a continuous plane; this makes the two sides of the sheet one, both of which can be traversed by travelling continuously in a straight line from any point on the strip. As a two-dimensional geometrical shape it is, in mathematical terms, 'non-orientable', an adjective which serves well to describe how – if sided by the *fall*; the synonymous *upon* and *from* – in seeking truth by travelling along the strip, it will never be arrived at, as it *is* the strip, the *sheet*, itself. It is this failure to arrive which is the source of Lacan's conception of the desire of *the drive*, which operates in accord with this Möbius movement, and keeps things in a purgatorial recirculation, in the Beckettian sense.[3]

The drive, as Žižek puts it, 'turns failure into triumph – in it, the very failure to reach its goal, the repetition of this failure, the endless circulation around the object, generates a satisfaction of its own'.[4] It is perhaps this satisfaction that Joyce was going after with the 'recirculation' of *Finnegans Wake*, in making of its first sentence the 'half-twist' of its last: its 'beginning' on its first page with 'riverrun' continuing on from the word 'ending' the book on its last, 'the' ('A way a lone a last a loved a long the'; sans full-stop, of course).[5] It would indeed be as a Möbius strip that *Finnegans Wake* might be best presented, and read, especially as it would be in accord with the author's wish for an 'ideal reader suffering from an ideal insomnia' in which the reading of the *Wake* could recur continuously.[6] The book becoming a Möbius strip – in which two becomes one – would thus make of it both the 'twone' – 'two'/'one'; two words here sutured by their shared zero, the letter 'o' – mentioned on its first page, and the 'onetwo' – 'one'/'two' – mentioned on its last.[7]

Thus, although the Möbius strip's traversability may appear to dissolve the two-sided structure into one single continuous side, in three dimensions it in fact remains structurally similar to the sheets so far discussed, in that the strip is still its sides', or side's, indivisible remainder, and in that it cannot be cut with scissors one side from the other (or, indeed, one side *from itself*): the initial sheet is still the shape's structuring principle; the shape can only be created from an original two-sided sheet-like structure, and if cut across and halved at any point, will return to it, unravelled. We can take the turning of *Finnegans Wake* into a Möbius strip as an example here: in his 'Joyce the Symptom' lecture Lacan argues that 'it is lucky that there is only one edition [of the *Wake*], which permits us to designate, when we cite, the good page, that is, the page that will never carry but the same number'; otherwise, if 'edited with different paginations – how would one find anything!'[8] This singular pagination existed for all editions of *Finnegans Wake* until the arrival of Danis Rose and John O'Hanlon's 2012 Houyhnhnm/Penguin 'restored' edition, which, whilst affecting cross-referencing, *à la* Lacan's prediction (though electronic aids have subsequently made this process all the more easy), also disallows it becoming a Möbius strip.[9] The new edition stands at 493 pages, whereas the classic pagination is 628; the simple fact is that to turn a book into a Möbius strip, its length in pages needs to be of an even number; in the *Wake*'s case, if pages 3–315 were printed on the recto side of a sheet and pages 316–628 on the verso – exactly back to back – and the half-twist applied the last page (628) would connect to the first (3), 'the' to 'riverrun', forming an endlessly readable strip.[10] Thus, for such a *readable* strip to be constructed, it must be formed out of an originarily two-sided sheet.

Ultimately, the Möbius strip here serves to exemplarily demonstrate the functioning of the unificatory/separatory principle by showing that its two sides can be both synonymous (*fall–fall*) and dichotomous (*upon–from*) at once. We could even go so far as to suggest that the Möbius strip – sided synonymously – presents *an other side* to the sheet – sided dichotomously – although these typically cannot be two sides of the same structure and therefore become inassimilable to the unificatory/separatory principle, except in rare instances where their dividing/uniting principle would be a concept *only* capable of occupying position A, such as *truth*, or *the unconscious*, for example.

Symptom

It is to the unconscious that we will now turn in delineating the functioning of the symptom – in its relation to *jouissance* – before going on to psychoanalytically situate the concept of the *sinthome*, and finally to bring it into relation with the Borromean knot. This will require an extensive reading of Seminar XXIII, *Le sinthome*, as well as interaction with key commentators on the work, which will take up the first part of this chapter. When we arrive at it we will initially take a heuristic approach to the *sinthome*, allowing us to postulate many conceptualisations of it over the course of this chapter, which we will attempt to bring together more thoroughly in the next. Indeed, 'preparatory to anything else' – as is Joyce's qualificatory phrase that opens the Eumaeus episode of *Ulysses* – we must let the *sinthome* do its own work.[11] Thus, before we assign to it a letter, siglum, or *matheme*, its own enigmatic position must excavate itself in the explorative work we are to produce on it; or – in Derridean terms – in relation to the *sinthome*, we must first do the 'writing *before the letter*'.[12]

It is important first off to recognise that our investigations herein must encounter two divergent strands of interpretation with regard to the analytic concepts of the symptom and the *sinthome*; that is, divergent *temporally*. In the delineation to follow we will attempt to recognise both, and to work within their commensuration, the first being the necessity to chart the trajectory the concept of the symptom takes in Lacan's thinking over the course of his teaching and practice, and the second being a readiness to allow of the conjunction of Lacan's varying pronouncements at different points in his career – so as to not get mired in a notion of *mutual exclusivity*, but instead to recognise these concepts' 'different inflections' – to arrive at definitions that are aware of their shifting nature as signifiers, and, indeed, aware of the shifting natures of their signifieds. To satisfy this first strand, and to provide an overview to the following disquisitions, we will quote at length from Luke Thurston's definition of the *sinthome* in Evans's Lacanian dictionary, which traces through time Lacan's thinking concerning the symptom:

> Before the appearance of the *sinthome*, divergent currents in Lacan's thinking lead to different inflections of the concept of the symptom. As early as 1957, the symptom is said to be 'inscribed in a writing process' (Ec, 445),

> which already implies a different view to that which regards the symptom as a ciphered message. In 1963 Lacan goes on to state that the symptom, unlike acting out, does not call for interpretation; in itself, it is not a call to the Other but a pure *jouissance* addressed to no one (Lacan, 1962–3: seminar of 23 January 1963; see Miller, 1987: 11). Such comments anticipate the radical transformation of Lacan's thought implicit in this shift from the linguistic definition of the symptom – as a signifier – to his statement, in the 1974–5 seminar, that the 'symptom can only be defined as the way in which each subject enjoys [*jouit*] the unconscious, in so far as the unconscious determines him' (Lacan, 1974–5; seminar of 18 February 1975).
>
> This move from conceiving of the symptom as a message which can be deciphered by reference to the unconscious 'structured like a language', to seeing it as the trace of the particular modality of the subject's *jouissance*, culminates in the introduction of the term *sinthome*. The *sinthome* thus designates a signifying formulation beyond analysis, a kernel of enjoyment immune to the efficacy of the symbolic. Far from calling for some analytic 'dissolution', the *sinthome* is what 'allows one to live' by providing a unique organisation of *jouissance*. The task of analysis thus becomes, in one of Lacan's last definitions of the end of analysis, to identify with the *sinthome*.[13]

The question that arises here is whether we should rigorously separate the concepts of symptom and *sinthome*, in moving *from* (Joyce-the-)Symptom *to* the *sinthome*, or whether we should view this trajectory as a kind of evolution of a singular concept. We have already encountered the suggestion of the *sinthome* being the symptom's *other side*, and thus, in the spirit of the principle of *enverity*, it will be between postulating the symptom as a completely unary entity or an entirely amorphous one – between its rigorous separation and absolute unification – that we will situate this discourse.

As Thurston highlights, Lacan remarks in Seminar XXII, *R.S.I.*, that 'the symptom is the way in which each person derives *jouissance* from the unconscious'.[14] It is on this *jouissance* that we will now concentrate in beginning to address the question of the symptom, and it is through this that we will begin to see how Lacan's varying notions of the symptom tie up. In Seminar VII Lacan is at pains to point out that 'we cannot avoid the formula that *jouissance* is evil[:] it is suffering because it involves suffering for my neighbour'.[15] In this reference to the 'neighbour' we first see the *intersubjective* effect of *jouissance* and the symptom, its effect in and on *civilisation*, in that the unconscious itself – which conveys *jouissance* through the symptom – '*is the discourse of the Other*', as Lacan maintains; its structure, language, and grammar is shared, in the big Other.[16] We should perceive here, too, *jouissance*'s *personal* effects, in that the 'neighbour' – in relation to the unconscious – should also be read as that which is in us, *and yet other*, at once; the fundamental *split* from which is created this particular *suffering*: subjectivity.

To unravel this statement further, however, we must first acknowledge the implications of the derivation of the English word 'suffering' from the French '*souffrance*', in its relation to *jouissance* and the symptom. As Alan Sheridan, the translator of Seminar XI, delineates: 'In French, the phrase '*en souffrance*' means 'in suspense', 'in abeyance', 'awaiting attention', 'pending'[, whilst] also mean[ing] 'pain', of course.'[17] In his *Inhibitions, Symptoms and Anxiety* Freud claims that 'a symptom is a sign of, and a substitute for, an instinctual satisfaction which has remained in abeyance; it is a consequence of the process of repression'.[18] In technical terms, Freud suggests that this repression arises in the ego when it – possibly 'at the behest of the superego – refuses to associate itself with an instinctual cathexis which has been aroused in the id'.[19] Thus, in the symptom and its *souffrance*, we are met again by the mechanism of deferral, but this time not in combination with difference – as in Derrida's *différance* – but rather with a certain similarity and familiarity; that of repetition.

In the repetition of a symptom there is found a certain comfort; the comfort of the ego keeping in abeyance an instinctual cathexis in the id for the appeasement of the superego. The wrath of the prohibitive superego is thus avoided through the manifestation of the symptom, but it would appear that through the particular formation that the symptom takes the superego is actually short-circuited rather than just merely obeyed. The subject is still in fact able to derive *jouissance* from the unconscious, via the symptom, as Lacan states; and, as Lacan teaches, in its symptomal manifestation the repressed is at once *the return of the repressed*, the original cathexis being able to betray itself through whatever parapraxis the symptom hooks onto.

Thus, in Freud's later topography – that of the id, ego, and superego – we see the symptom as the manifestation of repressed content (in the id) by the ego, made in deference to the superego. In effect – if we could discuss these constituents independently – if it could, the id would display its content uninhibitedly, but the ego realises that the superego would look down upon this, and thus it represses this content, by taking it into itself, which forces its recathexis – makes *it* (Lacan's word for 'id') *speak* – through another channel (the symptomal manifestation); a process effected by *jouissance*, and to this extent *jouissance* is repression's irreducible and inextricable *other side*. As Lacan states in Seminar III:

> [The] symptom acts as a language that enables repression to be expressed. This is precisely what enables us to grasp the fact that repression and the return of the repressed are one and the same thing, the front and back of a single process.[20]

It is in repression's expression – the simultaneous moment of repression and return – that *jouissance* is effected and inextricably cathected to the symptom.[21] If we continue to think repression and the return of the repressed in these Lacano-Machereyan terms – front and back, verso and recto (*envers, endroit*) – then we can postulate that it is in fact *jouissance* that is inscribed on either of these (Möbian) sides, and that the symptom is thus their *reading* (a reading *aloud*).

Thus, in the symptomal process the subject encounters *jouissance*. That is, despite – or because of – repression's best efforts, *jouissance* is nevertheless derived from the unconscious, through the symptom; the symptom smuggles it into the psyche, causing *souffrance*. This *souffrance* is at once both piquant pain and *enjoyment* (*jouissance*) (in the legal sense of 'enjoyment of rights', or, more desperately, of clinging onto property), in that it is the holding-in-reserve, the deferral or abeyance of the symptom's, and thus the *jouissance*'s, dissolution.[22] As Freud argues from the beginning of his psychoanalytic works, the subject feels a certain comfort in the symptom's repetition, in the putting off of its being reduced or dissolved. To describe this strange temporality of the symptom we could suggest that it is always-already *in lieu*.

Thus, the symptom can be construed as the means by which a subject gets its 'fix' of *jouissance*, but, like a fix of an addictive drug such as heroin, this fix only implies the necessity of the next, of its repetition; this is *jouissance*'s *souffrance*; as such, it embodies the doubled extremes of pleasure and pain at once, and is the combination of placeholding and *lack*. Thus, as well as the comfort found in the symptom's abeyance, in its repetition, we find also in its deferral, in its procrastination, its yearning and seeking, its very renewal. This rather Schopenhauerian connotation is arrived at by Adrian Dannatt in an article for the 'Joyce *avec* Lacan' issue of *lacanian ink*, in which he searches for a notion of *jouissance* in the specifically Irish context of the Celtic word 'craic', or the anglicised 'crack', describing it as what 'one continues looking for although one already knows that it is by its nature impossible to grasp', and likening it to the social phenomenon of the consistently-renewed search for *the craic*; 'a good time, a celebration, a satisfying social encounter, fun in fact', as well as to the sexual desire for '*the crack*', which he construes as a certain Platonic form; 'never 'a crack' but always 'the crack', rather than a specific vagina belonging to someone, a universal, generalized Ur-vagina, 'The Origin of the World' as painted by Courbet', and to the yearning for the impossibly ultimate 'orgasm beyond orgasm'; and finally to the drug crack cocaine, which, he suggests, 'in its repetitive, compulsive lack of completion [. . .] seems as good a definition as any of *jouissance*'.[23]

Thus, in these constituents' relation the symptom conveys *jouissance* (to the subject) from the unconscious, a *jouissance* which as we have seen can only in fact be the *promise* of *jouissance*. This impasse represents in effect what Zupančič frames as the 'Sadeian ethics of the Real', in that if *jouissance* was to be encountered in its fullest extreme it wouldn't be somatically sustainable by the subject: 'The problem is that the body is not made to the measure of enjoyment.'[24] In the notorious example of the Marquis de Sade:

> The basic problem that confronts [his] heroes/torturers is that they can torture their victims only until they die. The only regrettable and unfortunate thing about these sessions – which could otherwise go on *endlessly*, towards more and more accomplished tortures – is that the victims die *too soon*, with respect to the extreme suffering to which they might have been subjected. The enjoyment [*jouissance*] – which the victims seem to experience and

> which coincides, in this case, with their extreme suffering – encounters here an obstacle in the form of the 'pleasure principle' – that is, the limit to what the body can endure[.] If the body is to be equal to the task (or duty) of *jouissance*, the limits of the body have to be 'transcended'.[25]

This presents us with the realisation of death as the limit in the Real to the Imaginary body; that is, the image of the body as permanent, as everlasting, imagined as eternal, even 'transcendable' (in the belief that that which animates the body can transcend it). Thus, as Lacan states, 'the subject is not condemned to his consciousness, but to his body', in its very Real, in its terminable limit, and also in its *imaginary relation*, which fantasises an instance of *that which does not cease*; a universal constituent continually existent both in a manifestation of singularity (life) and in its aftermath ('afterlife'); that which has been supposed by so many postulations of concepts of a life after death.[26] These reflections on thanatology (the study of death), in relation to singularity, will be furthered in the next chapter, suffice to say that we see here that *jouissance*, siphoned by the symptom, is on the side of the death drive, and is thwarted in its extreme tendency by the pleasure principle.[27]

To render how the symptom's form of siphoning *jouissance* – which gives it its sustenance – operates, Lacan suggests in Seminar XXIII that 'it is in so far as it is hooked onto language that the symptom subsists'; thus, it is as a form of *jouis-sens* (*enjoy-meaning*) that it *enjoys* (in its *enjoy-meant*).[28] The symptom subsists by displaying itself through language, the language of parapraxis (from Freudian slips to nervous tics), which repeats itself until it is countered, but which in some cases remains unresolvable. For this reason, in the later Lacan there arises the concept of the subject coming to *assume their symptom*, to identify with it (at the end of analysis) and to operate with and within it with a certain confidence; that is to say, to *enjoy the symptom*. Lacan raises and discusses this issue specifically in relation to Joyce's symptomatology, and to the discourse of *Finnegans Wake*, in the first 'Joyce the Symptom' lecture, in which he advises:

> Read a few pages of *Finnegans Wake*, without trying to understand: *it* reads itself. It reads itself, but as someone remarked, someone in my vicinity, it reads itself because one can sense the presence of the *jouissance* of he who wrote it. We may wonder – or at least what the person in question wondered – is this why Joyce published it? [. . .] I wish, were he here, that I could convince him that he wanted to be Joyce the symptom, insofar as he gives the symptom its apparatus, its essence, its abstraction. Because if, as Clive Hart notes – one finds that, if one follows in Joyce's footsteps, one is, in the end, tired out – it only proves that your own symptoms are the only ones that carry interest for you. The symptom of Joyce is a symptom that does not concern you at all. It is the symptom insofar as there is no chance it will catch something of your unconscious. I believe that is the meaning of what that person said, who asked me about the reason for Joyce's publication.[29]

The postulation '*it* reads' [*ça se lit*] is the extension of Lacan's earlier formulation for the unconscious, '*it* speaks' [*ça parle*]. On these two postulations' relations to discourse we will focus in chapter 5, but in *its* reading (itself) in *Finnegans Wake* we begin to see the manifesting of Joyce's own *jouissance* in what Lacan comes to term Joyce-the-Symptom; the *making of his own name* in the symptom, the construction of it in his writing. This process Philip Dravers describes as:

> A dereliction of the name in Joyce in which autograph becomes a pure orthography, legible throughout, from *aperlogue* to *epellogue*, as "otherwise spelled, changeably meaning vocable scriptsigns." It is this that demonstrates the *intrajouissance* of Joyce in relation to the enjoyment inscribed in the ciphering of his symptom: hence *Joyce–le–symptôme*, Joyce who made a litter out of the letter and who, by courting the University as partner of his *jouissance*, sought in his own unique way to become the "all-hail hereafter."[30]

Dravers's concept of an 'autograph of pure orthography' I have elsewhere combined in the term '*orthograph*' – the signature of the process of 'auto-orthography' – in relation to the self-spellings of names of authors and in novels in the more contemporary literature of Audre Lorde and Jack Kerouac.[31] His statement here about the courtship of the University is derived from Joyce's famously stating of *Ulysses* that he had 'put in [it] so many enigmas and puzzles that it will keep the professors busy for centuries arguing over what [he] meant'; of the *Wake* he had told the bookseller Jacob Schwartz that he had chosen to write it in the style in which he was so as 'to keep the critics busy for three hundred years'.[32] In this, Joyce's name becomes guaranteed; it will be 'all-hailed hereafter' in its repetition through endless exegeses, in which its ciphering will be constantly renewed and recirculated, through its shifting meanings and its derelictions and renascences.

This flirtation with the academia thus co-opts the university discourse, but it does so seemingly from the position of the *objet a*; that is, the position of the analyst's discourse. For its readers, the *Wake* is able to present itself as the *a*, the cause of desire; of the desire *to know*. However, any *certain knowledge* in the text of *Finnegans Wake* is as unplaceable and bottomless as Freud's navel is in dreams, because of the endless deferrals, referrals, convolutions, and involutions of its language's, and letters', *jouissance*.[33] Thus, Joyce's *jouissance* is made available across the text, but it resists interpretation; or at least a singular, resolvable interpretation: *it* reads itself only, in itself. To this process the reader of the *Wake* must be secondary; thus, it is this '*intrajouissance*' of Joyce-the-Symptom that tires the reader out, in that its writing is *exhaustive* and *inexhaustible* at once, in its fissiparity and refract- and reflectivity.

Thus we meet again with Lacan's particular reading of the 'dumbillsilly' question in the *Wake*. The transliteration back into English that appears as 'Where is your gift, you imbecile?' seems to present the very question that Lacan is posing here to Joyce, though, paradoxically, *in Joyce's very own words*; that is, precisely: what does his *jouissance give* to the reader, if it cannot catch something of his or her unconscious? It is this question that will occupy a central place in chapters 5 and 6, although we make advances towards addressing it herein in this. As mentioned in the previous chapter, it is of course that Lacan's reading itself was only caught from Tindall's reader's guide to the *Wake*.

Thus we see that for Lacan Joyce's language is 'unsubscribed from the unconscious', as he describes it, and *exhausting* for the reader, in that it makes the reader work ceaselessly in deciphering its *ricorsi* – or recursions – of endless possible meanings (only to recipher them again), tiring him or her out; and in that *it cannot be read exhaustively* (except by itself, in its required somnambulant, Möbius-like insomnia), and is thus irreducible analytically.[34] Whilst it may seem to share similarities with the analysand's speech in analysis – in which symptoms are spoken by the analysand (of interest, ultimately, only to the analysand), as well as so many utterances 'of doubtful value to [. . .] the subject who communicates them' – the *Wake* operates a *discourse without speech*, in which its symptomal *jouissance* is found discoursing within itself, *intracoursing*, bubbling to the surface in *rejouissances* (such as in Lacan's rereading in French of the 'dumbillsilly' sentence, in which Joyce's, Tindall's, and his *jouissances* combine), and babbling up in its riverrun, as *lalangue*.[35] In that it is unsubscribed from the unconscious, uncathected in it, and *unhooked onto language* – to reverse Lacan's formulation for the symptom, in heading towards the *sinthome* – the *jouissance* that *reads itself* in Joyce-the-Symptom requires a process of *waking* (a *wake*) to be read: *waking the read*; a Joycéance. The concept of *rejouissance*, as a means of such waking the read, fits here, and will be explored further in chapter 5.

It is in its interest to the subject himself or herself that the symptom subsists, in the senses of the comfort that comes with it, discussed earlier, and of its delivery of *jouissance* through language – that is, of *jouis-sens* – but also in the assumptive sense that the later Lacan arrives at. His argument is that Joyce takes his symptom into himself, manifesting it within and utilising it creatively (with *artifice*), thus becoming Joyce-the-Symptom. It is *the name he makes for himself* through his art, and it becomes part of the mechanism to be put in place of the deficient (Name-of-the-)Father. As Véronique Voruz argues:

> It is Joyce's writing that offers Lacan his first insight into the possibility of transforming the symptom into something *positive*, a possibility that throws some light on his enigmatic phrase of 1976 to the effect that the concluding moment of an analysis may be an identification with one's symptom. Such a transformation – from symptom as cause of suffering to symptom as knotting of identity and enjoyment – is nowhere better illustrated than in artistic creation, which produces effects going well beyond the fleeting escape from the symptomatic grip produced by mere equivocation.[36]

As we have seen already, the process by which the *sinthome* functions – its discoursing of *lalangue* – is the other side of equivocation, but equivocation is also the 'only weapon' with which to combat the *sinthome*. There is thus in these functionings' separation the 'tendency towards reunion'; a unificatory/separatory force which strikes the balance between (Joycean) sanity and (Joycean) singularity.

Lacan's use of the term Joyce-the-Symptom, from the symposial 'Joyce the Symptom' talks onwards, becomes trajectorily synonymous with the *sinthome* (the former's use has all but disappeared from the *Sinthome* Seminar itself), but it is a concept we shouldn't risk completely conflating, as its differentiation from the *sinthome* is subtle, but important. Indeed, it is through the fact that Joyce-the-Symptom is a *part* of the knotting mechanism that suppletes the Name-of-the-Father that we come to the more irreducible role of the *sinthome*. The *sinthome* is the Real of the symptom, and thus its always-other side; it is that which is constitutive of the symptom and irreducible within it; the *lining* of (Joyce-)the(-)Symptom. Thus, it is this aspect of the symptom that Joyce assumes in becoming Joyce-the-Symptom.

In the subject-who-has-assumed-their-symptom it is thus the *necessity* of the *sinthome* that they have come to terms with. On the side of the symptom is its *comfort* – its compromise-formations, made of whatever contingent elements are required to maintain its equilibrium – but on the side of the *sinthome* is its constitutive *necessity*. In our discussion of Joycean sexuality to follow we will demonstrate these reflections with recourse to Lacan's four types of writing, but to display this now via the principle of *enverity* we show:

Joyce-the-Symptom

/ \

Symptom *Sinthome*

(*[contingent] comfort*) (*necessity*)

Figure 3.3 Unificatory/separatory principle (A: *Joyce-the-Symptom* < 1: *Symptom*, 2: *Sinthome*)

Voruz further argues that

> although Lacan's teaching may be marked by a number of failed attempts to treat the symptom completely, it is only with Joyce that [he] comes to accept irreducibility as *structural* and to envisage the symptom as a necessary residue of the very fact that we speak.[37]

This irreducible 'residue' – as Voruz calls it – is that which can be seen symptomally strewn all over Joyce's work, and at its most uninhibited, or *unhinged*, in *Finnegans Wake*; the *structural* position it occupies is that of *singularity*. It is Joyce's symptomal singularity that is the stress of the concept of Joyce-the-Symptom, and it is this singularity that fills the pages of the *Wake*; so singular is it in fact – so *particular* and peculiar to Joyce – that the book's very publication, its being put into the *public* realm, becomes a question for Lacan and his group.

'If the work of art, in its exaltation, as Freud would say, is supposed to uncover the repressed by all, by the many, it's precisely there that Joyce becomes a question', Josefina Ayerza argues;

> the huge concentration of puns in his writings doesn't provoke this effect, no laughter is on the side of the reader. It came to be known though, through the account of his wife Nora, that Joyce laughed thoroughly while writing [the] *Wake*. "You get to read it, but because you feel the presence of the *jouissance* of he who wrote that."[38]

This last quotation is of course another rendering of the sentence from the long passage from 'Joyce the Symptom' quoted earlier. The laughter of Joyce's *jouissance* is, then, present in the work, but it demands a certain kind of reader to acknowledge its structure: the reader of the University, whom Joyce co-opts and 'makes partner' to his *jouissance*; the reader for whom his or her own symptoms are not the only of interest, who, despite fatigue and the impossibility of the cessation of reading, will continue working on and deciphering the book *that does not cease to write itself*; the 'transferential addressee', in Derrida's words, who may not be an analyst, but who is *driven* by, and towards, the *jouissance* of Joyce-the-Symptom, and of the *Wake*'s *sinthomic* writing, by a drive which – in contrast to the homeostatic operation of the pleasure principle – 'consists of a push toward raising the level of tension', as Harari puts it.[39]

In respect to the *jouissance* encountered in Joyce-the-Symptom, Harari continues:

> *Jouissance* does not tend to reduce toward zero; [. . .] it is not a matter of the least possible *jouissance* – the ideal condition for the ethical and philosophical model of Epicurus, but of enjoying more and more, right up to the limit of death as the only unavoidable finality.[40]

Hence the distinction to be made here between *drive* and *desire*; although the *Wake* may animate the desire to know, in its role as *objet a* it must consistently thwart this in its semantic mis- and redirection, converting this desire into an unstoppable drive whose 'unavoidable finality' makes of it ultimately the *death drive*. However, it is this very drive that animates the *enjoyment* of the *Wake*; that of its guaranteed recurrence and inexhaustibility for the reader on this side of the death drive; that is, in life. The other side – that of '*it reads*' – is it in its 'undead' and *intrajouissant* recursive state, that of *its* very own *intrajouissant* death drive; and what are we separated from this death-driven *intrajouissance* by if not a *transparent sheet* (in the form of the *desire to know* that it inaugurates, in that of the *object meaning*, to the dignity of which we thus attempt to raise the *Wake*'s *jouis-sens*)?

Thus we see the irony in Anthony Burgess's statement that *Finnegans Wake* is 'one of the few books of the world that can make us laugh aloud on nearly every page', that he makes in the introduction to his abridged edition.[41] In appearing as it does in his truncated *A Shorter* Finnegans Wake – which has not nearly every page of the original in it – it precisely misses the truly *unending* nature of Joyce's *jouissance* across the work as a(n unending) whole; this irony, however, shares in that which Lacan identifies in the fact of the *Wake*'s very publication itself, and in the question of how Joyce could *finish* the *Wake*, and whether in fact he did. An analysis of if and why the work is funny, however – which runs the risk of undoing the jokes, as Freud warns of – will not be attempted here, but the processes by which its *jouissance* is displayed will be investigated in the dealings with its semantics and semiotics in chapter 5, suffice to say of the struggle to canonically place *Finnegans Wake*, which Derek Attridge speaks of in *Peculiar Language*; in terms of determining its literary 'serious-' or 'non-seriousness', the work's *singularity* should perhaps be read as *the* very singularity of literature itself (to play with Attridge's later title, *The Singularity of Literature*).[42] In Attridge's deliberating over the *Wake*'s canonical position as a 'central-' or 'limit-text' we should be prepared to put the *Wake*an discourse itself in position A in our principle, and the concepts of 'centre-' and 'limit-text' in positions 1 and 2.[43] Rather than this appearing a slightly facile solution to the problem of *Finnegans Wake*'s literary position, it should rather serve to demonstrate the precise position of singularity, as that which both spawns the categories into which it might then be put, and that which also deconstructs these conventions, especially when they begin to stagnate. In Walter Benjamin's words, which can easily be applied to the *singularity* of the *Wake*: 'A major work will either establish the genre or abolish it; and the perfect work will do both.'[44]

We must now look at Joyce-the-Symptom's process for the effectuation of at once establishing and abolishing genre. 'It may be in Joyce', Voruz states,

> that Lacan first discovers the possibility of a symptom functioning independently of the Other, a possibility that is, however, coupled with the realization that the symptom endures even after the subject is freed from his oppressive belief in the Other.[45]

We here see, in relation to the big Other, that Joyce certainly comes down on the side of *jouissance* in a binary that comes about in Lacan's late work, the functioning of which Zupančič explains in relation to subjective *responsibility*:

> Other/*jouissance*. In regard to the Other, I am not the author of my acts (i.e. the Other 'speaks/acts through me'); thus I may not be held responsible for them. However, there is something else which 'grows' from this act, namely, some *jouissance*. It is in this fragment of *jouissance* that we must situate the subject and his responsibility.[46]

Thus, the responsibility that Joyce takes for his work – the putting of it in his own name – is locatable on this plane of *jouissance*. His *jouissance*, however, is not just a fragment, leftover, indivisible remainder, or stain, a residue of the fact of speaking – of being spoken by the big Other, of speaking *into* the Other, in order to find its validation – but becomes the fundamental constituent of his subjectivity and his creative prowess (his *artifice*). It is his *jouissance* that he works on, and *enjoys*, in the *Wake*. Thus, he escapes the oppressiveness of being spoken by the big Other, which therefore entails being responsible *for it*, in all its temporal and temporary ideological fixations and fixities – 'the realm of what is considered acceptable or, in other words, prejudices', as Lacan calls them in Seminar VII – and becomes responsible for, and *to*, his own *jouissance* instead (in the further sense of responding *to it*).[47]

Thus, while 'man's desire is the desire of the Other', as Lacan puts it in Seminar XI – one of the meanings of which is that man has the desire for the Other *to exist* – Joyce's seems not to be, and this becomes an important critical and ethical crux in his work; that is, his non-observation of the Other's rule(s): his very *obversation* of this.[48] Further, to put this in the terms of the Master's discourse as elucidated in Seminar XVII, Joyce seems to not seek – at least with *Finnegans Wake* – the validation of a master signifier, S_1, which leaves this S_1 a little wan.[49] As Pierre Thèves puts it: 'In what Lacan calls the progress of the big Other' Joyce thus moves 'without guidance', without *its* guidance.[50] Therefore, in becoming disinvested from the mythical big Other, Joyce manages to avoid what Lacan calls in Seminar XXIII a 'trap of history', its 'captivating myth'; history of course being the 'nightmare from which [Joyce is] trying to awake', as he puts it in *Ulysses*.[51] In the *Sinthome* Seminar Lacan states that 'history is the greatest of fantasies. Behind history, the factual history historians are interested in, there is myth, and myth is always captivating'; indeed, he takes issue with Joyce's increasing entanglement of myths in his late works.[52] However, as Franco Moretti has noted:

> It is no longer possible to doubt that Joyce uses myth only to desecrate it, and through it to desecrate contemporary history: to parody Bloom with Ulysses, and Ulysses with Bloom; to create an order which gives greater relief to the absence of order, a nucleus gone haywire with irony and distortions.[53]

Thus, in Joyce's singular laughter in the composition of *Finnegans Wake* – that which fuelled the seventeen years of its production – he is read as not having looked for verification in the big Other; his work is thus divested of the Other, but this does not dissolve the symptom, nor does it *absolve* the *sin*thome (to re-evoke the Joycean ontology outlined in the last chapter; Joyce's statement that *sin* lays life upon one). Thus, we find in Seminar XXIII that the symptom (in those that have identified with its real, the *sinthome*) is to be located in the order of the Real; 'the identification with the symptom', in respect to its constitution of singularity – as Paul Verhaeghe and Frédéric Declercq state – is thus 'not a Symbolic or Imaginary one, but a Real identification, functioning as a suppletion (*suppléance*) for the lack of the Other'.[54] Without the big Other – having escaped it – the symptom still subsists, in something of a hyperactive form, as its *suppletion*.

The big Other is in fact inverted to a certain degree in this divestment; in Joyce's disinvestment from the unconscious. As Lacan states in Seminar XXIII: 'Meaning is the Other of the real.'[55] In *Finnegans Wake* this formulation is exemplified by the work's disinvestment from the big Other, in which it does not seek approval or verification, presenting in its language's 'little bits of Real' the Other of meaning; that is, something of the Real itself. It is in this singularity of *Finnegans Wake*, its unstable and paradoxical ability to present bits of Real semantically, through writing – a means typically of conveying meaning – that its genre is at once, and continually, established and abolished.

Thus, the Other can be inverted; in the Other, meaning is the inversion of the real, and vice versa; but, because of this, *there can be no Other of the Other*. Although Lacan visually demonstrates this inversion with recourse to the Borromean knot, which we will look at in the coming chapter, if we were to put it into the structure of the principle of *enverity*, into positions 1 and 2 would go the big Other, as both verifier of meaning, and its *inversion* in the real; that is, as the Other of meaning. Position A, however, would of necessity only represent the *lack of the Other*. 1 and 2 are thus synonymous as Other, even in their dichotomy; but this is due to them in fact not being sides, but rather only the 'inside-out' of one another; this is the very *logic of inversion*. It is for this reason that Lacan repeats here that neither is there, nor can there possibly be, an 'Other of the Other. In the place of the Other of the Other, there is no order of existence'; i.e., Other as meaning, and as real, *at once*, does not have an other side, or even a structuring principle; that is, one that could be located outside of the Real-Symbolic-Imaginary triad (or even – *extimately* – in the overlapping of the orders *inside* it), and which would occupy position A.[56] This is to precisely say that the Imaginary *is* imaginary; that the sides of the Other – Symbolic meaning and meaningless Real – correspond through a relation that can only be *imagined*, that is *imaginary*. It is for this reason – the lack of the Other, of an adjudicator, or auditor, as in Beckett's *Not I* – that we must fully assume our symptom and thus our responsibility; for, at base, there isn't *anOther* to whom we could impute it.

Sinthome

Thus, if Joyce-the-Symptom is Joyce's singularity – in its divestment from the Other, and disinvestment from the unconscious – then, for Lacan, the *sinthome* is the seat of this singularity. Verhaeghe and Declercq suggest that 'Lacan coins the *sinthome* to designate the idiosyncratic *jouissance* of a particular subject'.[57] If this 'idiosyncratic *jouissance*' is so much at stake in the concept of Joyce-the-Symptom it is so only in that it is *Joyce's* idiosyncrasy that is particular to it. Joyce's idiosyncrasy is a remarkable one, however, hence its importance to Lacan, in his making of it the very concept of Joyce-the-Symptom. It is that which causes Lacan's surprise at the fact of Joyce's refusal – 'such mental refusal!' – of psychoanalysis, in that Joyce assumed his symptom of his own accord, and in that he made (it) his own name: 'Joyce(-the-Symptom)'.

In the *sinthome*, however, this idiosyncratic *jouissance* is extended to individuals as such; that is, to any and every *particular subject*. Here, like the word 'certain', 'particular' encompasses antithetical meanings (it contains its own inverse), which become determined by whether it is preceded or not by a definite article (i.e., *this* particular subject, or *a* particular subject; *a* certain number, or *the* certain amount).[58] The importance of this antithetical quality – of having this double meaning at once in the one word – is that this is precisely what is to be found in the endlessly enigmatic concept of the *sinthome*: it is *the* (singular, *particular*) seat of singularity, of *particularity*, in an individual, and yet it encompasses all kinds of particular content; its content is always particular to the individual. To annex a phrase of Christine Froula's, *sinthomes* are what are 'infused from the first with a natural signature – unconscious, singular, ineluctable, inimitable; their destinations [are] unforeknown and unforeclosed' (precise connotations of which can be located in the instance of creation of singularity taken from Dante's *Divine Comedy* as our epigraph); because of this, *sinthomes* form something of what is 'in you more than you', as is Lacan's description of the *objet a* in Seminar XI.[59]

It is for these reasons that in defining the *sinthome* we run the risk of *being run away with* by it, of getting wrapped up in its ceaseless production of singularities, puns and contingent linkages, which are, nonetheless, necessary to the concept, *qua* what we have tried to precisely term the '*empty signified*'. In Lacan's own discourse on the *sinthome* he negotiates such association and precision to elucidate this particular concept in its own particular style(s). We will thus be careful in trying to navigate the *sinthome*'s course similarly, in concentrating on its form, and on its content; in running the gauntlet of the interpretations it has been given by Lacan and by his successors; in employing *Wake*an referentiality whilst remaining restrained in the wake of its connotations; and in utilising a language necessary to its contingency, aware always that like 'the word in poetry' – as the Russian formalist Viktor Shklovsky states – the *sinthome* 'is not just a word. It draws in its wake dozens of and thousands of associations. It is permeated with them, just as the Petersburg air during a blizzard is permeated with snow'.[60]

At the same time, we must keep in mind the pun's necessitous place in the conceptuality of both Lacan and Joyce; just as Joyce masterfully replied 'to the objection of triviality', aimed at his usage of portmanteau words in the *Wake*: 'Yes[,] some of the means I use are trivial – and some are quadrivial', so too did Lacan just as masterfully come back at the similar charge that he used 'just a bunch of plays on words', with: 'That's true[,] but I attach a great deal of importance to plays on words, as you know. They seem to me to be the key to psychoanalysis'; a truism it wouldn't have taken much reflection on the part of his interlocutor to have arrived at before formulating the assertion that quickly pales under the weight of its rejoinder.[61]

Beckett of course has Murphy state that 'in the beginning was the pun'.[62] Lacan bolsters this claim through demonstrating its originary importance in the work of Freud, and to the concept of the unconscious:

> A system of signifiers, a language, has certain characteristics that specify the syllables, the usage of words, the locutions into which they are grouped, and

> this conditions what happens in the unconscious, down to its most original fabric. If the unconscious is as Freud depicts it, a pun can in itself be the linchpin that supports a symptom, a pun that doesn't exist in a related language. This is not to say that symptoms are always based on puns, but that they are always based on the existence of signifiers as such, on a complex relationship of totality to totality, or more exactly of entire system to entire system, of universe of signifiers to universe of signifiers.[63]

Thus it is that in thinking the concept of the *sinthome* we will have to see its positioning – as the *empty signified* (which can allow a multiform universe of signifiers into it) – as *the place of the pun*, and its functioning as that of *punning itself*, allowing of the play involved in the concept, and in its trajectory, from Lacan's original pronouncements on it, through subsequent critical and clinical work. This very modality of the *empty signified* Moretti directly identifies in Joyce, claiming that:

> The difference between 'decadent poetics' and *Ulysses* can be summed up in the following formula: in the former a single signifier produces many signifieds, whereas in Joyce a single signified produces many signifiers. This reversal dissolves the demiurgic role of the author, who is placed on the same level as all other possible authors.[64]

This levelling of the author with all other possible authors is a process also involved in the *sinthome*, in that it is the seat of individuality in *all* individuals. We have postulated already that the *sinthome* to an extent is the symptom's *other side*, but this example of *enverity* is not as simple as all that in that the *sinthome* is resistant to the very concept of *the side*, or of being a side (we could say that it is sideless and infinitely-sided at once; that it is on all sides, but does not take a side, in its indefinite/definite particularity). Thus, we will give the slightly unsettling image of *flypaper* as that by which we can bring these concepts into the unificatory/separatory principle. If we imagine the two-sided sticky flypaper sheet, to one side we will see stuck the symptom; that is, further, the subject in his or her *enjoyment* of the symptom (their *suffering* if they haven't come to terms with it; their *identification* with it if they have come to assume their symptom). To the other side we will place Shklovsky's blizzard, though we should picture it slightly surreally as a blizzard made of flies, or of moths; as it is with the *sinthome* – to use a metaphor of Hunter Thompson's – that 'we are [always] like moths in a blizzard'; a blizzard, that is, *of moths*.[65] Here we begin to see emerge – as well as *the sinthome* in its singularity, as the very seat of singularity – the concept of a plurality of '*sinthomes*'; that is, their functioning as *points of jouissance*. These could be construed as a sea of 'bits of Real'; else we could envisage a picture of the *sinthome* permeating as a singular snowflake in a snowstorm dozens and thousands of *sinthome*-snowflakes deep.

Thus it is these *points of jouissance* that make up the discursive material (at base, *lalangue*) from which endless associations – from those involved in common communication to those flowing in *intrajouissant* punning – are formed. To put it precisely antithetically, ***the*** *sinthome* is also ***a*** *sinthome*; ***the*** *sinthome* – which is the ultimate symptom; that is, *ultimately the symptom* – is made of, based on, ***a*** *sinthome*, or any number of *sinthomes*. Thus, we can visualise these ruminations – in relation to the flypaper sheet which unites and separates the symptom and the *sinthome* – with the following diagram:

Symptom Flypaper *Sinthome*

(*Subject*) (*points of jouissance*)

Figure 3.4 Diagram of the symptom, the *sinthome*, and the flypaper sheet

It is in that such flypaper is translucent (opaquely transparent) that we are able to perceive faintly from the side of the subject (of the symptom) the impressions of the *points of jouissance* that stick to its other – *sinthomic* – side, which are then open to interpretation (interpretation which, if any way successful, could lead either to the resolution of the symptom, or to its assumption, by the subject). This goes to reinforce the symptom's position – in this dualistic-tripartite model – as the *empty signifier*, in that the *sinthomes* (as *empty signifieds*) at the cores of symptoms' messages are constituted by their subjects' socio-historical situationing, against which these messages (their *significations*) are matched in their analyses, leading in turn to their interpretation; their roles as *signifiers* thus becoming *filled.* Fundamentally, then, symptoms occupy the position of *signifier*, but are *empty* of any definitive particular content until it is given to them; i.e., initially, from a '*Stück*' – a little bit of Real that has got *stuck* – in the *sinthome* (which thus *fills* it, as *signified*), from which a multiplicity of connections with other moments in a subject's socio-historic positioning is produced.[66] Later, definitive content may be given to symptoms by their interpretation, in conjunction with said socio-historic positioning (or at least with the version of it that the subject gives in analysis).

In the case of *the sinthome*, as we have already argued, we must see it as the *empty signified*, in that it represents that area – the *sinthomic* side of the flypaper sheet (which acts in much the same way as the translucent waxed sheet does in Freud's writing-pad) – into which '*a sinthome*', a *point of jouissance*, a little bit (*Stück*) of the Real, gets *stuck*. We might see this most clearly in Joyce in Molly Bloom's soliloquy at the end of *Ulysses*, into which *sinthomic* matrix so many residues, and bits of (her) Real, stick, and are then enabled to repeat and radiate in their singularity because of the lack of any regular and restrictive diacritical demarcation or commonplace and constraining punctuation used in the passage's writing. We can take a particularly topical string of words from the episode as an example: 'White Arsenic she put in his tea off flypaper because they cant get on why they call it that if I asked him hed say its from the Greek'.[67] Here we can clearly see a chain of significations; Molly wonders at the word 'Arsenic' most likely because it contains the word 'arse', the organ of her husband's sexual fixation which she ruminates on recursively during her soliloquy; this brings her to think of Leopold himself (designated by 'him') – to whom she always returns in her thoughts – and his predilection for etymology, a residue from his explanation earlier in the day of the concept of 'metempsychosis' to her; the very process of etymology acting here like the *sinthome* itself in its drawing-out of a singular sense from a sea of meanings (or a babbling *lalangue* of '*jouis-sens*es').[68]

However much this may seem like precise psychoanalytic interpretation of Molly Bloom – that is, like 'applied psychoanalysis', a literary practice which Lacan denigrates at various points – it is in fact merely a step on the way to recognising the endlessness of interpretation that the *sinthome* puts fully on view; although Joyce indefatigably ties all his references up and makes them circulate in his writing's *intrajouissance*, there are still plenty of other inferences that can be made that may not accord with what had been specifically 'planted' by him, and which are yet no less valid for this reason; a phenomenon so often seen in Joyce Studies, from subtle conjectures to extravagant speculation.[69] Indeed, as Joyce himself said: 'Though people may read more into *Ulysses* than I ever intended, who's to say that they are wrong: do any of us know what we are creating?'[70] The depths of Joyce's work, then, are so plumbable that we may in fact never stop the act of interpretation (and to assume this, the *sinthome* of interpretation – that is, of *not ceasing* interpreting – may well present a viable *end* of analysis in itself). Thus, to employ a pun, we could say that this type of endless interpretation is precisely *a gaze constituted by the navel* (and the navel in this passage from *Ulysses* is perhaps what remains enigmatic here; our entry-word, 'flypaper' itself).

If we were here to make a distinction between Joyce the modernist and Joyce the postmodernist it would be in areas in *Ulysses* such as this that it would come into play in that we see the operation of the symptom – in all its conceptual rigour (its matching its manifestation against its socio-historic situation; thinking of 'Arsenic' as screening really thinking of 'arses') – leading into the operation of the *sinthome*, in its *varity*; that is, its connectivity to so many *inter*- and *intra*various *truths*, and *jouissances*.

The definition of the *sinthome* at which we are arriving we can see Žižek also leading towards in *Enjoy Your Symptom!*, in which he suggests that 'in contrast to symptom which is a cipher of some repressed meaning, sinthom has no determinate meaning; it just gives body, in its repetitive pattern, to some elementary matrix of *jouissance*, of excessive enjoyment'.[71] In this statement we are given much to work with. First, the *sinthome* – in relation to the symptom 'as a cipher of some repressed meaning' – is that which is on *the other side* of this meaning; its irreducible kernel of nonsense, which *sustains* its meaning. The *sinthome*, as the *empty signified*, is thus locatable here as the representative of 'meaning of meaning' – as Derrida calls it in 'Force and Signification' – that is, of 'infinite implication, the indefinite referral of signifier to signifier'; into this *empty signified* of the *sinthome* free-floating *points of jouissance* – signifiers in the specific sense that they *signify nothing*, as per Lacan's definition in Seminar III – cathect, as infinite-indefinite conveyors of signification (enjoy-meant).[72]

We could thus discuss the *sinthome, qua empty signified* (that is, the *sinthome*, as *one of its manifestations*, amongst the multitude) as the structure by which the signifier *slips into* the signified – as Lacan puts it in 'The Instance of the Letter' – or by which it *stuffs* the signified – as per the term used in Seminar XX. In that this combinatory of signification gets at the Saussurian concept of 'sign' – that is, of the signified and signifier together (in the algorithm of the former over the latter, separated by the bar; the hierarchy of which Lacan of course reverses in 'The Instance of the Letter') – we might here suggest the conjugation '*signthome*'. Indeed, Lacan himself equates sign and *sinthome* in Seminar XXIV, in stating that 'everything that is mental, when all is said and done, is what I write by the name of '*sinthome', s.i.n.t.h.o.m.e.*, namely, sign'.[73]

In Seminar III Lacan premonitorily discusses what would become *sinthomic* singularity in direct relation to the signifier:

> There is, in effect, something radically unassimilable to the signifier. It's quite simply the subject's singular existence. Why is he here? Where has he come from? What is he doing here? Why is he going to disappear? The signifier is incapable of providing him with the answer, for the good reason that it places him beyond death. The signifier already considers him dead, by nature it immortalizes him.[74]

The subject's singular existence here we could formulate as the '*signularity*' of the *sinthome* itself. The *empty signified* – which is as much Saussurian psychological concept as it becomes Lacanian somatic form[75] – is thus that which accepts a signifier into it, though this signifier, whilst animating the subject, must always remain enigmatic to him or her; it cannot answer the subject's existential questions any more than it can become assimilated *to* the subject's singular existence (it of course only *represents the subject to another signifier*). We could thus postulate the *sinthome* – as we will see Žižek doing to an extent momentarily – as something of a matrixial measure, a multi-possibilitous memic *blank*; the *empty signified* into which a signifier gets locked and is enabled to radiate *jouissance/jouis-sens*, to animate enjoyment/enjoy–meant, in something akin to the manner in which a prism spectralises and projects the light which enters it.[76] We might picture this with a reconceptualisation of the 'comb schema' – as Alfredo Eidelsztein calls it – from Freud's chapter on regression in *The Interpretation of Dreams*:

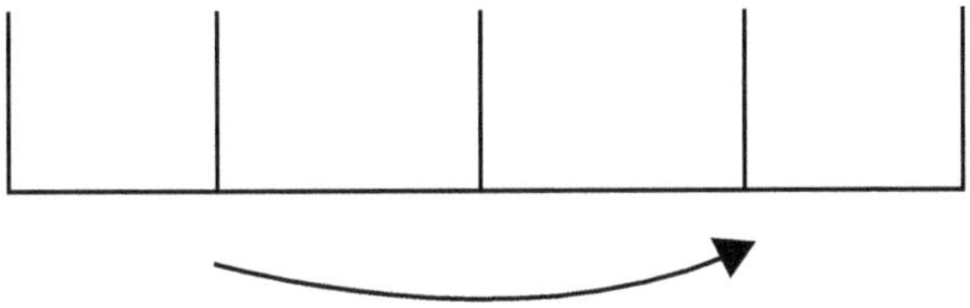

Figure 3.5 Freud's 'comb schema'[77]

Of course, in this one-dimensional Freudian topography, as Eidelsztein states, 'the vertical lines have no function in any dimension apart from the horizontal. It can only be crossed from left to right, in the same direction that we write', and as indicated by the arrow.[78] However, if we transposed the comb schema to three dimensions, we might be able to envisage the 'slots' between the vertical lines as *empty signifieds*, into which certain signifiers ('purely formal', until cathected in their combination's *signification*) become inserted. Thus, this is, to an extent, also a reconceptualisation of Saussure's famous schema of the two discursive 'waves' which constitute language – of signified ('the indefinite plane of jumbled ideas (*A*)') and signifier ('the equally vague plane of sounds (*B*)') – which come together through 'quilting points', as Lacan calls them, as pictured in Figure 3.6 (the hierarchy of which, to remain Lacanian, we here reverse):

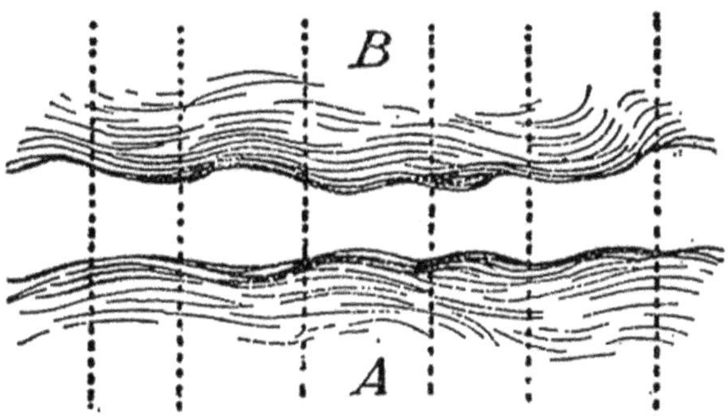

Figure 3.6 Saussure's 'discursive waves schema' (modified)[79]

In our reconceptualisation, we can now follow Lacan in his statements – made in Seminars XVI and III respectively – that 'it is not the signified that is within, it is very precisely the signifier', and that 'the signified is empty, the signifier is retained for its purely formal properties, which are used for example to form series'; series of representations that constitute the subject.[80] We can work with these postulates without the risk of departing from the structural anthropologist Claude Lévi-Strauss's assertion that 'the signifier precedes and determines the signified', as it is through its sliding into the signified that the signifier comes to determine it.[81] As Miller states, in Joyce's case such series formed through this process unfold from 'sources of reading, of the library. This is his life, those are his friends, his experiences, but like those of a novel, not of life. One cannot interpret them, because there is no function of truth: those who work on Joyce work in the dimension of exactitude'; the 'exactitude', that is, of tracing his references.[82] As a 'man of letters', Joyce's *corpus*; that is, his 'body's being (*l'être du corps*)', is both *being* (*l'être*) and *letter* (*lettre*) at once; homonymous, of course, in the French.[83]

A signifier – and subjective singularity rests on this contingency of there being *a certain* signifier, *amongst the multitude*, that sticks – locked into the signified thus drives the subject, creating in it its own *responsibility* (that is, both the radical accountability the subject must assume for himself or herself – in that the signifier does not provide an answer to the subject's questions – and the *response* to this fact that the subject continually gives, through its endless questioning).

Finally, our flypaper – one side of it, at least – represents in Žižek's earlier statement the process of repression itself; this is the process involved on the side of the symptom, and thus on that of the subject (the attempt at meaning's *exclusion*), whereas a certain *suppression* occurs from the side of the *sinthome* (in quashing *full exudation* of meaning – *sense* in all its sense *and* nonsense). This clearly shows the central *antagonism* inherent to the flypaper occupying position A in this structure, in which opposing forces – repression and suppression – are set going against each other. However, we must recall that Lacan proposes as a formula specifically for the subject – based on his reading of Freud – 'that it is repression that *produces* suppression'.[84] Repression – the attempt at exclusion of (a) *certain* meaning – is thus discovered as the fundamental constitutive feature of subjectivity.

This *certain meaning* is therefore representative of both *certain meanings* – those formed from moments in a subject's socio-historic situation, which are then matched against others, such as traumas, dreams, etc., which become repressed – and *certain meaning*; that is, the Real itself. This *certain meaning* (encompassing both of these instances) is thus locatable in the Real, which is repressed against by the subject, so as at once to *preserve* meaning for the subject by their *resisting* it; the subject unites itself to (its) meaning by separating itself from it (in its nonsensical entirety), the process of which we have seen in operation in the *originary screen*. Žižek hints at these connotations as he continues on from the quoted passage earlier: 'Although sinthoms do not have sense, they do radiate *jouis*-sense, enjoy-meant'; that is, the pure, death-driven *jouissance* of meaning, of (non)sense, which must only be obtained in little bits for it to *make any sense* to and for a subject: it is thus *against* sense that we erect our subjectivity.[85] Indeed, as are Lacan's last words of the *Sinthome* Seminar: 'There you have what I wanted to point out in this last session. One thinks against a signifier [. . .] one leans against a signifier in order to think. There you go, you are free.'[86] Unassimilable to the signifier the subject's existence erects itself *against* it; subjective thought is thus produced through this fundamental opposition, or *antagonism*, locatable in position A in the unificatory/separatory principle.

Further, in Žižek's definition we see in his very spelling of '*sinthome*' – which alters throughout his work – the concept's inconstancy at the level of content (the *content* even of its own orthography). Thus, as the *empty signified*, it can be filled by whatever *points of jouissance* come into it; by whatever gets stuck to it, or in it. We can see an analogy of this moment of the *filling* of the *empty signified* in Zupančič's elucidation of the origination of the Oedipus complex in the Oedipus myth itself, in which the protagonist – who doesn't have an Oedipus complex, but founds it by his *act* – 'answers [the Sphinx] with a single word, and he will become the hostage of this word, the truth of which he will attest to at a heavy price'.[87]

'What exactly does Oedipus do?' Zupančič asks; he does as the *empty signified* does: 'Pronounces a word, a signifier as a pure potentiality of a meaning that still has to come into being'; here we see the *sinthome* – as *empty signified* – in its position of *pronunciation, pronouncing* the ('purely formal') signifier which occupies it (the meaning of which will come into being through the subject's *singularity*).[88] In the Oedipus example, the *sinthomic* foundation here represents the impermeability (from one to another) of the sides of the *forced choice*, which was discussed earlier, in that from the side of this inaugural word's *contingency* – although it solved the riddle, it is not certain that it was the *only* order-word that would have – its *necessity* could not be seen; i.e., whatever the correct order-word pronounced, it always *would have* solved the riddle; and from the side of its *necessity* – the word *having had to have been* pronounced, and its consequences *having had to have come about* – its *contingency* was unviewable; i.e., in the fact that the oracle's prophecy concerning Oedipus actually only required the purely subjective enactment of these consequences. It is in such an interstice as this that we see the *sinthome*'s irreducibility; its positioning as a *forced choice*, or an 'ineluctable modality', to use Joyce's words.[89]

We will now continue with Žižek's interaction with the *sinthome* – a markedly singular (and varying) interaction, which inflects and furthers today's understanding of the concept – briefly, taking a tour through several of his references to it. In *The Fright of Real Tears* he locates the *sinthome* as *beyond* (human) meaning, as he sees in it an intrusiveness and insistence that resists any given '*frame of meaning*', the operation of which we see also in Joyce-the-Symptom's divestment from the big Other:

> When we pursue the work of interpretation far enough we encounter *sinthoms* (as opposed to symptoms, bearers of a coded message), formulations with no meaning guaranteed by the big Other, 'tics' and repetitive features that merely cipher a certain mode of *jouissance* and insist from one to another totality of meaning.[90]

Thus, the *sinthome* appears to be to Žižek something like a nontransplantable, but nevertheless living – and even *viral* – *organ without a body*; that which, however we unite/separate (our) reality, via the ontological *screen*, remains as a siphon of pure *jouissance*; *jouissance* being an element of the Real – or a Deleuzian 'intensity' within it – which would thus remain the same on either side of the screen, or without it (thus appearing as something of what Lacan at this stage in his teaching calls 'the One' – as opposed to the Other – which we will discuss further in chapter 5).

Thus, as Žižek states in *Organs Without Bodies* itself: 'The continuous proliferation of what Lacan called *sinthomes*, of the traces of affective intensities [. . .] should be interpreted not as an "allegory" with a fixed "deeper meaning" but as the 'pure "mechanic" intensity beyond meaning' (this 'beyond meaning' being 'meaning of meaning', as alluded to by Derrida; the infinite referrals of signification); that is, *jouissance* itself, in all its manifestations.[91] He goes on in this work to call the *sinthome* 'a figment of obscene enjoyment spreading like a virus', and asks: 'Could it be maintained that such intrusive *sinthomes* provide the zero-level, the elementary matrix, of memes?'[92] We will argue here that it is the *sinthomic* side of the flypaper sheet that is matrixial, as that onto which get stuck *points of jouissance* – or what we might loosely call (with Žižek) *sinthomes*; that is ' "anchors of familiarity," knots of potential meaning identified/recognized as "the same," independently of their actual meaning'.[93]

It is from the babble which Lacan called *lalangue* that these *points of jouissance* surface; that is, from that which 'preced[es] articulated language: the succession of Ones, signifiers of *jouis-sense* ("enjoy-meant")'.[94] It is these (primordial syllables, inaugural order-words) which get stuck – *initially* (i.e., before they *mean*) – in the *empty signified* of the *sinthome*. As Žižek claims in his first book (in English), *The Sublime Object of Ideology*: 'In so far as the *sinthome* is a certain signifier [we add: which becomes lodged in an '*empty signified*',] which is not enchained in a network but immediately filled, penetrated with enjoyment, its status is by definition 'psychosomatic', that of a terrifying bodily mark'.[95] This bodily mark, then, is the *sinthome* at its basest, or most carnal; that is, as that which is constitutive of our very psychosomatic bearing. It is thus at once the *being* stuck in the subject's body, and the subject's realisation of their being *stuck in the body*; this again is precisely the mechanism of the constitutive *forced choice*: meaning being *being*'s *being* means that the subject (the *being*) – insofar as he or she *means* – is stuck in, consigned, or condemned to, being(/meaning); that is, in, or to, the body that *is*, and that is, *insofar as it means*. Lacan marks this element of the *sinthome* with the syllable '*lom*', which we will discuss momentarily.

If the concept of the *sinthome* seems currently to be morphing in front of our very eyes, it is because it is in itself necessitously amorphous and pliable, inaugurally contentless, but immediately filled by fissiparous signification; it brings into itself multiform possibility and contingency; it is, as Žižek states, a concept 'containing a set of associations (synthetic-artificial man, synthesis between symptom and fantasy, Saint Thomas, the saint . . .)', certain of which we have begun to explore; others which we will come to.[96] It is indeed that which allows Lacan to go on something of a punning spree; in 'Joyce le Symptôme I' he etymologically takes 'symptom' back to its first spelling, as 'sinthome' (evidenced in the Bloch and von Wartburg etymological dictionary), to give the concept its *rebirth* from this point, much in the way that Joyce does with his (re)use of certain words in the Oxen of the Sun episode of *Ulysses*.[97] Commenting on Joyce's use at one point in the episode of Edmund Burke's writing style in his narration Jeri Johnson suggests that

> fertility for Joyce came in recirculation and recycling, not purifying and sterilizing. It came in the recognition that to reuse Burke was to renew Burke not kill him (nor was it to reinstall him in a position of prior authority; Burke once used by Joyce is no longer the same Burke).[98]

Thus, the *sinthome*, once used by Lacan, is no longer – nor can it be – the same 'sinthome'. Nonetheless, Lacan traces its etymological trajectory in his inaugural symposial talk to its updating to 'symptomate' by the doctor – and writer of *Gargantua and Pantagruel* – François Rabelais.[99] Thereafter, in the first session of the *Sinthome* Seminar, Lacan delineates a series of associations that can be made from the *sinthome*; first, he alludes to 'the fault my *sinthome* has the advantage of beginning with, the English sin', which – as we have seen – as well as the Bible, is indeed what Joycean ontology begins with.[100] He then goes on to situate the *sinthome* in relation to 'the in(si)stance of the letter' – as Thurston has it – warning that, however rigorously its writing may be handled, this 'will do nothing but displace the *sinthome*, or rather multiply it' (as we should be beginning to recognise); thus, the associations continue into the coining of the pun 'sinthomaquinas' ['*sinthomadaquin*'] (from St Thomas Aquinas, the theologian to whom Joyce pledged his aesthetic fidelity), which reduces to Joyce becoming simply the '*saint homme*' ('saint man', in the universal sense), which, 'contrary to what appears at first glance, given [Joyce']s detachment from politics, produces what [Lacan then] call[s] sint'home rule' (this element of course relating to the long-held desire in Irish politics for Home Rule, which dominated political life in the country from the late nineteenth century to the outbreak of the Irish War of Independence, ensuing from 1919 to 1921, and eventually resulting in the Anglo-Irish Treaty which established the Irish Free State, but only after the Government of Ireland Act of 1920 had partitioned the country into the six-county North and the twenty-six-county South).[101] 'Sint'Home Rule' finally turns into '*sinthome roules*', which are described by Lacan as 'roulettes which Joyce brings together'; an apposite description not only of the (quasi-arbitrary) operation by which the *sinthome* works, but also of that by which Joyce's writing – which is here precisely *sinthomic* – works too.[102] The roulette wheel here further comprises for us an image of thirty-seven *empty signifieds* – if we include the zero – into one of which a signifier – in this case, the ball – will drop, in an image similar to Freud's 'comb schema'.

As we suggested earlier, we must be cautious about getting carried away with, or by, the proliferation of puns and portmanteau concepts that arise at this point in Lacan's work, especially in the two 'Joyce the Symptom' symposial talks, and in the early stages of the *Sinthome* Seminar. Lacan charges through a litany of such concepts in these sessions, many of which are explicated exceptionally by Harari in his book on the Seminar – thus becoming stepping-stones towards a conceptualisation of a post-Joycean psychoanalysis – whereas for other commentators they have served somewhat as stumbling blocks or pitfalls.

Despite ostensibly moving on from what could be considered the 'structuralist' teaching of his earlier Seminars – into a supposedly more aleatory 'post-structuralist' phase – Lacan's concepts here precisely work structurally, in that they receive a large part (but perhaps *not all*) of their particular meaning from the structure of the seminarial work – or working-through – from which they arise. We might cite – from the 'Joyce the Symptom' lectures – the '*escabeau*' (Joyce's linguistic 'stepping-stool') that becomes the '*S.K.beau*' (which thus may not only emphasise the initials apparent in phonetic elements of words, but also perhaps pertain to the *siglic* couple in *Finnegans Wake*, '**S**' and '**K**'); the '*eaub-scène*' (combining 'obscene' with '*eau*' ['water'] and '*beau*' [the 'beautiful'], if the first syllable is rearranged); and the '*faunesque*' and '*faunetique*' (the entering of a faun – such, perhaps, as Flann O'Brien's Pooka MacPhellimey – into phonetics), as examples of these concepts.[103] We will concentrate on only one such instance, however – which could be argued to be encompassing of all the others – the abovementioned writing of '*l'homme*' as '*lom*' (a reduction not possible in English, as the word 'man' – which doesn't require the definite article – is already at its most monosyllabically irreducible).[104] Lacan first uses the word in the first symposial lecture – after which it becomes central to the second – in a passage that traces the reflections on the symptom and the *sinthome* that have been delineated thus far:

> It's insofar as the unconscious is knotted to the *sinthome*, which is what there is of the singular in each individual, that one can say that Joyce, as someone wrote somewhere, identifies himself with *the individual*. He is the one who has gone to the extreme of incarnating the symptom in himself, thus escaping any possible death and being reduced to the very structure of Man, if you'll permit me to write it very simply as *l.o.m.*[105]

This structuration of the 'man' as '*lom*' thus reduces it to an irreducible syllable that connotes at once the definite and indefinite individual, definite and indefinite *man*, and the assumption of the latter *into* the former; that is, the assumption by *an* individual of *the* irreducible *sinthome* of individuality, by *a* 'man' of *the* '*lom*', by *Joyce* of *the* symptom. Not only this, but we here see, too, precisely the assumption of the definite (article) into the indefinite; that is, the assumption of the word 'the' ('*l*'') into whatever man (*homme*), as '*lom*'. This is a process Lacan perhaps picks up from the title *Finnegans Wake*, which likewise does away with an apostrophe, making the single, possessive 'Finnegan's' into the plural *every-men* of 'Finnegans'.[106]

The word 'the' (though it is 'a word that is not a word', as Joyce says) which undergoes this subsumption here is of course the last of *Finnegans Wake*, and – it could be argued – to an extent the first of the Creation; and it is to the Creation that Lacan turns his attention in the first session of the *Sinthome* Seminar. As Joyce commented, concerning his choice of the final word in the *Wake*:

> I have found the word which is the most slippery, the least accented, the weakest word in English, a word which is not even a word, which is scarcely sounded between the teeth, a breath, a nothing, the article *the*.[107]

At the beginning of Genesis we find the Hebrew word '*ruah*', which Alan Bass defines in a note to Derrida's use of it in 'Force and Signification':

> The Hebrew *ruah* [רוּח], like the Greek *pneuma*, means both wind or breath and soul or spirit. Only in God are breath and spirit, speech and thought, absolutely identical; man can always be duplicitous, his speech can be other than his thought.[108]

Something of this originary *breath* or *spirit* – the 'power' of Dante's 'prime mover', which Joyce takes up in the *Wake* (in a particularly *sinthomic* passage) as: 'The first mover, that father I ascend fromming knows, as I think, caused whom I, a self the sign' – thus comes into man, but it does so through (the) original 'sin'*thome*.[109] Thus, in this rendering of the Creation, 'non-duplicity' *errantly* comes into man – from the Name-of-the-Father, the God of Genesis (in position A here) – separating 'speech' and 'thought' into positions 1 and 2 in the principle of *enverity*.

'*Ruah*' itself is a particular Hebraic expression that is almost untranslatable, hence the widely-varying translations through which it is rendered: as 'Spirit' in the King James Version of the Bible; as 'wind' in the New Revised Standard Version; as 'breath' in the Knox translation; and as 'power' in the Good News Bible. The word in fact connotes something of an exhalation, orally pronounceable – onomatopoeically written – as '*thuh*': 'The'.[110] It is perhaps this 'the', then – this '*ruah*' – that prompts Lacan in Seminar II to suggest that 'it isn't inconceivable that even the *fiat*, the most primary of creative speeches, is *secondary*'.[111] The *fiat* uttered by God in Genesis is indeed preceded by this *speechless speech* – this *discourse without speech* – of the *ruah*, just as the 'riverrun' of *Finnegans Wake* is in fact preceded by the 'the' of its last page, although the former occupies the most primary of positions in the book. The '*ruah*' – at the point at which it is articulated in the Creation – is, however, not yet holy; the word 'holy' does not appear until Gen. ii. 3, when God 'hallows' the seventh day of Creation, separating the Sabbath as the day of rest.

The word 'holy', from the Hebrew 'qadash', means to consecrate, or to set apart, to separate; therefore, according to the Creation story, all is one in God, all is *atonement*; 'at-one-ment', as is the word's derivation (and thus 'at-one-*meant*'. It is thus here – as Lacan repeats at this stage in his teaching – that 'there is a One'). This atonement cannot be truly 'in the beginning', however, for there can be no true beginning, without an other. Thus it is that this 'the' that is a word and not a word fills something of the role of the *originary screen*, or the *coincedentia oppositorum* that gives rise to the unificatory/separatory principle; it is at once a word and not a word of weakness and of power, of Spirit and of breath, of nothing and of creation, and of ataraxy and of *jouissance*; the *jouissance* that then gets split when this word that is not a word gets hallowed and becomes *the Word*; that is, split between *jouis-sens*, 'enjoy-meant', and the (subjective) response to it of '*j'ouïs-sens*', meaning 'I hear meaning'.[112]

Joyce's single use of the word '*ruah*' in the *Wake* situates it – importantly, after a 'the' – in a Judeo-Christian assemblage which eclectically retells the Creation story, from the viewpoint not only of the Bible, but also of the conjugal bed, and of *Finnegans Wake* as a whole: 'The incident was an accident for here the ruah of Ecclectiastes of Hippo outpuffs the writress of Havvah-ban-Annah – to pianissime a slightly varied version of Crookedribs confidentials'.[113] The passage is laced with sexuation, sexual innuendo, and religious imagery. The main female correspondent of the *Wake*, ALP, or Anna Livia Plurabelle, is given at once her proper name, 'Annah', and shown also to be Eve, in 'Havvah'; 'Hawah' being Hebrew for 'Eve'. The hendiadys of 'Havvah-ban-Annah' is yet more remarkable, however, for the fact that it implicitly alludes to the male correspondent, HCE, or Humphrey Chimpden Earwicker – as well as to the necessity of male correspondence in (pro)creation – by its bawdy play on the Cockney-tinged 'have a banana', euphemistically referring to the male member, which the next word, 'pianissime', does yet more explicitly.[114] Creation is thus seen to be double: fe/male, but its multifarity stretches further than that; at once we have creation from the 'outpuff' of the '*ruah*' and from the 'crooked rib' of Adam, and this is varied in itself to become again a reference to the part played by the *privates* of the male and female – their 'confidentials' – in (pro)creation; and even the parts played by these *privates* are double, representing here sex *and* waste: '***Pianiss***ime' (penis); '***pi***ani***ss***ime' (piss).

To return to '*lom*', as a whole, however; whilst the word 'man' is of course gendered – which inevitably brings into it certain significations – '*lom*' should nonetheless be dealt with as the point of irreducibility within the subject himself or herself. Indeed, something of this is seen in Lacan's privileging of another moment in Joyce in which Adam is made androgynous: 'Adam was of course, in the joke made precisely by Joyce, a *madame*'.[115] This reference is to the palindrome that Joyce has Lenehan speak in *Ulysses*: 'Madam, I'm Adam'.[116] Thus, this sentence takes into itself both *first man* – Adam – and *first woman* – as a Madam – as well as the irreducible singularity of the individual – the '*I*' itself – which separates and unites the palindromic reversals and reprisals – the '*envers*' – involved in the initial *bungle* that is God's Creation (Lacan's word is '*bouffonnant*', or even, later, '*bévue*').[117]

To this '*lom*', however, we can reattach the apostrophe – to make '*l'om*' – to thus connote the only phoneme that both the symptom and *sinthome* share (the 'om'); the syllable that Lacan reattaches to the 'symptom' in place of the lopped-off 'bol' of 'symbol' (which he commences because of his first talk originally being mis-billed as 'Jacques the Symbol'); and, last, an irreducible point in both the religions of Hinduism and Buddhism.[118] 'Om' – known by the symbol ॐ – is the sacred Sanskrit syllable meditated on by practitioners of these religions, and is described in the Māṇḍūkya Upaniṣad as that which encompasses the four conditions of Atman – 'the Self' – which are 'outward-moving consciousness' (waking life); 'inner-moving consciousness' (dreaming life); 'silent consciousness' (sleeping life); and 'supreme consciousness' ('Atman'; 'the eternal Word OM').[119] The Upaniṣad goes on to state that 'the Word OM as one sound is the fourth state of supreme consciousness. It is beyond the senses and is the end of evolution'.[120] The *sinthome*, the fourth ring that ties up those of the Real, Symbolic, and Imaginary – and which Žižek describes as 'beyond meaning', and Lacan as that which comes to be assumed at the end of analysis – is thus seen to fit with the connotations it is given when referentially brought into conjunction with the 'om' of '*lom*'.

This 'om' of '*lom*' may stretch also to the 'omo' that is read in the facial features by Dante in *The Divine Comedy*, which derives from the Italian '*uomo*' (or the Latin '*homo*') – meaning precisely 'man' – and refers to the graphic patterning of the eyes, eye sockets, and nose on the face.[121] From this indelible sigla of the face written with letters (and thus further constitutive of the 'man of letters') we come to the very irreducibility of the *body*, and of the *bodily*, itself, which we have begun to address throughout the work so far, and which Lacan makes central to his reflections in 'Joyce le Symptôme II', in which he announces that 'what is significant [. . .] is to be aware of the fact that MAN [*LOM*] has a body'.[122] To tie this in with the *sinthome*, Lacan seems here to imply that in that *man*, or, rather, *the subject* – as a concept-*of*-him-or-itself – is a concept-*to*-him-or-itself, bodilily – unfilled, that is, on the imaginary plane, precisely like the *empty signified* – it is the signifier (or, in Saussure's original terms, the '*sound–image*'; that is, an *environmental* entity, if we consider the environment to which this term refers to be a *langscape*) that comes to fill it – or him – with *signification*.[123] This seems indeed to be why Miller re-stresses that Lacan also designated the subject with the small '*s*' of the signified right up to the end.

To the body and the bodily senses – which Lacan of course stresses we are 'condemned to' – we find references abounding in Joyce, particularly in relation to the characters of Leopold Bloom in *Ulysses* and Shem in *Finnegans Wake*, but it is on the beginning paragraphs of the Proteus episode of *Ulysses*, centring on Stephen Dedalus, that we will now concentrate. Here Dedalus explores the limits of his own body, and of its *sensibility* (in the Lockean sense of relating to the bodily senses), formulating the 'ineluctable modalities' of the visible and the audible, and conducting empirical experimentation by which he tests these:

> Ineluctable modality of the visible: at least that if no more, thought through my eyes. Signatures of all things I am here to read, seaspawn and seawrack, the nearing tide, that rusty boot. Snotgreen, bluesilver, rust: coloured signs. Limits of the diaphane. But he adds: in bodies. Then he was aware of the

> bodies before of them coloured. How? By knocking his sconce against them, sure. Go easy. Bald he was and a millionaire, *maestro di color che sanno*. Limit of the diaphane in. Why in? Diaphane, adiaphane. If you can put your five fingers through it, it is a gate, if not a door. Shut your eyes and see.[124]

How ineluctable Stephen proves the visible here to be in that even its negative – its *other side* – inescapably consigns him to its modality: 'Shut your eyes *and see*.' The necessity of course is for Stephen *to have seen*, prior to the experiment of closing one's eyes, to arrive at the same realisation as John Locke that such 'ideas, *which have admittance only through one sense*[,] have no [other] postern to be admitted by; no other way to bring themselves into view, and be perceived by the understanding' than the *one sense*.[125] We thus begin to see through Stephen's 'limit[ing] of the diaphane in bodies' – that is, limiting the *transparency* in bodies, in general, and in his own body, in his closing-off sense experiments – precisely the entrance of that 'opaque *jouissance*' that the *sinthome*, in its bodily relation, exudes, through its exclusion of *sense*. Thus, in the relation of *sinthome* and *sensibility*, to inadvertently pun on Jane Austen, we are met with the sustentative point at which what accords to the *senses*, what is *sensible*, bodily, somatic, is *sensed* psychically, subjectively; the *sinthome*, then, in its imaginary relation (of the *ego* in relation to the body), represents the locus of the *split* that unites the body and mind *psychosomatically*; that is, as the result of the fragilely enantiomorphic sense of wholeness and fragmentation that comes about from the formation of the ego in the imaginary at the mirror stage.

Notes

1 Jacques Lacan, *The Seminar of Jacques Lacan, Book XVII: The Other Side of Psychoanalysis* [1969–1970], ed. by Jacques-Alain Miller, trans. by Russell Grigg (New York: W. W. Norton, 2007) p.135.

2 Lacan orally signs off the session of 10 February 1976 of the *Sinthome* Seminar:

> Since I have got to this point at this time, you must have had your fill of it (*votre claque*), and even your Jacques'Laques, since besides I would add to it the *han*! which would express the relief that I experience at having got through today; I reduce my proper name to the most common noun.

See Jacques Lacan, *Le seminaire XXIII: Le sinthome* [1975–1976], texte établi par Jacques-Alain Miller (Paris: Éditions du Seuil, 2005) p.89; Jacques Lacan, *Seminar XXIII: Joyce and the Sinthome, 1975–1976*, trans. by Cormac Gallagher (London: Karnac, unofficial translation, n.d.) session VI, p.15. As Geert Lernout explains, Lacan 'assumes that his audience will have had enough, *avoir votre claque*, even their *jaclaque* and he himself will only add *han*, "an expulsion of breath accompanying a violent action"'. See Geert Lernout, *The French Joyce* (Ann Arbor: University of Michigan Press, 1992) p.75. Harari further clarifies that 'the pun on his name also alludes to *la claque*, a "slap": the irony is that the audience will be obliged to applaud him, even though they might *en a eu leur claque*, be "fed up to the back teeth" with him'; that is, the audience must – to use Jacques Derrida's play on his own shared first name – '*J'accepte*' (i.e., '(I) accept Jacques'). See Roberto Harari, *How James Joyce*

Made His Name: A Reading of the Final Lacan [1995], trans. by Luke Thurston (New York: Other Press, 2002) p.157; Jacques Derrida, *The Post Card: From Socrates to Freud and Beyond* [1980], trans. by Alan Bass (Chicago: Chicago University Press, 1987) p.26. 'Not accidentally,' Lernout states, 'Lacan's obsession with his name' stems from Joyce's with his, famously encapsulated in his signing of a letter to Harriet Shaw Weaver, of 15 December 1926, with the pun 'Jeems Jokes'. See Lernout, *The French Joyce*, p.75; James Joyce, *Selected Letters of James Joyce*, ed. by Richard Ellmann (London: Faber and Faber, 1975) p.316. To describe Lacan's language Žižek of course adopts the term 'Lacanese'.

3 For the Beckett, see chapter 2, note 27.

4 Slavoj Žižek, *Less Than Nothing: Hegel and the Shadow of Dialectical Materialism* (London: Verso, 2012) p.498.

5 James Joyce, *Finnegans Wake* [1939], ed. by Robbert-Jan Henkes and others (Oxford: Oxford World's Classics, 2012) p.628, 15–16.

6 Ibid. p.120, 13–14.

7 Ibid. p.3, 12; p.628, 5.

8 Jacques Lacan, 'Joyce le Symptôme' [1975], in *Le seminaire, Livre XXIII: Le sinthome* [1975–1976], ed. by texte établi par Jacques-Alain Miller (Paris: Éditions du Seuil, 2005) p.165 (trans. by Benanav).

9 See James Joyce, *The Restored* Finnegans Wake, ed. by Danis Rose and John O'Hanlon (London: Penguin Classics, 2012).

10 Provided we removed Joyce's locating and dating of his composition ('PARIS, 1922–1939'), there would of course be some blank space between the last and first words 'the' and 'riverrun'; space, however, that would be open to so much symbolic interpretation.

11 See James Joyce, *Ulysses* [1922], ed. by Hans Walter Gabler and others (New York: Vintage Books, 1986) 16.1, p.501; James Joyce, *Ulysses: The 1922 Text*, ed. by Jeri Johnson (Oxford: Oxford World's Classics, 1998) p.569.

12 See the first section of Derrida, *Of Grammatology*, entitled 'Writing Before the Letter'.

13 Luke Thurston, '*Sinthome*', in Evans, *An Introductory Dictionary of Lacanian Psychoanalysis* (London: Routledge, 1996) p.191.

14 Jacques Lacan, '*R.S.I.* Seminar (1974–1975)', ed. by Jacques-Alain Miller, *Ornicar?* 4 (p.106). Quoted and translated by Marie Walshe in Marie Walshe, 'Enjoying the Symptom: A Faithful Suffering?' *The Letter: Irish Journal for Lacanian Psychoanalysis*, 31 & 32 (Summer/Autumn 2004) 52–66 (p.52). For an alternative translation, see Jacques Lacan, *The Seminar of Jacques Lacan, Book XXII: R.S.I., 1974–1975*, trans. by Cormac Gallagher (London: Karnac, unofficial translation, n.d.) session VI, p.98.

15 Jacques Lacan, *The Seminar of Jacques Lacan, Book VII: The Ethics of Psychoanalysis*, 1959–1960, ed. by Jacques-Alain Miller, trans. by Dennis Porter (London: Routledge Classics, 2008) p.227.

16 Jacques Lacan, *The Seminar of Jacques Lacan, Book XI: The Four Fundamental Concepts of Psychoanalysis* [1964], ed. by Jacques-Alain Miller, trans. by Alan Sheridan (New York: W. W. Norton, 1981) p.126 [my emphasis].

17 Alan Sheridan, 'Footnote 1', in Lacan, *Seminar XI: The Four Fundamental Concepts of Psychoanalysis*, p.56.

18 Sigmund Freud, *'Inhibitions, Symptoms and Anxiety'* [1926], trans. by Alix Strachey, in *SE*, XX, p.91.

19 Ibid.

20 Jacques Lacan, *The Seminar of Jacques Lacan, Book III: The Psychoses, 1955–1956*, ed. by Jacques-Alain Miller, trans. by Russell Grigg (New York: W.W. Norton, 1993) p.60.

21 We take the liberty here of extending the meaning of 'cathexis' – the investment or concentration of mental energy – to encompass a further process of the *grafting* of this energy *on* or *to* a psychical phenomenon, such as a symptom, for example.

22 Further to this legal sense of *jouissance*, see Alan Sheridan's definition in his glossary to the shorter *Écrits*:

> JOUISSANCE (*jouissance*). There is no adequate translation in English of this word. 'Enjoyment' conveys the sense, contained in *jouissance*, of enjoyment of rights, of property, etc. Unfortunately, in modern English, the word has lost the sexual connotations it still retains in French. (*Jouir* is slang for 'to come'.) 'Pleasure', on the other hand, is pre-empted by '*plaisir*' – and Lacan uses the two terms quite differently. 'Pleasure' obeys the law of homeostasis that Freud evokes in 'Beyond the Pleasure Principle', whereby, through discharge, the psyche seeks the lowest possible level of tension. '*Jouissance*' transgresses this law and, in that respect, it is *beyond* the pleasure principle.

See Alan Sheridan, 'Translator's Note', in Jacques Lacan, *Écrits: a selection*, trans. by Alan Sheridan [1977] (Abingdon: Routledge Classics, 2001) p.xiii.

23 Adrian Dannatt, 'The Crack', *lacanian ink*, 11 (1995) 34–39 (pp.34–38). There is of course in sexual anatomy also the prevalent desire for the 'crack' between the muscles of the *gluteus maximus*, which is a favourite area of Leopold Bloom's in *Ulysses*, as his wife Molly well knew: 'If he wants to kiss my bottom I'll drag open my drawers and bulge it right out in his face as large as life he can stick his tongue 7 miles up my hole as hes there my brown part'. See Joyce, *Ulysses*, 18.1520–1522, p.642; Joyce, *Ulysses: 1922*, p.730. In mentioning Courbet Dannatt is making reference to the fact that Lacan owned the original of '*L'Origine du monde*'.

24 Alenka Zupančič, *Ethics of the Real: Kant and Lacan* (London: Verso, 2000) p.81.

25 Ibid. pp.80–81. Joyce had notably more literary investment in the writer who could be said to be the other side to Sade – Leopold von Sacher-Masoch – the action of whose *Venus in Furs* granted him becoming the namesake of the concept of masochism, as Sade had become of sadism.

26 Jacques Lacan, 'Réponses à des étudiants en philosophie sur l'objet de la psychanalyse' (trans. by Paul Verhaeghe and Frédéric Declercq), *Cahiers pour l'Analyse*, 3 (May–June, 1966) 5–13 (p.8). Quoted in Paul Verhaeghe and Frédéric Declercq, 'Lacan's Analytic Goal: *Le Sinthome* or the Feminine Way', in *Re-Inventing the Symptom: Essays on the Final Lacan*, ed. by Luke Thurston (New York: Other Press, 2002) p.77, note 14 (translation theirs). For the passage in *Television*, see p.110.

27 The pleasure principle being the homeostatic state that maintains life against its drive towards death (by short-circuiting the *death drive*). See chapter 1, note 96.

28 Lacan, *Le seminaire XXIII: Le sinthome*, p.39; Lacan, *Seminar XXIII: Joyce and the Sinthome*, session II, p.13.

29 Lacan, 'Joyce le Symptôme', in *Le seminaire XXIII: Le sinthome*, p.165 (trans. by Benanav).

30 Philip Dravers, 'In the Wake of Interpretation: "The Letter! The Litter!" or "Where in the Waste is the Wisdom?"' in *Re-Inventing the Symptom*, p.168. Dravers is here quoting Joyce, *Finnegans Wake*, p.118, 27–28, and William Shakespeare, *Macbeth*, in *Complete Works of Shakespeare, Volume III: Tragedies*, Act I, Scene V, 51, p.398.

31 See Daniel Bristow, 'New Spellings: Auto-orthographies in *Zami* and *Vanity of Duluoz*', *Life Writing*, 11th ser., 3 (2014) 275–292 (p.283).

32 Ellmann, *James Joyce*, p.521, p.703.

33 See Lacan, *Seminar XVII: The Other Side of Psychoanalysis*, p.106, for discussion of the position of analyst.

34 Lacan, 'Joyce le Symptôme', in *Le seminaire XXIII: Le sinthome*, p.164 (trans. by Benanav): '*Désabonné à l'inconscient*'; Collins and Hecq translate this more literally as 'unsubscribed' – or 'unsubscribing' – '*to* the unconscious'.

35 Lacan, *Seminar III: The Psychoses*, p.29.
36 Véronique Voruz, 'Acephalic Litter as a Phallic Letter', in *Re-Inventing the Symptom*, p.119. See, for example, Jacques Lacan, *The Seminar of Jacques Lacan, Book XXIV: L'insu que sait de l'une-bévue s'aile à mourre, 1976–1977*, trans. by Cormac Gallagher (London: Karnac, unofficial translation, n.d.) session 1, p.4: 'Knowing how to deal with your symptom, that is the end of analysis'.
37 Voruz, 'Acephalic Litter as a Phallic Letter', in *Re-Inventing the Symptom*, p.116.
38 Josefina Ayerza, 'To resume again . . .', *lacanian ink*, 11 (1995) 3–6 (p.4).
39 Harari, *How James Joyce Made His Name*, p.109.
40 Ibid.
41 Anthony Burgess, 'What It's All About', in James Joyce, *A Shorter* Finnegans Wake, ed. by Anthony Burgess (New York: The Viking Press, 1968) p.xxvii.
42 See Derek Attridge, *The Singularity of Literature* (Abingdon: Routledge, 2004).
43 See Derek Attridge, *Peculiar Language: Literature as Difference from the Renaissance to James Joyce* [1988] (London: Routledge, 2004) 2 edn. pp.231–232.
44 Walter Benjamin, *The Origin of German Tragic Drama* [1925], trans. by John Osborne (London: Verso, 1998) p.44.
45 Voruz, 'Acephalic Litter as a Phallic Letter', in *Re-Inventing the Symptom*, p.116.
46 Zupančič, *Ethics of the Real*, p.106, note 23.
47 Lacan, *Seminar VII: The Ethics of Psychoanalysis*, p.309. As Harari comments, in Althusserian terms: 'Being responsible implies having to give a response. The etymology of the term is often forgotten: responsibility comes from responding. When I am interpellated, then, I can respond to the extent of my *savoir-faire* ['know-how']'. See Harari, *How James Joyce Made His Name*, p.115.
48 Lacan, *Seminar XI: The Four Fundamental Concepts of Psychoanalysis*, p.235.
49 For more in relation to Joyce and the four discourses, see my forthcoming essay: 'Seminars XVII and XVIII with XXIII: On a University Discourse that Might not be Joycean'.
50 Pierre Thèves, '*Où est ton cadeau, espèce d'imbécile?*' *Psychoanalytical Notebooks*, 13 (2005) 35–45 (p.40). This is Thèves's reading of a passage he excerpts from the French of the *Psychoses* Seminar: '*Une interrogation de l'Autre comme tel*', which is rendered in English by Grigg as 'an investigation proceeding in the direction of the Other as such'. See Lacan, *Seminar III: The Psychoses*, p.289. We can commensurate these disparate takes by suggesting that investigation towards the Other is guided by the *progress* of the Other, from which Joyce abstains. The progress of the Other is one that desires destination, whereas Joyce's work desires remaining *in* progress.
51 Lacan, *Le seminaire XXIII: Le sinthome*, p.124; Lacan, 'Le Sinthome', p.48; Joyce, *Ulysses*, 2.377, p.28; Joyce, *Ulysses: 1922*, p.34.
52 Lacan, *Le seminaire XXIII: Le sinthome*, p.124; Lacan, 'Le Sinthome', p.48.
53 Franco Moretti, 'The Long Goodbye: *Ulysses* and the End of Liberal Capitalism', trans. by Susan Fischer, in *Signs Taken for Wonders: On the Sociology of Literary Forms* [1983] (London: Verso Radical Thinkers, 2005) p.192.
54 Verhaeghe and Declercq, 'Lacan's Analytic Goal', in *Re-Inventing the Symptom*, p.69.
55 Lacan, *Le seminaire XXIII: Le sinthome*, p.134; Lacan, 'Le Sinthome', p.53.
56 Ibid. In the Borromean knot of Real, Symbolic, Imaginary, the inexistent place of the Other of the Other would be located between Real and Imaginary.
57 Verhaeghe and Declercq, 'Lacan's Analytic Goal', in *Re-Inventing the Symptom*, p.69. See also on Lacan's conceptualisation of singularity Mari Ruti, *The Singularity of Being: Lacan and the Immortal Within* (New York: Fordham University Press, 2012). However, we tend to avoid the binary she seems to set up between singularity and normativity within.
58 On this topic see Sigmund Freud, 'The Antithetical Meaning of Primal Words' [1910], trans. by Alan Tyson, in *SE*, XI, pp.153–161.

59 Christine Froula, 'Scribbling into Eternity: Paris, Proust, "Proteus"', in *Renascent Joyce*, ed. by Daniel Ferrer, Sam Slote, and André Topia (Gainesville: University Press of Florida, 2013) p.111. See Dante Alighieri, 'Purgatorio XXV', in *The Divine Comedy* [1308–1321], trans. by C.H. Sisson (Oxford: Oxford World's Classics, 1998) p.308.
60 Viktor Shklovsky, *Knight's Move* [1923], trans. by Richard Sheldon (Normal: Dalkey Archive Press, 2005) p.70.
61 See Ellmann, *James Joyce*, p.546, and Lacan's off the cuff remark at a press conference in Jacques Lacan, 'The Triumph of Religion' [1974], in *The Triumph of Religion, Preceded by Discourse to Catholics*, trans. by Bruce Fink (Cambridge: Polity, 2013) p.80.
62 Samuel Beckett, *Murphy* [1938], in *The Selected Works of Samuel Beckett*, ed. by Paul Auster, 4 vols (New York: Grove Press, 2010) I, p.42.
63 Lacan, *Seminar III: The Psychoses*, p.119.
64 Moretti, 'The Long Goodbye', in *Signs Taken for Wonders*, p.264, note 28.
65 Hunter S. Thompson, *Hey Rube: Blood Sport, the Bush Doctrine, and the Downward Spiral of Dumbness: Modern History from the ESPN.com Sports Desk* (New York: Simon & Schuster, 2005) p.58: 'The world is getting weirder and weirder. Huge things are happening at speeds too high to measure, or even fathom, in the brain of a normal human. We are like moths in a blizzard.'
66 Aijaz Ahmad argues that

> if we do not *choose* our own 'bits' of reality, those 'bits' will then be chosen for us by our class origin, our jobs, the circuits of our friendships and desires, our ways of spending our leisure time, our literary predilections, our political affiliations – or lack of them[; that is,] there are no neutral 'bits', not even of not-knowing.

See Aijaz Ahmad, *In Theory: Classes, Nations, Literatures* [1992] (London: Verso Radical Thinkers, 2008) p.138. Whilst the emphasis on the modulatory effect of 'bits' on subjectivity is quite in accord with and very close to our postulations above, it is yet *choice* – a capitalist category if ever there was one – that is still accorded primacy here: if we do not knowingly *choose*, then we are yet determined by things we 'not-knowingly' choose, things we have nonetheless chosen, but without knowing it. There is thus here a presupposition that we can *choose* to choose our own 'bits', or we can choose not to (and therefore leave it up to predestination to do the rest, however unknowingly). This deadlock is what the methodology here being put forward in regard to the *sinthome* is able to challenge, in that it posits a subjectivation as *ineluctable modality*, rather than chosen modality (that is, consciously or not). A subject's later modulations might then be open to being taken up in Badiouian terms of effects of eventality.
67 Joyce, *Ulysses*, 18.240–241, p.613; Joyce, *Ulysses: 1922*, p.696.
68 For Bloom's definition of 'metempsychosis' see ibid. 4.341–342 p.52; ibid. p.62: 'Metempsychosis, he said, frowning. It's Greek: from the Greek. That means the transmigration of souls.'
69 On Lacan's view on 'applied psychoanalysis' see Luke Thurston, *James Joyce and the Problem of Psychoanalysis* (Cambridge: Cambridge University Press, 2004) p.9:

> As early as 1958, Lacan had brusquely dismissed the old tradition of 'applied psychoanalysis': [. . .] it was not that Lacan had many doubts about the general interpretative possibilities that Freud's discovery entailed; rather, he was concerned that those possibilities should not be obliterated by a lazy disregard for the real *structural* differences between various kinds of linguistic event.

70 James Joyce, quoted in Arthur Power, *Conversations with James Joyce*, ed. by Clive Hart (Chicago: University of Chicago Press, 1974) p.103.
71 Slavoj Žižek, *Enjoy Your Symptom! Jacques Lacan in Hollywood and Out* [1992] (Abingdon: Routledge Classics, 2008) p.22.

72 Derrida, 'Force and Signification', in *Writing and Difference* [1967], trans. by Alan Bass (London: Routledge Classics, 2001) p.29. This phrase comes from the title of the 1923 book co-authored by C. K. Ogden and I. A. Richards, *The Meaning of Meaning: A Study of the Influence of Language Upon Thought and of the Science of Symbolism*, which Lacan also discusses in Seminar XVIII.

73 Lacan, *Seminar XXIV: L'insu que sait de l'une-bévue s'aile à mourre*, session 11, p.117 [my emphasis]. Regarding the sign in Saussure, it is important to remember that the 'two terms' from which it is made – the *signified* [*signifié*] and the *signifier* [*signifiant*] – 'have the advantage of indicating the opposition that separates them from each other and from the whole of which they are parts', and thus *unificatory/separatorily*; i.e.: sign, A, signifier, 1 and signified, 2. See Ferdinand de Saussure, *Course in General Linguistics* [1906–1911], ed. by Charles Bally and others, trans. by Wade Baskin (Glasgow: Fontana/Collins, 1974) rev. ed., p.67. This translation is generally preferable for technical terminology to the newer one quoted in chapter 1.

74 Lacan, *Seminar III: The Psychoses*, pp.179–180.

75 We may here perceive a risk in this theory of the *empty signified* of its beginning to concern 'things-in-themselves' rather than being true to the Saussurian notion of purely concerning *concepts*. However, in precise Kantian terms, it is rather that both the signifier and the signified operate on the plane of *phenomena*, as opposed to on that of *noumena*; that is, of *things-in-themselves*, or *in-the-world* – that are not directly approachable through our intellection or intuition – i.e., as Kant puts it:

> A **noumenon** [is] a thing which can never be thought as an object of the senses, but only as a thing in itself[;] all the rest to which sensible intuition does not extend is called noumenon [. . .] we cannot understand the possibility of such noumena, and the domain beyond the sphere of appearances is (to us) empty.

See Immanuel Kant, *Critique of Pure Reason* [1781], trans. and ed. by Marcus Weigelt, based on the translation by Max Müller (London: Penguin Classics, 2007) p.260. We can therefore run with the signified to these lengths because of our realisation of its role as an element and functor of a purely *phenomenal* linguistic structure (inclusive of the register of the somatic *imaginary*), rather than its concerning impossible-to-reach concrete *noumenal* things-in-themselves.

76 To provide an analogy for this irreducible animating feature of the *sinthome* we might evoke the character of Arnold Rimmer in the UK sci-fi TV show *Red Dwarf*, who – as a computer-generated hologram – is *projected* by a 'light bee' that floats 'inside' him, as a certain 'floating signified' which contains all the signifiers of his personality and subjectivity within it.

77 See Freud, *The Interpretation of Dreams*, in *SE*, V, p.537. Figure 3.5 appears in Alfredo Eidelsztein, *The Graph of Desire: Using the Work of Jacques Lacan*, trans. by Florencia F. C. Shanahan (London: Karnac Books, 2009) p.29.

78 Ibid.

79 Saussure, *Course in General Linguistics*, trans. by Baskin, p.112. See Lacan, *Seminar III: The Psychoses*, p.261, for his discussion of this schema in relation to the signified and signifier.

80 Jacques Lacan, *The Seminar of Jacques Lacan, Book XVI: From an Other to the other, 1968–1969*, trans. by Cormac Gallagher (London: Karnac, unofficial translation, n.d.) session I, p.6; Lacan, *Seminar III: The Psychoses*, p.255.

81 Claude Lévi-Strauss, *Introduction to the Work of Marcel Mauss* [1950], trans. by Felicity Baker (Abingdon: Routledge, 1987) p.37.

82 Jacques-Alain Miller, 'Lacan with Joyce: The Seminar of the Clinical Section of Barcelona' [1996], *Psychoanalytical Notebooks*, 13 (May 2005) 7–32 (p.24).

83 See Jacques Lacan, *The Seminar of Jacques Lacan, Book XX: Encore: On Feminine Sexuality, the Limits of Love and Knowledge, 1972–1973*, ed. by Jacques-Alain Miller,

trans. by Bruce Fink (New York: W. W. Norton, 1998) p.5, for usage of the phrase 'the being's body', which, as Fink points out, could also be translated as 'the being of the body, being qua body, the body qua being, and so on' (footnote 18).

84 Lacan, *Television*, p.28 [my emphasis].
85 Žižek, *Enjoy Your Symptom!*, p.226.
86 Lacan, *Le seminaire XXIII: Le sinthome*, p.155; Lacan, 'Le Sinthome', p.63.
87 Zupančič, *Ethics of the Real*, p.204.
88 Ibid. p.206.
89 Joyce, *Ulysses*, 3.1, p.31; Joyce, *Ulysses: 1922*, p.37.
90 Slavoj Žižek, *The Fright of Real Tears: Krzysztof Kieślowski Between Theory and Post-Theory* (London: British Film Institute, 2001) p.98.
91 Slavoj Žižek, *Organs Without Bodies: On Deleuze and Consequences* [2004] (Abingdon: Routledge Classics, 2012) p.5.
92 Ibid. p.128.
93 Ibid. p.129.
94 Ibid.
95 Slavoj Žižek, *The Sublime Object of Ideology* (London: Verso, 1989) p.76.
96 Ibid. p.75.
97 Lacan, 'Joyce le Symptôme', in *Le seminaire XXIII: Le sinthome*, p.162.
98 Jeri Johnson, 'Explanatory Notes', in *Ulysses: 1922*, p.907.
99 Lacan, 'Joyce le Symptôme', in *Le seminaire XXIII: Le sinthome*, p.162.
100 Lacan, *Le seminaire XXIII: Le sinthome*, p.13; Lacan, *Seminar XXIII: Joyce and the Sinthome*, session I, p.4.
101 Ibid. pp.14–15; Lacan, 'Le Sinthome', p.3.
102 Lacan, *Le seminaire XXIII: Le sinthome*, p.15; Lacan, 'Le Sinthome', p.3. There is as we can see a veritable symphony of resonances extractable from the *sinthome*, to demarcate which we could conjure the conjugated '*sinfon*'.
103 See Lacan, 'Joyce le symptôme II', in *Joyce avec Lacan*, pp.31–36. He discusses the '*faunesque*' in the first 'Joyce le symptôme' talk (at *Le seminaire XXIII: Le sinthome*, p.166), before coining '*faunetique*' in the second. For '**S**' and '**K**' see Roland McHugh, *The Sigla of Finnegans Wake* (Austin: University of Texas Press, 1976) pp.122–132. McHugh's work here 'permit[s] **K** and **S** in *FW*, theoretically at least, to be conjoined', as he puts it (p.123). Although it is known that Lacan received most major new releases in the field of Joyce studies from Jacques Aubert, as *The Sigla* came out in 1976 we cannot comment on where Lacan may have derived knowledge of the **S/K** sigla from, if indeed these letters' instance in his conjugation is not pure coincidence. A bibliography in itself – of material that commentates on, or has been spawned from these concepts – could easily be constructed here, suffice it to point to a few examples, such as the chapter 'The punning of reason: meaning, nonsense and the limits of psychoanalytic reason' in Dany Nobus and Malcolm Quinn, *Knowing Nothing, Staying Stupid: Elements for a Psychoanalytic Epistemology* (Hove: Routledge, 2005) pp.63–83; Shelly Brivic, *Joyce Through Lacan and Žižek: Explorations* (New York: Palgrave MacMillan, 2008) p.37; and Hervé Castanet, *S.K.beau* (Paris: Editions de La Différence, 2011). For the Pooka MacPhellimey, see Flann O'Brien, *At Swim-Two-Birds* [1939] (London: Penguin Classics, 2001).
104 In opposition to this is Lacan's writing: "~~The~~' Woman', with the definite article struck through, which is discussed in the next chapter.
105 Lacan, 'Joyce le Symptôme', in *Le seminaire XXIII: Le sinthome*, p.165 (trans. by Collins).
106 Concerning this, Lernout cites Jean-Louis Houdebine's inferred scepticism over whether Lacan had ever 'actually read the texts' of Joyce, stating that 'his repeated misspelling of the title of Joyce's last work [. . .] points in th[e] direction' of his having not. See Lernout, *The French Joyce*, p.76. By this misspelling he is no doubt

referring to the insertion of a rogue apostrophe into '*Finnegans*'. This is an issue that has plagued many subsequent essays – written from predominantly psychoanalytic, rather than literary, perspectives – that fill certain journals, and that deal with this period in Lacan's thinking. However, it would be beyond naïve to postulate that Lacan hadn't advanced to the point of knowing the correct title of Joyce's last work (or of the correct name of his biographer, which Lernout diligently cites being written as 'Richard Helmann [*sic*]': see ibid. p.75); if these mistakes originally appeared so in Seminar XXIII's publication in *Ornicar?* under the editorship of Miller, they had gone by the time of its 2005 official Seuil edition. It must be remembered that the words of the sessions of the Seminar had come out of Lacan's mouth (prompted by written notes), to be transcribed by a stenographer, then to have been established by Miller, a process Lacan coined the term '*stécriture*' for. See Roudinesco, *Jacques Lacan*, p.319. Whilst a '*Finnegan's*' may be unacceptable in most Joycean instances, in such Lacanian cases it might not be entirely amiss for 'the publisher [to] ask the reader's indulgence for typographical errors unavoidable in the exceptional circumstances', as is Sylvia Beach's inscription at the beginning of the 1922 text of *Ulysses*.

107 See Ellmann, *James Joyce*, p.712, footnote. This is Ellmann's translation of Louis Gillet's recounting Joyce's words in his *Stèle pour James Joyce*. The original reads: '*J'ai trouvé le mot le plus glissant, le moins accentué, le plus faible de la langue anglaise, un mot qui n'est même pas un mot, qui sonne à peine entre les dents, un souffle, un rien, l'article* the.' See Louis Gillet, *Stèle pour James Joyce* (Marseille: Éditions du Sagittaire, 1941) p.151.

108 Alan Bass, 'Translators note (24) to 'Force and Signification', in Derrida, *Writing and Difference*, p.384.

109 Joyce, *Finnegans Wake*, p.483, 27–29.

110 I am indebted to Fr Gerard Deighan, whose course of lectures on the Pentateuch and the Biblical Foundations of Israel, at the Milltown Institute of Theology, Philosophy and Spirituality, Dublin (Winter semester, 2006) provided this reference. Lacan plays on the *ruah* himself – adding to it an oblative inflection – in Seminar X, claiming that 'nothing could be more beautiful than the awakening of Being with the *Ruach*, the passing breath of the Eternal', which – he claims – Ernest Jones knew 'a bit more about[,] tell[ing] us what sort of wind is involved here. It's anal wind.' See Jacques Lacan, *The Seminar of Jacques Lacan, Book X: Anxiety* [1962–1963], ed. by Jacques-Alain Miller, trans. by A.R. Price (Cambridge: Polity, 2014) p.298. After the next sequential reference to this Seminar, this will become the version that will be referred to in the shortened form of *Seminar X: Anxiety*.

111 Jacques Lacan, *The Seminar of Jacques Lacan, Book II: The Ego in Freud's Theory and in the Technique of Psychoanalysis, 1954–1955*, ed. by Jacques-Alain Miller, trans. by Sylvana Tomaselli (New York: W. W. Norton, 1991) p.312.

112 Lacan first plays on the homonymy of '*jouis*' ('enjoy') and '*j'ouïs*' ('I hear') in his Seminar on anxiety, before developing it further by also linking it to the '*responsability*' of *jouissance*, as *j'ouïs-sens*: '"God commands me to enjoy *(de jouir)*" – this is textually in the Bible – it is all the same the word of God. [. . .] a God who demands something of you and who in Ecclesiastes gives you the order "enjoy (*jouis*)". That is really something! Because to enjoy when ordered to do so, is all the same something which everyone senses that if there is a source, an origin of anxiety, it ought all the same to be found somewhere there. To this order "*Jouis!*", I can only answer one thing, which is: "*J'ouis* (I hear)". Of course, but naturally I do not enjoy so easily for all that.' See Jacques Lacan, *The Seminar of Jacques Lacan, Book X: Anxiety, 1962–1963*, trans. by Cormac Gallagher (London: Karnac, unofficial translation, n.d.) session VI, p.10. For an official translation, see Lacan, *Seminar X: Anxiety*, p.80.

113 Joyce, *Finnegans Wake*, p.38, 28–31.

114 For further reference, see Roland McHugh, *Annotations to Finnegans Wake* (Baltimore: The John Hopkins University Press, 1980) p.38.

115 Lacan, *Le seminaire XXIII: Le sinthome*, p.13; Lacan, *Seminar XXIII: Joyce and the Sinthome*, session I, p.4.

116 Joyce, *Ulysses*, 7.683, p.113; Joyce, *Ulysses: 1922*, p.132. As Kiberd indicates, we see a similar instance of particular individuality meeting irreducible *sinthomic* individuality in the construction: 'Siopold!' (Joyce, *Ulysses*, 11.751, p.227; Joyce, *Ulysses: 1922*, p.265), which he describes as 'a conflation of Leopold, Simon and Lionel (whose part Simon sings), as if to suggest a collective orgasm in which individual identity is quite unimportant'. See Declan Kiberd, *Ulysses and Us: The Art of Everyday Living* (London: Faber and Faber, 2009) p.173. Against this totalising collective notion, however, we should stress that it is here only through the maintenance of irreducible parts of the individuals involved – that is, parts of their names – that this collectivity can be brought about (i.e., it is manifested precisely as it is resisted).

117 As Gallagher explains, this word that appears in the title of Seminar XXIV is a 'play on *Unbewusst* ['unconscious' in German,] and *une-bévue* cannot be reproduced in English. 'Something of a-bungle' or similar expressions miss the point. A practical solution', he suggests, 'would be for readers to add *une-bévue* or simply *bévue* to their Lacanian vocabulary.' See Cormac Gallagher, 'Translator's Note', in Lacan, *Seminar XXIV: L'insu que sait de l'une-bévue s'aile à mourre*, p.1.

118 See Lacan, 'Joyce le Symptôme', in *Le seminaire XXIII: Le sinthome*, p.164: 'Why would they print *Joyce the Symptom*? Jacques Aubert communicates it to them and then they put out *Jacques the Symbol*. For them, of course, it's all the same. From the sym that *ptoms* to the sym that *bols*' (trans. by Collins). For the 1929 drawing, 'Symbol of Joyce' by Constantin Brancusi, see Ellmann, *James Joyce*, p.ii.

119 *The Upanishads*, trans. by Juan Muscaró (London: Penguin Books, 1965) p.83.

120 Ibid. p.84. Lacan comments on the word 'that buddhist monks murmur all day long, AUM, [that] there must be something radical in the order of the signifier here'. See Lacan, *Seminar III: The Psychoses*, p.279.

121 Dante, 'Purgatorio XXIII', in *The Divine Comedy*, p.298. See also David Higgins, 'Commentary and Notes', in ibid. p.621.

122 Lacan, 'Joyce le symptôme II', in *Joyce avec Lacan*, p.32 [trans. by Hecq].

123 The centrality of this is further seen in Saussure when he claims, in terms particularly resonant of the unificatory/separatory principle, that 'the linguistic entity [here, the subject precisely as a *l'être*, as a *man of letters*] exists only through the associating of the signifier with the signified[.] Whenever only one element is retained, the entity vanishes; instead of a concrete object we are faced with a mere abstraction.' *Enverity*, it is being claimed, is necessitous. See Saussure, *Course in General Linguistics*, trans. by Baskin, pp.102–103.

124 Joyce, *Ulysses*, 3.1–9, p.31; Joyce, *Ulysses: 1922*, p.37.

125 John Locke, *An Essay Concerning Human Understanding* [1689], ed. and abridged by Kenneth P. Winkler (Indianapolis: Hackett, 1996) p.41.

Chapter 4

Joyce's knots

Death and sex before the *Wake*

Knots

As far as the role of the Imaginary Order in Joyce's life and work is concerned we must now look to Lacan's sustained interaction with the 'Borromean knot' in the sessions of Seminar XXIII; which, as Adrian Price has pointed out, should in fact topologically rather be called a 'link', knot being 'a misnomer, as Lacan apparently came to realise sometime over the 1975 Christmas break'.[1] However, as the designation 'Borromean knot' has retained currency in subsequent Lacanian studies it will be used here, for purposes of familiarity. Lacan introduces the Borromean knot, which is so called because of its having been the heraldic emblem of the Borromeo family, in Seminar XIX, going on to discuss it at certain points in the Seminars up to his year on Joyce. In his introduction to it he demonstrates that in the case of these three rings it is 'only because of the third [that] they hold together'.[2]

As is shown in Figure 4.1 the three rings of the Borromean knot are interlinked in such a manner so that if any one ring is severed the chain of three will become entirely undone and fall apart. In this demonstration of the knot, taken from Seminar XXIII, Lacan has labelled each ring with a letter representing the orders of the Real, Symbolic, and Imaginary; we can see that if we cut the upper-left ring (R) and slip it out of the equation it would leave the bottom ring (S) sat on top of the upper-right ring (I), unattached to it by any link; the same would occur if we were to cut either of the other two. Thus, it is only via the third that the Borromean knot ties up.

As the topological model by which the consistence and continuity of the three orders is demonstrated the Borromean knot therefore seems unsurpassable as a representation not only of the three orders' interdependence, but also of their constitutive proneness to the oscillation highlighted in chapter 1, in that no ring can take a privileged position in the knot; if any one is severed the consequence – of the knot's disintegration – is the same; i.e., no one ring can occupy position A in the principle of *enverity*, as no one isolable ring completely supports another two – their support is precisely triadic; the structure of the (at least) three is needed for the knot to consist. Whilst this is the case; in this triadic structure – as

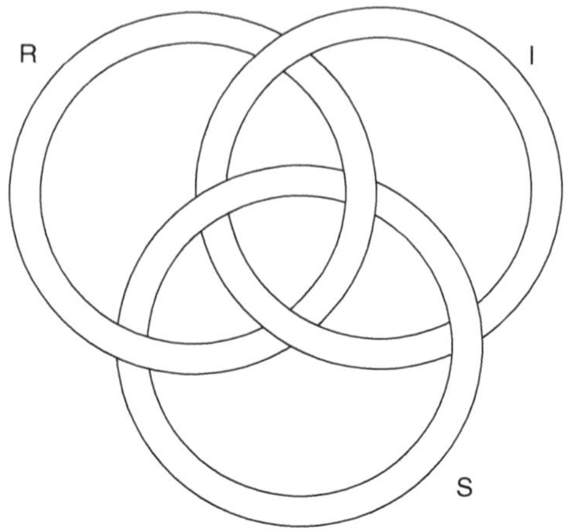

Figure 4.1 The Borromean knot ['*Le nœud borroméen*'][3]

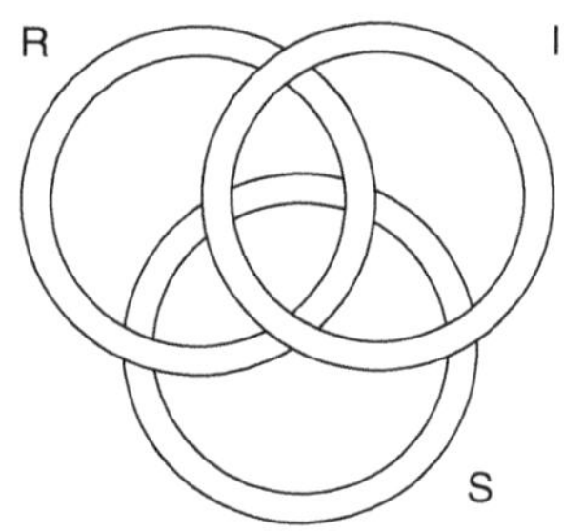

Figure 4.2 The three rings, separated ['*Les trois anneaux séparés*'][6]

Dravers points out – there is nonetheless a unificatory/separatory operation always at work, in that 'in securing the relation between two, the third term also keeps them apart, thereby ensuring that the two are free to play across each other's surfaces without becoming directly interlinked'.[4]

This is how the unconscious structure of the three orders thus appears in the ideal, archetypal subject. As Lacan elucidates – particularly in Seminar XXIII – however, this is not to be taken as the universal case for all subjects' unconscious psychical makeups; they can vary to the extent of necessitating a fourth – reparative – term: namely, the *sinthome*.[5]

Thus, as follows, we show the three rings of Real, Symbolic, and Imaginary entirely untied (Figure 4.2), and subsequently their repair via the fourth term of the *sinthome*, as a supplementary knot which ensures that they cannot come apart again (Figure 4.3):

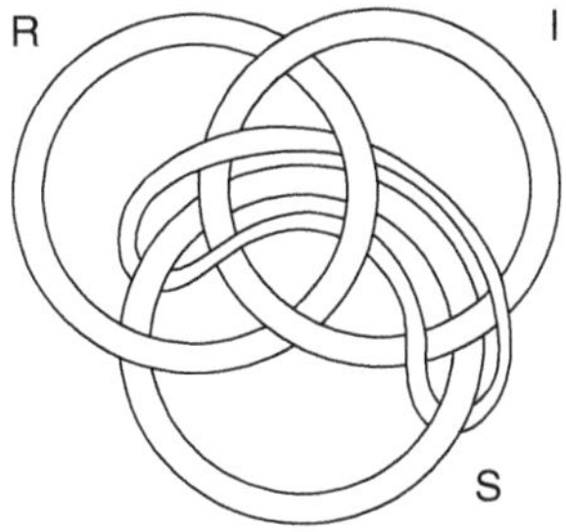

Figure 4.3 The three rings tied by the *sinthome* ['*Les trois anneaux lies par le sinthome*']

In the particular case of Joyce, Lacan determines that it is the Imaginary Order that has suffered a certain deficiency in his psychality. In a peculiar formation particular to Joyce (in this instance) the Imaginary in his orderly triad is only 'wedged' in its place, because of a fault in the knot in which the Symbolic and Real are directly linked to one another. This direct linking of the Real and Symbolic rings, which are unattached directly to the Imaginary, in effect means that the Imaginary ring gets clasped between the Symbolic and the Real, thus exerting a certain pressure on it, which – with enough force – could cause it to be pushed out and to slide away. This fault in the knot's linkage is shown in Figure 4.4 – 'the failed knot' – in which an arrow points out the gap through which the Imaginary could come to escape from the triad:

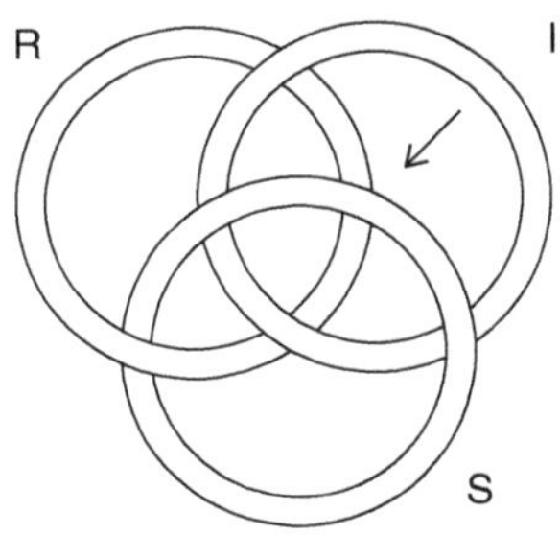

Figure 4.4 The failed knot ['*Le noeud raté*'][7]

As Dravers explains:

> The fault in the knotting peculiar to Joyce is located at the intersection between the Symbolic and the Real, where the Symbolic, instead of passing under the Real in a way which would have allowed the knot to hold together in a Borromean fashion, passes over it. In this way the symbolic knots itself directly to the real without the intervention of the imaginary as a third term.

> At the same time this leaves the imaginary precariously wedged in place between the real and the symbolic, without being secured at the level of the knot. Thus, instead of being knotted to the real through the mediation of the imaginary, the symbolic is tied directly to the real, so that when the imaginary is put under pressure it slips away, as shown.[8]

This of course has particular repercussions for Joyce, as it would for any subject who displays such a fault in their triadic knotting, because – as Lacan puts it – 'the imaginary relationship, well, it has no place. It has no place in this case'.[9] We will explore the implications of the possibility of the sliding-away (and of the re-knotting) of the imaginary order in the following section, suffice to show first how Lacan postulates that Joyce's particular *sinthome* is employed to repair this fault. Joyce deploys it correctively as an '*Ego*' (as the name he makes for – and of – himself); that is, as a self-made *Ego* (and thus not as the ego that is reinforced by, say, a practitioner of the school of ego-psychology, to which Lacanianism had been opposed from the start). Joyce's *sinthome, qua Ego*, is thus formed on the basis of his art, on that of his know-how with *artifice*:

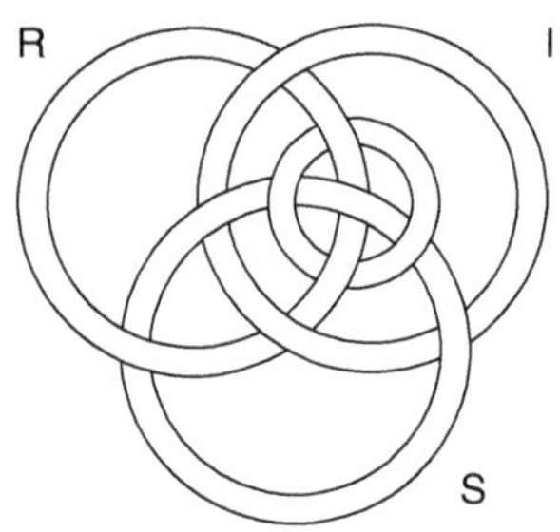

Figure 4.5 The corrective ego ['*L'ego correcteur*'][10]

Thus, as depicted in Figure 4.5, the *sinthome* – as 'the ego corrector' – specifically links again the symbolic and the real, at the point at which it is ensured that the ring of the imaginary can no longer slip out. Via the implementation of the 'ego corrector' *sinthome* Joyce's knot is retied, and whilst the original fault is still singularly perceivable, Joyce's knot nonetheless becomes consistent and continuous, in its *singularity*; that is, via the very singularity of the *sinthome*, which – as Žižek perspicaciously puts it – is 'the knot tying the world together'.[11]

Joycean thanatology → Joycean sexuality

We will now attempt to determine certain of the consequences that result from the earlier elucidations of some of Lacan's clinical responses to the life and work of James Joyce, concerning the symptom, the *sinthome*, and the three Orders' Borromean knotting; this, specifically in relation to the topics of death and sex, and how these are dealt with by Joyce in his works.

Cessation

First, however, we will assess how Lacan deals with Joyce's own death. In the first 'Joyce the Symptom' speech he claims that were he still alive Joyce would be close to 'a hundred years old, and [that] it is not useful to continue life so long'.[12] He appears here to be making oblique reference to Freud's invocation of George Bernard Shaw in a preface to his last major work, *Moses and Monotheism*. Freud here states:

> I do not share the opinion of my contemporary Bernard Shaw, that human beings would only achieve anything good if they could live to be three hundred years old. A prolongation of life would achieve nothing unless many other fundamental changes were to be made in the conditions of life.[13]

Whilst this speculation concerns modifications to the biological bases of life – so as to produce results in its psychical functioning conducive to what could be classified 'achievement' – it also, in its context, gets at the particular manifestation of life as led by Moses, in which it was at the cusp of death that his achievement came to fullest fruition; his death (or murder, according to Freud) occurring at the approach to the promised land. This Mosaic biographical narrative is one employed both by Ellmann in his presentation of Joyce – that of his leading his followers to the promised land of *Finnegans Wake*, yet dying before he could fully accompany them into its environs (and before he could be on hand for the at least three hundred years of its exegesis) – and by Lacan in his of Freud:

> Throughout his life, Freud followed the paths that he opened up in the course of this experience, attaining in the end something that one could call a promised land. One cannot say, however, that he entered into it. You need only read what can be considered to be his testament, 'Analysis terminable and interminable', in order to see that if there was one thing that he was aware of, it was that he hadn't entered into it, into the promised land.[14]

The centrality of the Moses narrative to the thanatographies put forward here further bolsters Freud's claim that a doubling or tripling of a lifespan or life expectancy (exponentially expandable to *immortality* itself) would have no positive effect, for the reason of the *fundamentality of death* to life, and to the making of life *a life*.

Žižek precisely postulates 'the border of death as the ultimate (im)possibility of a human life'.[15] Not often a utiliser of the grammatical insertion of parentheses to indicate two similarly-weighted possible readings of a word – that is, with or without the bracketed part – (a practice more commonly associated with deconstruction, of which Žižek is always sceptical), his specifically ambiguous statement precisely points here to the double movement of death, as at once *completing* a human life – rendering its narrative 'whole', finished, ready for biographisation, making life 'possible' (only after the cessation of its *live* possibility) – and, in effect, '*incompleting*' life, in making it *non-all, not-whole, for the subject*; i.e., giving it no *subjective* definitiveness, but leaving it opening out onto the utterly *unknowable* of the plane of death (in the Levinasian sense).[16] In this respect the 'achievement' of life only comes *afterwards*, through retrospection, even *retro-activation*. Without the necessitous fulfilment/incompletion of death, life's prolongation would lead only to prolonging the wait for *the moment of death itself*, despite this moment entailing – as Žižek states – 'the collapse of the structure of meaning and care' (at least, for the subject who dies). Thus, expanding on and explaining the preceding, Žižek elucidates consequences of Martin Heidegger's concept of *Dasein*, or Being-towards-death:

> The historical totality-of-meaning into which we are thrown is always already, "constitutively," thwarted *from within* by the possibility of its utmost impossibility. Death, the collapse of the structure of meaning and care, is not an external limit which, as such, would enable *Dasein* to "totalize" its meaningful engagement; it is not the final quilting point that "dots the i" of one's life span, enabling us to totalize a life story into a consistent, meaningful narrative. Death is precisely that which *cannot* be included in any meaningful totality, its meaningless facticity is a permanent threat to meaning, its prospect a reminder that there is no final way out. The consequence of this is that the choice is not a direct choice between success and failure, between authentic and inauthentic modes of existence: since the very notion that one can successfully totalize one's life within an all-encompassing structure-of-meaning is the ultimate inauthentic betrayal, the only true "success" *Dasein* can have is to heroically confront and accept its ultimate failure.[17]

In a manner, such acceptance concerns the imaginary order. In his book *Event*, Žižek claims that 'in the imaginary dimension' there is a 'confus[ion of] reality and imagination'.[18] Indeed, because the imaginary interacts with the play of images, this confusion arises within it (and can become exacerbated; Žižek gives the example of the lunatic as a subject who has overidentified with the imaginary); however, as the order that maintains link *and* separation at once – through its particular form of registration; what Klotz calls the link *of* separation – the imaginary is in part essential to the realisation and acceptance of death, as it is to that of life, as it preserves *the image* of the body (only by which image we can know our own body at all), and thus of its cessation, as well as of its thriving.

The imaginary – and thus this relation to the body – is the order that Lacan maintains is only 'wedged' in place in Joyce's psychical knot, and that is liable to slipping out; that is, until this instability is countered (however provisionally) by the deployment of the *sinthome*. The example Lacan gives from Joyce's writing is that of the scene in *A Portrait of the Artist as a Young Man* of Stephen's beating by his fellow schoolchildren after his proclaiming that Byron is the greatest of the poets over Tennyson:

It was the signal for their onset. Nash pinioned his arms behind while Boland seized a long cabbage stump which was lying in the gutter. Struggling and kicking under the cuts of the cane and the blows of the knotty stump Stephen was borne back against a barbed wire fence.

—Admit that Byron was no good.
—No.
—Admit.
—No.
—Admit.
—No. No.

At last after a fury of punches he wrenched himself free. His tormenters set off towards Jones's Road, laughing and jeering at him, while he, torn and flushed and panting, stumbled after them half blinded with tears, clenching his fists madly and sobbing.

While he was still repeating the *Confiteor* amid the indulgent laughter of his hearers and while the scenes of that malignant episode were still passing sharply and swiftly before his mind he wondered why he bore no malice now to those who had tormented him. He had not forgotten a whit of their cowardice and cruelty but the memory of it called forth no anger from him. All the descriptions of fierce love and hatred he had met in books had seemed to him therefore unreal. Even that night as he stumbled homewards along Jones's Road he had felt that some power was divesting him of that suddenwoven anger as easily as a fruit is divested of its soft ripe peel.[19]

Lacan claims of this scene:

> As Joyce testifies, having been beaten up by his four or five friends, there is something which simply slips away, like the skin of a fruit[.] This shows that he [Stephen] did not experience *jouissance*, but rather – this is something which is valid psychologically – he had a reaction of disgust, and this disgust relates to his own body[,] in the relation to his own body as foreign.[20]

It is in such cases as this violence sustained to the body that the Imaginary ring in Joyce – locatable in that of his characters – comes away, nullifying the typical relation; it is even in such moments, as Lacan suggests, that Joyce's particular *sinthome* – the *Ego*, or 'corrective ego' – (temporarily) ruptures, allowing the imaginary to slip out: 'The rupture of the ego sets the imaginary relation free. It is easy to imagine that the imaginary will bugger off – if the unconscious allows it, and it incontestably does.'[21] (It is thus in the rupturing of the *sinthome* that its other side – its functioning as symptom – disappears also, as, as Lacan points out, no *jouissance* is derived from the unconscious when the imaginary relation is lacking.)

Lacan finds this particularity of Joyce's knotting everywhere in Joyce's writing, especially, as he states, in

> the 'epiphany', the famous Joycean epiphany, which one encounters at every turn. Please note this, when he gives a list of his epiphanies: that they are always distinguished by the same thing, that they are the result of a mistake, namely that the unconscious is linked to the real.[22]

The unconscious – which here stands in the place of the symbolic – is directly interlinked with the real (as depicted in Figures 4.4 and 4.5), causing the 'wedging' of the imaginary between them, which is liable to slip away, and which does slip away in instances of 'Joycean epiphany'.

In the collection of Joyce's early writing experiences and experiments known as the *Epiphanies* we see just such renderings, in which the imaginary relation is to an extent perceivably excluded from the triadic knot because of the strength of the link between the symbolic and the real in Joyce's writing. Concerning the tragic death in youth of his brother George – after whom Joyce named his only son – Joyce wrote four sequential epiphanies (numbers 19–22), the first and last of which we will now concern ourselves with.[23] Number 19 runs:

[Dublin: in the house in Glengariff Parade: evening]
Mrs Joyce – (*crimson, trembling, appears at the parlour door*) . . . Jim!
Joyce – (*at the piano*) . . . Yes?
Mrs Joyce – Do you know anything about the body? . . . What ought I do? . . . There's some matter coming away from the hole in Georgie's stomach. . . . Did you ever hear of that happening?
Joyce – (*surprised*) . . . I don't know. . . .
Mrs Joyce – Ought I send for the doctor, do you think?
Joyce – I don't know. . . . What hole?
Mrs Joyce – (*impertinent*) . . . The hole we all have. . . .here (*points*)
Joyce – (*stands up*)[24]

Here we are met with Joyce's open admission that he does not know about the body, in so many ways the locus of the imaginary order. In the devastating scene, his twice-given response of 'I don't know' to his mother's pleas is the demonstration of the stupefaction brought on by this non-identification with the imaginary (its having been forced out of the triadic knot – even if only temporarily – by the trauma). This inability of Joyce to be able to identify imaginarily is enough to stoke up Mrs Joyce's 'impertinence' in her reply to him. His final act in the scene is then to stand up; no (imaginary) resolution is offered. This lack of resolution, which renders the scene so poignant and pertinent, is that which also demonstrates its lack at the level of the imaginary, its lack of *affect*; we are left only with a stark real and certain of its symbolic traces, linked only with one another (rendering the writing's unconscious effects on the reader), without being tied in by the imaginary (bypassing the writerly attempt to render a conscious affect in the reader). This lack of affect of the imaginary order is found directly in the epiphany following on from the death and funeral scenes, number 22:

[Dublin: in the National Library]
Skeffington – I was sorry to hear of the death of your brother. . . . sorry we didn't know in time. . . . to have been at the funeral. . . .
Joyce – Oh, he was very young . . . a boy. . . .
Skeffington – Still. . . . it hurts. . . . [25]

Joyce here has to be told that his brother's death hurts by Skeffington, to whom Joyce's response must have appeared at some level inadequate, *inaffective.* This is of course not to suggest that Joyce was cold towards his brother's death – he made his son his brother's namesake in his brother's honour after all – nor that the response in his epiphanies is completely psychologically incongruous – the mechanical words to Skeffington are no doubt typical subjective effects common to such a traumatic event – but that, in both epiphanies, the strain on the imaginary, and at points the *Ego-sinthome*'s detumescence and the ring's slipping out, is clearly discernable; that is, in Joyce's inability to comprehend or connect with the body, and in the disconnect from affect not only in the dialogue itself but in the very truncated form it takes in its writing, the form of the *epiphany.*[26]

Whereas the lack of the imaginary relation in the previous two instances causes *the real* to come starkly into view, in the last story in *Dubliners* – 'The Dead' – it is the *symbolic effects* of death that take precedence. In the story, Gabriel Conroy has attended a Christmas soirée at his aunts' house in Dublin with his wife Gretta, and delivered there a speech to the congregated guests sat around the dinner table, before having bestowed upon him the honour of carving the goose. Entertainment for the evening has been provided at the piano, but as leaving-time approaches Gretta Conroy is enraptured by a song sung to its accompaniment by the tenor Bartell D'Arcy. Back in their room at the Gresham Hotel Gretta is distant and the instance of the song is evoked at a key moment:

> 'Tell me what it is, Gretta. I think I know what is the matter. Do I know?'
>
> She did not answer at once. Then she said in an outburst of tears:
>
> 'O, I am thinking about that song, "The Lass of Aughrim".'
>
> She broke loose from him and ran to the bed and, throwing her arms across the bed-rail, hid her face. Gabriel stood stock-still for a moment in astonishment and then followed her. As he passed in the way of the cheval-glass he caught sight of himself in full length, his broad, well-filled shirt-front, the face whose expression always puzzled him when he saw it in a mirror, and his glimmering gilt-rimmed eyeglasses. He halted a few paces from her and said:
>
> 'What about the song? Why does that make you cry?'[27]

At the moment at which the source of Gretta's discomposure is revealed Gabriel catches sight of himself disconcertingly in the mirror and feels puzzled by his facial expression reflected in it. The (dis)connection of the imaginary – and its mirror stage – thus comes in at the moment at which its intensity begins to shatter the coordinates of the scene, and of the relations between husband and wife (it may be that here the imaginary exerts too much force of its own and thus begins to come away).

Gretta reveals that she is 'thinking of a person long ago who used to sing that song'; that is, her young beau, Michael Furey.[28] Gabriel charges her with having wanted to return to Galway to see him, but she intercedes. "He is dead,' she said at length. 'He died when he was only seventeen. Isn't it a terrible thing to die so young as that?"[29] All the while Gabriel had been trying to arouse the affections of Gretta in their hotel room, but comes to feel

> humiliated by the failure of his irony and by the evocation of this figure from the dead, a boy in the gasworks. While he had been full of memories of their secret life together, full of tenderness and joy and desire, she had been comparing him in her mind with another. A shameful consciousness of his own person assailed him. He saw himself as a ludicrous figure, acting as a pennyboy for his aunts, a nervous, well-meaning sentimentalist, orating to vulgarians and idealizing his own clownish lusts, the pitiable fatuous fellow he had caught a glimpse of in the mirror.[30]

Whilst identification with the imaginary is brought to its fullest pitch here in Gabriel – in reducing himself even more in his mirror-image, and even to the extent of his imagining what is taking place in Gretta's imagination – the imaginary nonetheless loses out to the symbolic in that the fact of Michael Furey's death (its *real*, the cessation of the subject Michael Furey) is not met by any imaginary apperception on Gabriel's part; i.e., only the symbolic effects of Michael Furey's love affair with Gretta, and of the impressions that his death has left on her, seem to register in Gabriel's psyche; the dead boy's threat to the couple's relationship – amatory and sexual – seems unaffected in Gabriel's mind by Furey's actual *no-longer-existing*. Furey here seems to occupy the imaginary of Gretta – provoked by the reminder of him through the song 'The Lass of Aughrim', and exacerbated by her confession: 'I think he died for me' – but Gabriel appears somewhat unable to register this imaginary relation; that is, to match it with anything similar in his own mentality.[31] Ellmann argues that Gabriel has no similar experience to counterpose Gretta's with – her 'emotional intensities [are] outside of his own experience' – but it is perhaps that he has not this *mode* of emotionality itself.[32] Thus, rather than the dead per se, Furey takes on something of the role of the *undead* here, his re-emergence a continual threat to Gabriel, and to his relations with his wife; through his death, and its symbolic continuance, he seems to become *unkillable* to Gabriel. Thus, despite the cessation of Furey's singularity, its remnants in Gretta's imaginary – and thus its continuing symbolic effect between the pair – seizes Gabriel with terror.

The character of Michael Furey corresponds to a real-life figure that preoccupied Joyce greatly in his relations with his own wife Nora, Michael Bodkin, who held a similar position in her history to that which Furey does in Gretta's in 'The Dead'.[33] The preoccupation with Bodkin is discernable in that he doesn't only get transmuted into the character of Furey, from Oughterard in Galway, in 'The Dead', but is also referenced in the notes for the character of Bertha in *Exiles*, given his proper name and proper place in Galway, Rahoon – 'Bodkin died. Kearns died. In the convent they called her the man-killer [. . .] She weeps over Rahoon too, over him whom her love has killed' – and as the centrepiece of the poem 'She weeps over Rahoon' from *Pomes Penyeach*, which begins: 'Rain on Rahoon falls softly, softly falling,/where my dark lover lies.'[34]

Whilst this line directly chimes with the last refrain of 'The Dead' – 'his soul swooned slowly as he heard the snow falling faintly through the universe and faintly falling, like the descent of their last end, upon all the living and the dead' – it also hints at the cloudiness of the imaginary order for Joyce; its having made the lover of the other 'dark', alike to the indiscernible lady of the sonnets, and to how a reflection may appear in a mirror; that is, *in a glass darkly*.[35] The symbolic dead, then, for Joyce – epitomised in this figure of Bodkin and of Furey, from Oughterard and from Rahoon – is a figure whose effects (despite the subject himself's cessation) carry so much weight as to disturb to a troubling degree any successive formation involving the affected. In contrast, the dead in relation to the Real – which Joyce presents in all its unyielding starkness in the *Epiphanies* – through its traumatic absurdity forecloses a certain affective interaction. In both cases, because of the strength of their interlinking and mutual support, it is either the real or the symbolic that comes to fill the entire narrative field to the detriment of the other orders; this is due to their intermediary – the imaginary – escaping the triad at these points, and, through its not being linked correctly to the other rings in the Borromean manner, being unable to provide the mediation that could otherwise be expected of it.

Thus, a pure concept of death would, as Žižek points out, entail 'the collapse of the structure of meaning and care'. Subjective death would therefore entail the complete cessation of singularity, the utter disintegration of all subjective coordinates, with no possibility of their reunification in some kind of afterlife. To think this pure concept of death it is necessary to see the subjective life as a *particular* utterly devoid of any connection to *the universal*, a perception which renders the fullest realisation of the concept of *singularity*. Thus, once the conditions conducive to the production of the particular subjective singularity have occurred in the world, then after its life the cessation of this subjective singularity would be its absolute finality. Its cessation of consciousness might be anatomically likened to the detachment of a hangnail from a cuticle, with the subject's world of affect feeling to the body as how that of a removed fingernail does to a finger; the particular – its subjectivity – would thus cease fully, and would not dissolve its parts back into the universal, as in most religious conceptions. Such a rendering as this is thus representative of the manner in which the poet Fernando Pessoa – under the heteronym Alberto Caeiro – saw nature itself: 'Nature is parts without a whole.'[36]

This version of death would perhaps then be the manifestation of the final of the two deaths between which Lacan places such subjects as Antigone, who first suffers a 'symbolic death' at the hands of Creon, and then her *actual* death, enclosed in a walled chamber. Because of the particularity of the positioning of Joyce's Imaginary Order it is between these two deaths that he seems to place the dead subject itself, but, interestingly, between these *from either direction*; i.e., in the case of the actual death of George Joyce he presents it in its real in the epiphanies as devoid of the ability to symbolically *mean* (that is, as unhooked onto *meaning* by the imaginary); it stays between the two deaths, having entered from the real, but not having passed into the symbolic. In the case of the death of Michael Furey, or Bodkin, its symbolic effects are continually felt; they do not pass over into *actual* death, or complete *cessation*: his death remains in the symbolic, and does not pass into the real.

Thus, the particular thanatological reflections on (pure) death which posit it as the cessation of singularity are not readily locatable in Joyce. This is not due to there remaining in Joyce remnants of religiosity (which his atheism certainly counters), but rather to the particularity of his psychical knot, and the place of the imaginary within it. Nonetheless, it is here the case that the concept of pure death cannot be fully imagined *beyond anyone's imagination*; its thanatology cannot sincerely be subsumed into the psychoanalytic or subjective realm. As Freud himself puts it:

> We cannot, indeed, imagine our own death; whenever we try to do so we find that we survive ourselves as spectators. The school of psychoanalysis could thus assert that at bottom no one believes in his own death, which amounts to saying: in the unconscious every one of us is convinced of his immortality.[37]

Ricorsi

We will thus turn from death to the death drive, and at the same time from thanatology to sexuality (theoretically utilising Lacan's Seminar XX herein in particular). We see this very structure of the movement *from* death *to* sex throughout Joyce's work, most prevalently in *Ulysses*, which – as a '*life in the day of*' – begins with a funeral (Patrick Dignam's) and ends with a birth-giving (Mina Purefoy's).[38] Although we might be expected to associate Eros – Freud's term for the psychosexual aspect of life (from the Greek god of love) – with sexuality, and Thanatos – the term applied in contrast by Wilhelm Stekel to the death drive (from the Greek daemon of death) – with death, we will look to the element of *necessity* in the *sinthome* – which Lacan characterises with the formula: 'That which doesn't cease being written' (*ne cesse pas de s'écrire*) – as the thread by which to find our way through positing the contrary.[39] Drawing on pronouncements made late in Seminar XXIV, Harari suggests that here

> Lacan's new definition of the *sinthome* [is] as [something] "not ceasing to write itself" [*ne cessant pas de s'écrire*], which it is clear can only correspond to what he terms "the necessary." A moment later he states that the "varity of

> the *sinthome*" is what "the analysand says awaiting verification." This *varity* is thus posited at the expense of *the* truth – as an inflection of the necessary. "That which does not cease to write itself" alludes to a theoretical constellation that returns inexorably, incessantly. In the last instance, the necessary is that which must not be gotten rid of; if it comes away, it must be tied back in – it's necessary, one cannot hide it[;] it is a question of "Without that – entailed by my way of dealing with it – I cannot live. It is necessary for me." A nodal category, in sum.[40]

Here we see elucidated the necessity of *assuming* the *sinthome*; its varity (subjective variety) – despite blocking and troping the subject's *truth* (its verity) – is demonstrated nonetheless to be necessitous to the subject, in providing it the ability to *live*; that is, to retain its ownmost subjectivity itself. As suggested earlier, the *sinthome* thus encompasses *necessity*, in opposition to the comfort-compromise *contingency* of the symptom, Lacan's formula for which is 'that which ceases not being written' (*cesse de ne pas s'écrire*).[41] Lacan interposes these two terms with two others: the possible, 'that which ceases, being written' (*cesse, de s'écrire*) – as he puts it in Seminar XXIII, with the insertion of the caesura – and the impossible, 'that which doesn't cease not being written' (*ne cesse pas de ne pas s'écrire*).[42]

Thus, the *impossible* – the domain of the Real – as that which doesn't cease not being written is that which can never be known, that which will always remain unknowable, impossible, Real; unwritten and unsymbolised. If, however, a little bit of Real were to be rendered, through some *contingency*, its not-being-written (its impossibility) would cease. Thus, in its *becoming-possible* – the *possible* always being a *becoming*, for once it is realised it is no longer *potential* (possible) but *real* – this piece of the Real ceases (*as Real*), in being written. Finally, the *necessary* is that which all along doesn't cease being written; a writing that doesn't meet cessation. This *sinthomic* writing is what propels the subject (in its life); and, in its utter unstoppability, becomes *beyond the subject* (surviving its death); that is, it is on the side of the ceaseless death drive. How this aspect of the death drive fits into the sexual can be elucidated through a close reference to the series of erotic letters that Joyce sent to Nora in 1909, which we will commence momentarily.

Firstly, however, we should approach how Lacan came to frame sexuality. As Jacqueline Rose states, in his late works Lacan came to theorise that

> 'There is no sexual relation' – this became the emphasis of his account. 'There is no sexual relation' because the unconscious divides subjects to and from each other, and because it is the myth of that relation which acts as a barrier against the division, setting up a unity through which this division is persistently disavowed. Hence the related and opposite formula 'There is something of One' (the two formulas should be taken together) which refers to the fantasised unity of relation '*We are as one*.[']][43]

Georges Bataille precisely states that 'in that he is an erotic animal, man [become]s a problem to himself'; this is certainly so in the wake of the impossibility of the sexual relationship.[44] It is in this lack or impossibility of the sexual relation that we can see the principle of *enverity* again at work in what Rose calls the 'division' between two subjects *to* and *from* each other, and in their inability to properly become One (the pre-analytic formula 'there is a One' having become 'there is something of One'; that is, bits of it, it being divided, or split). However, Lacan suggests that Joyce's relation to Nora *is* sexual. 'What is Joyce's relation to Nora?' he asks; 'oddly enough, I'd say it is a sexual relation, even though I say there's no such thing. But it's a funny kind of sexual relation.'[45] As Harari clarifies, Lacan claims that Nora

> fitted [Joyce] like a glove turned inside out. What does this mean? Take a glove, turn it inside out and put the other hand inside it: it adjusts marvelously well, fitting exactly. This is how well Nora "fitted" Joyce, for Lacan; thus she was the only woman of his life: *The* woman, as he constantly tells her in his letters.[46]

(However, in a 1975 essay by Moustafa Safouan, the inverted glove is located on the plane of female fantasy; he argues (no less enigmatically) that 'merely by turning inside out like a glove [the woman] would turn into the still form of her rivalry, which also represents the most intimate and inadmissible nucleus of her identity'.[47] This is perhaps the aspect of Nora that Joyce desired in his – sometimes urophilic and coprophilic – 'dirty letters'; that is, 'the glove turning inside out, the possibility of an eversion of what lies deepest in inner secrecy', as Lacan puts it in Seminar X.)[48]

Yet Lacan suggests that in terms of gender identification the '*woman* does not exist', which can be read – according to Jacqueline Rose and Juliet Mitchell, at least – as meaning not that *women* do not exist, nor that *a* woman does not exist, but that the concept '*The* Woman' in and of itself does not exist, as it is a fantasmatic image that has been created and maintained (in all its idealised and degraded forms) in a predominantly male, phallic, and patriarchal economy.[49] In this we see that women have lost out over time to a societal and cultural manifestation that has privileged the male (gaze) and the male fantasy of '*The* Woman' (one particularly found in the movement of courtly love, for example, as Lacan suggests in Seminar VII), a consequence of which is that, as Joyce's brother Stanislaus 'put it so pithily, in the final analysis men always blame women for being exactly what men have made of them', a no-win situation inscriptions of which can be found in so many male-imposed dictates, customs and laws the world over.[50]

Thus, in his later formulation Lacan writes '~~*The*~~ Woman', cancelling the definite article. 'Furthermore', he states,

> she is incorrectly called *the* woman, since, as I have stressed before, once the *the* of *the* woman is formulated by means of a not all, then it cannot be written. There can be no *the* here other than crossed through.[51]

This *the* in French is the feminine '*la*' and by its femininity it thus encompasses both the '*The*' that gets crossed through in Rose's translation of the formula ('~~*The*~~'), and the word 'Woman' itself, which gets crossed through in Fink's ('~~Woman~~'). However, contrary to the *the* ('*l'*') of *l'homme*, this sexed *the* does not get subsumed into the general subject (as in '*lom*'), but remains as an instance of what Lacan calls 'outsidesex [*hors–sexe*]'.[52]

Thus earlier we are seemingly met with two mechanisms by which Lacan operates, which bear striking resemblance to two Derridean trademarks: the method of '*sous rature*', and the designation of the impossibility of an '*hors-texte*'. The first of these refers to the process of *erasure*, which Gayatri Chakravorty Spivak explains as operating through the double recognition that 'since [a] word is inaccurate, it is crossed out[, yet] since it is necessary, it remains legible'.[53] Here, however, the word '*the*' ('*la*') is marked (with a strikethrough) as precisely *impossible*: '~~*la*~~'; its remaining legible representing the *misrecognition* of its supposed necessity.

The latter Derridean instance comes from the infamous phrase in *Of Grammatology*, '*there is nothing outside of the text* [there is no outside-text: *il n'y a pas de hors–texte*].'[54] The impossibility of there being an outside-text thus here becomes compatible with Lacan's assertion that there is no sexual relation (*il n'y a pas de rapport sexuel*) in that Lacan qualifies this by stating 'that the sexual relationship cannot be written': sex must remain *outside* [*hors-sexe*]; that is, outside the text [*hors-texte, ce qui ne cesse pas de ne pas s'écrire*], the place – in both thinkers' schemas – precisely of *impossibility*.[55]

These reflections therefore raise questions concerning the kind of '*the*' that actually ends the *Wake*. In Philippe Lavergne's 1982 French translation of the *Wake*, the work ends: '*Au large vire et tiens–bon lof pour lof la barque au l'onde de l'*', thus with the neutral '*l'*' preceding the translation of 'riverrun', '*erre-revie*'.[56] Lavergne's translation thus preserves the 'unaccented' and 'weak' nature of Joyce's choice of English word, *fading* as it does (in the manner of Lacan's reformulation of Ernest Jones's concept of aphanisis) into the white of the last page, and into the '*erre-revie*' of the first, in a move away from, or to become the other side of, meaning. Indeed, as Lacan describes the process of aphanisis in Seminar XI: 'When the subject appears somewhere as meaning, he is manifested elsewhere as 'fading', as disappearance [. . .] hence the division of the subject'.[57] This unificatory/separatory procedure is here perceivable in the double-movement of the *Wake*'s last word; at once signalling a nothingness (the remainder of the blank page) and the commandment for the reinsertion into meaning (the return to the first page); the '*l'*' – with its apostrophe – perfectly emphasising both the lack/absence and the implied continuance. In Stephen Heath and Philippe Sollers's earlier translation of the last chapter, however, it is the masculine '*le*' that has the last word.[58] Yet, as it is the female correspondence – ALP – that is prevalent at the end of the work, it is perhaps the feminine '*la*' that should be the preferable article to this. In its fullness, and completely unbarred (not even constrained by a full-stop), the word ('*la*') would in the Lacanian sense thus denote the *impossibility of impossibility* in the *Wake*; that is, the almost-absolute freedom of enunciation in its enunciated content: its attaining to *discourse without speech*.

Albeit, as we can see in his letters, Joyce does indeed create a fantasmatic image of '*The* Woman', but he also manages to construct something of a sexual relation, as Lacan attests. In his letter to Nora of 15 December 1909 he depicts an image of her which he subsequently gets off on, but it is an image he nevertheless looks to Nora for validation of; it is perhaps this, which represents again something of the lack of the imaginary relation in Joyce, that qualifies the sexual rapport between the two, in that it is due to the missing imaginary that Joyce needs Nora to fully join in in the fantasy, to make their fantasies one (it is known that Nora wrote back in kind, but her side of the correspondence is lost). Further, as we have gathered from our investigations into the composition of *Finnegans Wake* so far, we know that Joyce was able to inscribe *jouissance* into his writing (no doubt the masturbatory and idiotic *jouissance* that according to Lacan is ultimately *male*, but perhaps also something further ('*beyond phallic*'), able to touch that of the female and bring it into a shared, sexual, *jouissant* relation).[59]

In the abovementioned letter to his wife Joyce describes to her, and to himself

> the idea of a shy beautiful girl like Nora pulling up her clothes behind and revealing her sweet white girlish drawers in order to excite the dirty fellow she is so fond of; and then letting him stick his dirty red lumpy pole in through the split of her drawers and up up up in the darling little hole between her plump fresh buttocks.
>
> Darling, I came off just now in my trousers so that I am utterly played out.[60]

Thus, this sexual relationship between the couple – the sexual relation that occurs here when the partners are absent from each other – is based fundamentally on reading and writing, locating the fantasy in the symbolic order. Indeed, concerning sex's real in this letter Joyce claims that 'it is all nonsense, too, dear, about buggering you. It is only the dirty sound of the word I like'.[61] However, in an earlier letter of 6 December 1909 Joyce does seem directly attracted to the Real in his desire to 'glory [. . .] in the very stink and sweat that rises from [Nora's] arse', to smell her farts and 'the perfume of [he]r drawers as well as the warm odour of [he]r cunt and the heavy smell of [he]r behind'; all of this suggesting a fascination with the other's body – in contrast to the repulsion he felt towards his own – and a direct desire for the unseemly as well as the beautiful involved in sex, which – whilst these fascinations in themselves are not uncommon paraphilias – perhaps comes about here because of the precarity of the imaginary in Joyce's psychical knotting.[62]

These erotic love letters' temporality is thus such that they encompass both Freudian *Nachträglichkeit* (deferral or 'afterwardness': retroactivation) and the repetition compulsion of the death drive at once. Joyce 'comes off' over the written sexual relation, which is at once a coming-off over his own writing of the letter, his own reading of it, the knowledge of Nora reading it and *enjoying* it, and of her replying, and the deferral of the projected acts themselves, which are at once fantasised at that moment and scheduled for realisation in a future moment, at which point sexual potency will recur, as its 'playing out' – no matter how total, or 'utter', it may feel – always remains *not-whole*; that is, for Joyce, his sexuality is constantly and continually *being written*; reinscribing and repeating, like the desire of the drive. Joyce's *sinthomic* drive is thus always in the process of *writing itself*.

Such *ricorsi* as this is what sustains the sexual in Joyce, this Italian word for 'recursion' being that from Vico with which Joyce elected to represent the circular and circulative structure of *Finnegans Wake*; a work which precisely *doesn't cease being written*, in that with every subsequent restarting and rereading elements of its impossible contingently become possible and thereafter necessary; and this, recursively. Such recursive continuality as this is apparent not only in the sexuality of the *Wake* – which will be discussed further at points in the next chapter – but across all aspects of Joyce's writing, and deep within its very structuration. For example, we find in Joyce's maxim in *Ulysses* – that 'love loves to love love' – the endlessness and circularity of the repetition involved in amatory and sexual desire.[63] In *A Portrait of the Artist as a Young Man*, likewise, it is the Deleuzian 'dark precursor' of a 'mysterious' and suggestive word – 'smugging', an obscure activity that other schoolboys have been caught doing by the schoolmaster – that sets the sexual going in Stephen, to be continually returned to, *reread*, and reawoken through (unconscious) retroactivation.[64]

Even in terms of the continuity of structure; subsequent to *Dubliners*, Joyce sought to excise all inverted commas denoting speech from his works – punctuation marks which he described as 'perverted commas' in a letter to Harriet Shaw Weaver of 11 July 1924 – so as both to free up the scansion of the text and to meld all of its moments into a more fluid continuity.[65] These fluidities perhaps achieve their apogees in the last passages of *Finnegans Wake* and in the Penelope episode of *Ulysses* (both of which are notably feminine), this latter being an episode which Lacan's discourse in his discussion of feminine sexuality seems at times to mimic or emulate, particularly in the later sessions of Seminar XX, in which he at points puns elaborately on words like 'soul' ('*âme*'), finding it in all sorts of other words, not least in its homonymy with love ('*aime*'); or refers to a sexual(ised) statue – 'The Ecstasy of St. Teresa' by Gian Lorenzo Bernini – replicating Molly Bloom's ruminations on the penises of 'those statues in the museum' in her soliloquy; or indeed refers narcissistically back to himself, championing his own *Écrits* as 'the best thing you can read'; all dumbshow equivalents of the no doubt sexually-cathected processes taking place continually in the unconscious.[66] Although implicit at this stage, it is perhaps then that Joycean sexuality had a part to play in giving form to the 'string of psychological peaches' that are Lacan's reflections on feminine sexuality and the limits of love and knowledge in Seminar XX, and to the work that followed on from this, in which the writer became an increasingly important staple in the psychoanalyst's thinking.

Thus, to conclude, in relation to thanatology and sexuality, although death ultimately entails the cessation of subjective singularity, Joyce dared to embrace its radically impossible and paradoxical *step beyond* ('*pas au-delà*' in French, which means both 'step/not beyond' at once, as in Maurice Blanchot's title) in which he encountered the realm of sexuality and the drive (that *which doesn't cease not being written* in conjunction with that *which doesn't cease being written*), and thus their *ricorsi*'s specific relations to writing and reading.[67] In effect, then, a post-Joycean psychoanalysis must encompass the ability to apprehend a subjectivity that has come to assume the *sinthome* such an encounter entails.

Notes

1 See Adrian Price, 'In the Nebohood of Joyce and Lacan', *Lacanian Compass Express*, 2nd ser., 14 (December 2014) 1–24 (p.8).
2 Jacques Lacan, *The Seminar of Jacques Lacan, Book XIX: . . .Ou pire/. . .Or worse, 1971–1972*, trans. by Cormac Gallagher (London: Karnac, unofficial translation, n.d.) session V, p.13.
3 See '*Le nœud borroméen* [The Borromean knot]', in Lacan, *Le seminaire, Livre XXIII: Le sinthome* [1975–1976], texte établi par Jacques-Alain Miller (Paris: Éditions du Seuil, 2005) p.20. All knot images are from redrawings made by Sally Nall.
4 Philip Dravers, 'Joyce & the Sinthome: Aiming at the Fourth Term of the Knot', *Psychoanalytical Notebooks*, 13 (2005) 93–116 (p.100).
5 At this point it will be worthwhile addressing a sustained objection to the Borromean topology made by Žižek, specifically concerning the place within it of sexuation. He states:

> the reason Lacan, in his later teaching, turned to the theme of knots was precisely in order to think the [sexual] non-relationship as embodied in a paradoxical element[.] Here enters the Borromean knot, consisting of three circles intertwined in such a way that no two are directly connected but are held together only through the third, so that if we cut the third knot, the other two will also be disconnected – in short, there is no relationship between any two circles. What is this third circle? The *objet a*? The *sinthome*? The symbolic order itself? Here Lacan, at the very end of his teaching, reached a deadlock to which, in an authentically tragic mode, he openly confessed
>
> > The metaphor of the Borromean knot is, in its most simple state, inadequate. It abuses the metaphor, because there really is no thing which supports the imaginary, the symbolic, and the real. What is essential in what I am saying is that there is no sexual relationship. That there is no sexual relationship because there is an imaginary, a symbolic, and a real, this is what I did not dare to say. But I nonetheless said it. It is evident that I was wrong, but I simply let myself slide into it. This is disturbing, it is even more than annoying. It is even more annoying that it is not justified. This is how things look to me today, and this is what I confess to you. All right!
> >
> > [*Le séminarie, Livre XXVI: La topologie et la temps*, 1978–1979 (unpublished)]

Two things should be noted here. First, retroactively, one can see where the obvious mistake lay: the Borromean knot works as a metaphor only if we think the three circles as simultaneous, intertwined on the same surface. (The only way to save this model would be to add a fourth element holding the three together, which Lacan did with his notion of the *sinthome* holding together the ISR triad.) Second, why was Lacan, by his own confession, wrong to say that there is no sexual relationship because there is an imaginary, a symbolic, and a Real? Because the three are not given simultaneously as a triad [. . .] In Lacan's triad of imaginary-symbolic-Real, or in Freud's of ego-superego-Id, when we focus on one term, the other two get condensed into one (under the hegemony of one of them). If we focus on the imaginary, the Real and the symbolic get contracted into the imaginary's opposite under the domination of the symbolic; if we focus on R, I and S get contracted under the domination of S.

What Lacan is struggling with here is how to formulate or formalize an impossible/Real object which keeps the two sexes apart and, simultaneously, is the only thing, a third thing, which indirectly connects the two. Insofar as this object is an obstacle to the identity of each sex, this means that every sex is grounded by its immanent impossibility. The inadequacy of the Borromean metaphor is that it makes it appear as if, when the third circle is cut off, the two other circles (the two sexes) simply wander off, each going its own way – as if the two sexes have some kind of consistency outside of their constitutive difference.' See Slavoj Žižek, *Less Than Nothing: Hegel and the Shadow of Dialectical Materialism* (London: Verso, 2012) pp.798–800.

Whilst Žižek's complicating criticism should always be kept in mind, it should be noted in response first that the anti-metaphoricity of Lacan's stance in Seminar XXVI is as open to being read as demarcating the knot's non-metaphoricity itself (its *mathematisation*) as it is of metaphorical failure inhibiting the supposed desire for a '*correct*' metaphor; i.e., the topological – or mathematised – knot is precisely *not* a metaphor, but a representation in the real. Second, our unificatory/separatory principle may be able to intervene here at the level of the called-for *simultaneous connector and divider* (*of the sexes*). Despite – as we have previously noted – the orders/rings being open to oscillatory indetermination, whichever is the '*third ring*' in the triad necessarily operates as position A, not only uniting and separating, but *constituting* the other two rings, which in themselves would be unsustainable without it (or without the *sinthome*, supplementarily). Their possible hegemonisation appears therefore to be a risk only of their metaphorical representation, not of their topological constitution.

6 See '*Les trois anneaux séparés, puis lies par le sinthome, quatrième* [The three rings as separate, and as secured by the fourth ring of the sinthome]', in Lacan, *Le seminaire XXIII: Le sinthome*, p.20.

7 See '*Le noeud raté* [The failed knot]', in ibid. p.151.

8 Dravers, 'Joyce & the Sinthome', p.109.

9 Lacan, *Le seminaire XXIII: Le sinthome*, p.151; Jacques Lacan, *The Seminar of Jacques Lacan, Book XXIII: Joyce and the Sinthome, 1975–1976*, trans. by Cormac Gallagher (London: Karnac, unofficial translation, n.d.) session XI, p.12.

10 See '*L'ego correcteur* [The corrective ego]', in Lacan, *Le seminaire XXIII: Le sinthome*, p.152.

11 Žižek, *Less Than Nothing*, p.232.

12 Lacan, 'Joyce le Symptôme', in *Le seminaire XXIII: Le sinthome*, p.162 (trans. by Benanav, modified).

13 Sigmund Freud, 'Moses and Monotheism' [1939], trans. by James Strachey, in *SE*, XXIII, p.54, note 2. Lacan discusses this note explicitly in *The Seminar of Jacques Lacan, Book III: The Psychoses, 1955–1956*, ed. by Jacques-Alain Miller, trans. by Russell Grigg (New York: W. W. Norton, 1993) pp.243–244, in which he draws from Freud's text the sense of his own interpretative translation of the statement '*mé phunaï*' ('it's better *not have been born*') in *Oedipus at Colonus*, as 'it would be better *not to have been born like this*.'

14 Jacques Lacan, *The Seminar of Jacques Lacan, Book I: Freud's Papers on Technique, 1953–1954*, ed. by Jacques-Alain Miller, trans. by John Forrester (New York: W.W. Norton, 1988) p.15.

15 Žižek, *Less Than Nothing*, p.894.

16 Levinas describes death as 'not unknown but unknowable'. See Emmanuel Levinas, 'Time and the Other' [1947], in *Time and the Other [and Additional Essays]*, trans. by Richard A. Cohen (Pittsburgh: Duquesne University Press, 1987) p.75. Whilst this notion might be contrasted with the category of the 'unknown known' – in which we can postulate the knowledge of death as the ultimate *disavowed* knowledge ('I know well that all my subjective coordinates will simply cease, but all the same I don't believe it . . .') – the *state of death* itself *is* unknowable, in that it will never become known to the subject, as the subject's subjectivity – that is, its means of *knowing* – itself will have ceased.
17 Žižek, *Less Than Nothing*, p.529.
18 Slavoj Žižek, *Event* (London: Penguin, 2014) p.119.
19 James Joyce, *A Portrait of the Artist as a Young Man* [*1916*], ed. by Jeri Johnson (Oxford: Oxford World's Classics, 2000) pp.68–69.
20 Lacan, *Le seminaire XXIII: Le sinthome*, pp.149–150; Jacques Lacan, 'Le Sinthome: Jacques Lacan's *Seminar XXIII*, 1975–6', ed. by Jacques-Alain Miller, *Ornicar?* 6–11 (1975–1976) p.60 [translation modified].
21 Lacan, *Le seminaire XXIII: Le sinthome*, p.155; Lacan, 'Le Sinthome', p.63.
22 Lacan, *Le seminaire XXIII: Le sinthome*, p.154; Lacan, 'Le Sinthome', p.63.
23 See Richard Ellmann, *James Joyce: New and Revised Edition* (Oxford: Oxford University Press, 1983) pp.93–94 for more on the event of George's death.
24 James Joyce, 'Epiphanies' [1901–1904], in *Poems and Shorter Writings*, ed. by Richard Ellmann, A. Walton Litz and John Whittier-Ferguson (London: Faber and Faber, 1991) p.179.
25 Ibid. p.182. Joyce's friend, Francis Sheehy Skeffington, met his own abrupt end on 12 May 1916 when, 'although he had taken no part in the [Easter] rising, [he] was arrested and shot without trial'. See Donal McCartney, 'From Parnell to Pearse: 1891–1921', in *The Course of Irish History*, ed. by T. W. Moody and F. X. Martin (Blackrock: Mercier Press, 2001) p.256.
26 Through deploying Salvador Dalí's mechanism of *paranoia-criticism* we can perhaps see the further unconscious pervasiveness of the body in Joyce's thoughts by interpreting in the speech he offers in reply to Skeffington the enunciation 'body' in the enunciated 'boy'.
27 James Joyce, 'The Dead', in *Dubliners* [1914] (London: Penguin Modern Classics, 1973) p.215.
28 Ibid.
29 Ibid. p.216.
30 Ibid. pp.216–217.
31 Ibid. p.217.
32 Ellmann, *James Joyce*, p.248.
33 See ibid. pp.248–249, for example.
34 See James Joyce, 'Entries in a Notebook, Now at Buffalo', in *Poems and* Exiles, ed. by J.C.C. Mays (Harmondsworth: Penguin Twentieth-Century Classics, 1992) p.347, and James Joyce, 'She weeps over Rahoon', in *Pomes Penyeach* [1927] (London: Faber and Faber, 1966) p.16.
35 Joyce, 'The Dead', in *Dubliners*, p.220.
36 Fernando Pessoa [Alberto Caeiro], '47 On an incredibly clear day' [1914], in *Fernando Pessoa & Co. Selected Poems*, ed. and trans. by Richard Zenith (New York: Grove Press, 1998) p.65. As Richard Zenith explains, Pessoa was 'famous for splitting himself into a multitude of literary alter egos he dubbed "heteronyms" – more than mere pseudonyms, since he endowed them with biographies, religious and political views, and diverse writing styles'. The line quoted from the poem above 'was, according to Pessoa, Caeiro's greatest, truest verse'. See Richard Zenith, 'Introduction', in Fernando Pessoa, *A Little Larger Than the Entire Universe: Selected Poems*, ed. and trans. by Richard Zenith (London: Penguin Classics, 2006) p.xiii and p.xxix.

37 Sigmund Freud, 'Reflections on War and Death' [1915], trans. by A. A. Brill and Alfred B. Kuttner (New York: Moffat, Yard and Company) p.41. I prefer this translation over that from the *Standard Edition*. For reference, however, see Sigmund Freud, 'Thoughts for the Times on War and Death', trans. by E. C. Mayne, in *SE*, XIV, p.289.
38 As Clive Hart also reminds us, in *Finnegans Wake* 'Book III begins with death (403) and ends with a birth (590)' also, reversing and inverting the major events of Book I. See Clive Hart, *Structure and Motif in Finnegans Wake* (London: Faber and Faber, 1962) p.67.
39 See Jacques Lacan, *The Seminar of Jacques Lacan, Book XX: Encore: On Feminine Sexuality, the Limits of Love and Knowledge, 1972–1973*, ed. by Jacques-Alain Miller, trans. by Bruce Fink (New York: W. W. Norton, 1998) p.59: 'The necessary – what I propose to accentuate for you with this mode – is that which doesn't stop *(ne cesse pas)* what? – being written *(de s'écrire)*.'
40 Roberto Harari, *How James Joyce Made His Name: A Reading of the Final Lacan* [1995], trans. by Luke Thurston (New York: Other Press, 2002) pp.122–123.
41 See Lacan, *Seminar XX: Encore*, p.94: 'It is in this "stops not being written" *(cesse de ne pas s'écrire)* that resides the apex of what I have called contingency.'
42 See Lacan, *Le seminaire XXIII: Le sinthome*, p.13 (my modified translation), and *Seminar XX: Encore*, p.59.
43 Jacqueline Rose, 'Introduction – II', in Jacques Lacan and the école Freudienne, *Feminine Sexuality*, ed. by Juliet Mitchell and Jacqueline Rose, trans. by Jacqueline Rose (New York: W. W. Norton, 1985) p.46. In the concluding quotation, Rose refers to Lacan, *Seminar XX: Encore*, p.47.
44 Georges Bataille, *Eroticism: Death and Sensuality* [1957], trans. Mary Dalwood (London: Marion Boyars Publishers Ltd., 2006) p.274.
45 Lacan, *Le seminaire XXIII: Le sinthome*, p.83; Lacan, 'Le Sinthome', p.38.
46 Harari, *How James Joyce Made His Name*, pp.164–165.
47 Moustafa Safouan, 'Feminine Sexuality in Psychoanalytic Doctrine', in Lacan and the école Freudienne, *Feminine Sexuality*, p.128.
48 Jacques Lacan, *The Seminar of Jacques Lacan, Book X: Anxiety* [1962–1963], ed. by Jacques-Alain Miller, trans. by A. R. Price (Cambridge: Polity, 2014) p.236.
49 See Lacan, *Seminar XX: Encore*, p.7. Rose's translation of Lacan's statement stresses the definite article (which in French is feminine: '*la*'): '*The* Woman does not exist'. See her explanation of the sentence in Rose, 'Introduction – II', in Lacan and the école Freudienne, *Feminine Sexuality*, p.48.
50 See Declan Kiberd, *Ulysses and Us: The Art of Everyday Living* (London: Faber and Faber, 2009) p.203.
51 Jacques Lacan, 'A Love Letter (*Une lettre d'amour*)', in *Feminine Sexuality*, p.151. This translation is preferable to our discussion, over Fink's, but for reference see Lacan, *Seminar XX: Encore*, p.80.
52 Lacan, 'A Love Letter (*Une lettre d'amour*)', in *Feminine Sexuality*, p.155. Fink uses the translation 'beyondsex' in Lacan, *Seminar XX: Encore*, p.85.
53 Gayatri Chakravorty Spivak, 'Translator's Preface', in *Of Grammatology* [1967], ed. by Jacques Derrida, trans. by Gayatri Chakravorty Spivak (Baltimore: John Hopkins University Press, 1997) p.xiv. See ibid. p.23, for further elucidation of the concept by Derrida himself.
54 Ibid. p.158.
55 Lacan, *Seminar XX: Encore*, p.35.
56 James Joyce, *Finnegans Wake*, traduit de l'anglais, présenté et adapté par Philippe Lavergne (Paris: Gallimard, 1982) p.924.
57 Jacques Lacan, *The Seminar of Jacques Lacan, Book XI: The Four Fundamental Concepts of Psychoanalysis* [1964], ed. by Jacques-Alain Miller, trans. by Alan Sheridan (New York: W. W. Norton, 1981) p.218.
58 See Joyce, '*Finnegans Wake*, 17ème et dernier Chapitre', traduction de Stephen Heath et Philippe Sollers, in *Tel Quel*, n°54, été 1973: '*Allez voir le seul dernier l'aimé le long le*'.

59 For these Lacanian references see Lacan, *Seminar XX: Encore*, p.81 and p.74.
60 James Joyce, *Selected Letters of James Joyce*, ed. by Richard Ellmann (London: Faber and Faber, 1975) pp.189–190.
61 Ibid.
62 Ibid. p.184.
63 James Joyce, *Ulysses* [1922], ed. by Hans Walter Gabler and others (New York: Vintage Books, 1986) 12.1493, p.273; James Joyce, *Ulysses: The 1922 Text*, ed. by Jeri Johnson (Oxford: Oxford World's Classics, 1998) p.319.
64 Joyce, *A Portrait of the Artist as a Young Man*, p.35. As Deleuze describes: 'Different intensities [. . .] are preceded by an invisible, imperceptible dark precursor, which determines their path in advance.' See Gilles Deleuze, *Difference and Repetition* [1968], trans. by Paul Patton (London: Continuum, 1994) p.92.
65 James Joyce, *Letters of James Joyce III*, ed. by Richard Ellmann, 3 vols (London: Faber and Faber, 1966) III, p.99.
66 See Lacan, *Seminar XX: Encore*, p.84 and p.76, and Lacan, 'A Love Letter (*Une lettre d'amour*)', in *Feminine Sexuality*, p.147, for example; and Joyce, *Ulysses*, 18.540–541, p.620; Joyce, *Ulysses: 1922*, p.704.
67 See Maurice Blanchot, *The Step Not Beyond* [1973], trans. by Lycette Nelson (Albany: State University of New York Press, 1992). As Nelson puts it in her introduction: 'The step beyond is never completed, or, if it is completed, is never beyond' (p.xvii).

Chapter 5

Waking the read

The indelible sigla of *Finnegans Wake*

Reading the Wake: *writing*

(↘) . . .waking 'The Dead'. *Waking the Read*. . . .**Read**/Reed. . .Reading the *Wake*. . .

(👂) Said aloud (by the author), this chapter's title could initially be heard as 'Waking the Red', rendering its pun ostensively redundant – though in fact only dormant – via this pronunciation; that is, at least until it is spelt out: *R-E-A-D*. (👓) Read aloud (by the reader), the title could be construed as being 'Waking the Read', in the present tense (pronounced as 'reed'), which suggests a more immediate involvement than 'read' (pronounced as the past participle). Hearing the title as 'Waking the Re(e)d' may – through how it's received by the ear – evoke notions of musicality, even of botany, as well as hint at its reverse, 'Reading the *Wake*', but it would negate the consonance of the phraseological pun on the commonplace 'waking the dead'; a pun which doubles back on itself in referring to the final story of Joyce's first major work, *Dubliners*, with a reference to which the first line of this chapter starts, so that its beginning re-stages the circularity involved in the reading of the *Wake*. . .[1] (↖)

Thus, in the opening segment we employ the use of certain sigla that are unique to *writing* (that is, that can be read, but not read aloud *as such*). They are: pointed arrows indicating the direction of reading (downwards from left to right, and then at the end pointing diagonally back up to the start again); symbols denoting an ear – when discussing how a word is to be heard – and eyeglasses – when discussing how it is to be read (that is, visually; the use of touch in Braille, for example, is an instance we omit here); and the word 'Read' with the letters 'R', 'e', and 'd' in bold type, which if we imagined were coloured red would ensure that the word 'read' could only be read as the past participle, through a rebus-like instance of confluential advertence (*two* significations, in this case, combining to evoke *one* pronunciation: the letters within the word that denote the colour red coloured red, and the word 'read' itself, making it only possible for 'read' to be read as the past participle).

We also here encounter the 'Babelian confusion' that Derrida singles out in his essay 'Two Words for Joyce', in which he takes as the object of his study the two words – put together by Joyce in *Finnegans Wake* – 'he war'. Discussing the different pronunciations that can be given to the latter of these, he highlights that

> the Babelian confusion between the English *war* and the German *war* cannot fail to disappear – in becoming determined – when listened to. It is erased when pronounced. One is constrained to *say* it either in English or *else* in German. It cannot therefore be received as such by the ear. But it can be read.[2]

Thus, it is through some of these (post-)Joycean stylistic means employed in the construction of this chapter's opening gambit that we begin to see the processes of writing and reading occupying central places in the discursive techniques that Joyce utilises in his late works, and how their interactions can be played upon, transmuted, and adapted to open up further possibilities of sensory perception; possibilities which we will focus on herein.

Joyce, in the *Wake*, indicates the reverse side of the process highlighted by Derrida earlier. If pronounced, his question in the text, which in full is: 'Can you rede (since We and Thou had it out already) its world?', would undoubtedly be heard by an English-speaker to contain the present tense verb, 'read'.[3] Like 'war' – which contains the English 'war' and the German '*war*' (meaning 'was', and pronounced '*var*') – '*rede*', whilst it is pronounced aloud by the English speaker-reader, and *silently* contextualised in the process of reading, as the present tense 'read', it also connotes, orthographically, the German word for 'speech'.[4] Thus, when spoken – and Joyce always insisted that aloud was how *Finnegans Wake* was intended to be read – this word for 'speech' implies that which is often viewed as its opposite: writing, which we most often think of as that which can be read (though, as 'was well said of a certain German book' – according to Edgar Allan Poe – 'that "*er lasst sich nicht lesen*" – it does not permit itself to be read', so has been claimed of *Finnegans Wake*).[5]

Three components thus arise out of these initial reflections: language, the system and construction of words that can be *said* or *read* (or both, in being *read aloud*); speech, that which *says* words, and which is restrained by their pronunciation, and constrained to the usually *singular* meaning that results from pronunciation (although this is of course not always the case, as certain pronunciations bring back in that element of 'Babelian confusion': the same pronunciation of the different words 'where' and 'wear' in English, to give a simple example);[6] and writing, that which deploys the permanent traces of letters in its construction, but which allows ambiguity to seep in via its orthography, in that even *singular* words it constructs can be polyvalent enough to produce two or more connected or unconnected meanings (in one language, such as with 'read' – pronounceable as 'red' or 'reed' – or translingually, such as in Derrida's example of 'war' from Joyce given earlier). Underpinning and interrelating all of these is 'the economy of *discourse*, the relationship between meaning and meaning', as Lacan puts it (such as found in 'the relationship between the [delusional's] discourse and the common organization of discourse', for example), which we will come to in full after briefly dealing with the earlier components one by one.[7]

We could argue that a bit of the real of language emerges throughout *Finnegans Wake* through what Derrida describes as the book's own displaying of its 'Babelian underside'; that is, its displaying of what Lacan calls *lalangue*.[8] Miller describes '*lalangue* [as that] which is distinguished from language in that it is precisely without law. Language is thus conceived as a superstructure of laws that capture *lalangue* as that which is without law'.[9] Thus, this '*lalangue*' – which is as Babelian for its confounding of tongues as it is for its baby-like babbling, which Lacan intended with the '*lala*' sound inherent in it – is something of language's *other side*, its *lining*, and (part of) the Real from which the Symbolic arises. As Lacan himself puts it in Seminar XX, in a 'hypothesis' that relinks the subject of the unconscious and the signifier with *lalangue*:

> My hypothesis is that the individual who is affected by the unconscious is the same individual who constitutes what I call the subject of a signifier. That is what I enunciate in the minimal formulation that a signifier represents a subject to another signifier. The signifier in itself is nothing but what can be defined as difference from another signifier. It is the introduction of difference as such into the field, which allows one to extract from *lalangue* the nature of the signifier *(ce qu'il en est du signifiant)*.[10]

In *lalangue*, then, 'there is something of a One' (not a solid or concrescent One, which encompasses '*All*', but an undifferentiated Oneness, awaiting compartmentalisation). *Lalangue*, as part of the Real, can represent only 'something of a One' because, as Lacan puts it in Seminar XXIV:

> The very idea of the Real involves the exclusion of all sense. It is only insofar as the Real is emptied of sense that we can grasp it a little[,] which obviously brings me to not even give it the sense of the One – but one must hang on to something – and this logic of the One is indeed what remains, what remains as existence.[11]

Through *difference* a signifier is thus 'extracted' from this 'something of a One' of *lalangue* and thereafter *established*. Indeed, 'in language', as Saussure – whom Lacan is following here – claims, 'there are only differences *without positive terms*', and so language positivises terms – makes of them *signifiers*, even *master signifiers* – through *difference*, by extracting them from *lalangue*.[12] As Lacan puts it in Seminar XVII:

> All signifiers are in some sense equivalent, if we just play on the difference of each from all the others, through not being the other signifiers. But it's for the same reason that each is able to come to the position of master signifier, precisely because its potential function is to represent the subject for another signifier.[13]

The subject is thus the *between* of signifiers whose potentials have been positivised. Further, if we see the field of *lalangue* (as situated in the Real) as also the place of undifferentiated *points of jouissance*, then it would be from here that the *sinthome* (as *empty signified*) would extract such a *point* and bring it into itself in the *sinthomic* rendering of the process of subjectivation (see Figure 5.1).

Thus it seems that in terms of Joyce's last work, it can only really be *between* language and *lalangue* that we can come to situate the *Wake* (which in fact unificatory/separatorily positions it in A, as the antagonism between language and *lalangue*, as sides 1 and 2). Whilst *lalangue* might have been utilised to a greater extent in the *Wake*'s composition than in the composition of other (generally more conventional) books, and whilst *lalangue*'s constitutive flux will have been drawn on in the book's *work in progress* (that is, in its genetic changeability over its seventeen-year gestation), its final textual establishment – although this is something that is to an extent editorially in flux too, though no longer on the part of the author – in effect *languafies*, or '*superstructures*', it, to use Miller's term for the procedure of language; captures it in a linguistic law, though a law that is far closer to the lawlessness encompassed by *jouissance* than to the more linguistically strictured type found in most conventional texts. It is this process of *capturing* that the text of the *Wake* renders the structure and schema of through its linguistic practice (which also hints at the very quilting points involved in *discourse*), and it is this that we will investigate through close readings in the third section of this chapter.

Moving nominally on from language to speech, however; as a work intended to be read aloud, speech is thus integral to *Finnegans Wake*, as it is to psychoanalysis, in which the analysand speaks and interpretation is established through the return of their message to them 'in an inverted form', as Lacan puts it.[14] A similar process is able to take place in the reading of the *Wake* aloud, in that the trying of an 'unreadable' word out loud will establish it as a sound, in which might be *heard* a meaning that can better contextualise it in its order on the page than the inward reading alone would possibly be capable of (and thus, hallucinatorily). Thus the words, when spoken – in both the psychoanalytic session and the reading aloud of the *Wake* – are able to construct a *system* (from that of language to that of discourse) that is beyond them individually. Indeed, as Lacan admits in Seminar II (in a proto-Deleuze/Guattarian moment): 'The most complicated machines are made only with words.'[15] In Seminar III, the following year, he takes this further, and brings it back to *the other side* of language; that is, to the fundamental underpinning of *lalangue*, which at this point remained unnamed as such:

> What is important is to understand what one is saying. And in order to understand what one is saying it's important to see its lining, its other side, its resonances, its significant superimpositions. Whatever they may be – and we can include every misconstrual – there is no element of chance. Whoever reflects upon the organism of language must know as much as possible and construct as complete a catalogue as possible, not only concerning a word but also a turn of phrase or a locution. Language operates within ambiguity, and most of the time you know absolutely nothing about what you are saying.[16]

That the instance even of misconstrual is without the element of chance is something already detectable in Joyce, and can be seen in an anecdote concerning the *Wake*'s composition. Because of Joyce's failing eyesight he would often have to dictate his work in progress, and one of his stenographers during this process was Beckett. As Ellmann recounts:

> In the middle of one such session there was a knock at the door which Beckett didn't hear. Joyce said, 'Come in,' and Beckett wrote it down. Afterwards he read back what he had written and Joyce said, 'What's that "Come in"?' 'Yes, you said that,' said Beckett. Joyce thought for a moment, then said, 'Let it stand.'[17]

Although this story was told to Ellmann by Beckett, the phrase 'come in' itself does not appear to appear *as such* in *Finnegans Wake*; however, Hugh B. Staples conjectures that the instance had occurred, and can be located in the 'what is that?' in the section known as 'The Mime of Mick, Nick and the Maggies' in part II of the *Wake*.[18] Thus, in this semi-mythical anecdote, although through chance a misconstrual may have been inserted into the stenographed text, in Joyce's decision to let it stand the *undecidability* of that chance is excised in the phrase's establishment in its writing; it thus receives its positioning retroactively, through the quilting point that had arisen in the subsequent discourse with Beckett, concerning its placement in the text. To put it in Lacan's precise formulation from Seminar XXIII, chance is here 'that which ceases, being written': chance moves from impossible to possible; that is, it resides in the order of the Real *until* it is written; or, as Lacan puts it in Seminar XXIV:

> What I call the *impossible, is the Real*, [it] limits itself to non-contradiction. The Real is the impossible to simply write, or in other words, does not cease not to be written. The Real, is the possible waiting to be written.[19]

Thus we see in this instance speech finding itself occupying writing, but in a way that is disjunctive to the intentions of both the dictator (the writer speaking, Joyce) and the transcriber (the amanuensis writing, Beckett). This speech has therefore found its insertion into writing through a discursive disjunction, a structural misconstrual that has rendered a former 'impossible' possible, and which has thus led to a juxtaposition that has become archived in the text of the *Wake*, but which – like Lautréamont's 'fortuitous encounter upon a dissecting-table of a sewing-machine and an umbrella' – has subsequently *lost* the *impossible* of its chance element.[20]

In Seminar XVI Lacan claims that 'writing, far from being a transcription, is a different system, a system to which eventually there is attached what is cut up in a different support, that of the voice'.[21] Here, we indeed see the voice being 'cut up' *into* the system of writing, in a way that seems anticipatory of the 'cut-up technique' deployed by the artist Brion Gysin and Beat writer William S. Burroughs; a technique that the latter describes in a manner that renders well the mediation between impossible and possible that this instance has given rise to, that 'when you cut into the present the future leaks out'; that is, that it ceases *not being written.*[22]

It is Derrida's claim in *Of Grammatology* that *writing* is to be precisely found 'before speech and in speech'.[23] If taken in conjunction with his later statement in that work – that '*there is nothing outside of the text*' – we might see the instance of Joyce's 'what is that?' making it into the *Wake* as demonstrative of the fact that the knock at the door, and its answer, were not outside the text at all, but concatenatively *underwriting* the very text itself – as what Derrida calls 'archē-writing' (a kind of '*Ur*-writing') – in being instances of the impossible contingently becoming necessary through the *realisation* of the possibility dwelling within them.[24]

The concept of 'archē-writing,' Derrida suggests, is:

> At first the possibility of the spoken word, then of the '*graphie*' in the narrow sense, the birthplace of 'usurpation,' denounced from Plato to Saussure, this trace is the opening of the first exteriority in general, the enigmatic relationship of the living to its other and of an inside to an outside: spacing.[25]

Here we see writing as a *spacing* in which the text comes to be, through such a contingency as that described earlier. Alike to *différance*, archē-writing is a site of differing and deferring originariness *before the letter*, and in this it perhaps comes closest to Lacan's concepts of *lalangue* and the *sinthome*, although Lacan does not set off from these, but rather (re)turns to them via his investigations into the letter, into speech, into language, and into the symptom. However, what is primarily essential for Lacan is that there is something *to be read* – the unconscious – which 'passes through the writing whilst surviving there intact', a formulation we will return to.[26] Thus, these concepts are distinct, and yet connected, as Jean-Luc Nancy begins to uncover in his discussion of Derrida's concept in his essay 'Blank Opening':

> Writing, the writing he names 'arche-writing', is not the graphic notation of a saying full of sense. It is this: that the arche *is* writing, in other words, the senseless adventure of 'sense'.
>
> The being of this *is*, if it is well understood (and this is what Heidegger was able to understand), is never a substantive but always a verb. Writing is a verb, that is, an opening. An opening of sense at the point where sense opens itself, broaches itself, ventures itself. An opening that is therefore *blank* – 'a textual blank' – and consequently unveiling nothing like another land or another regime. Unveiling nothing, but opening that nothing itself.[27]

This 'textual blank' thus heavily suggests the *sinthome* conceptualised as the *empty signified.* As an opening that opens onto nothing – unveiling nothing and opening it up – this 'blank' provides the *spacing* for a signifier (an element which also starts by *signifying nothing*, as Lacan suggests) to lodge into it and radiate its *jouis-sens*, and thus inaugurate 'the senseless adventure of 'sense'', in Nancy's words. This, however, is only one side of archē-writing – its conceptualisation as that which spawns *sinthomic* textual blanks, matrixial measures of *spacing* – one which suggests its *other side*, which we can construe as its conceptualisation as that which spawns the *objet petit a*. In this, its *opening* suggests the operation of *hole-making*; that is, a piercing of the originary unificatory/separatory screen, which makes a hole through it *into* (*and thus from*) *nothing*, thus evoking *lack* itself, which is then positivised by the subject as an unidentifiable *object* – the missing jigsaw piece, the always-already 'lost' object, which is denoted by Lacan by an instance of writing, the letter (and the *exemplary* letter), '*a*' – which is endlessly sought to fill this hole, and thus to (imaginarily) 'complete' the subject.

We must thus now turn (back) to the *sinthome* – in conjunction with its instance and insistence in writing; that is, the effects of its 'lettering' – before moving onto the particular letter of the *lost object*, '*a*', and its instances within the Joycean text. As Patricia Gherovici points out – and as we have already discussed –

> Lacan adapts the classic [Aristotelian] philosophical definition of 'necessary as that which cannot cease being', and changes it for 'necessary as that which does not cease being written'. The *sinthome* is what does not cease to be written, it turns and returns.[28]

In this way, the *sinthome* – as it is deployed in writing – is able to make connections, *lateral* connections, connections out of the ordinary (that is, *extraordinary* connections in *Finnegans Wake*, and connections *from* – or *out of* – the *ordinary* in *Ulysses*), between disparate phenomena, that can open up and inaugurate new and unusual conjunctures. As Deleuze and Guattari's rousing call goes in *Anti–Oedipus*, in terms of these kinds of connections: 'We must set up units of production, plug in desiring-machines.'[29] The *sinthome* is thus a *plug* of this type; that is, not in the sense of that which *blocks* or *stops* – which its other side, the symptom, comes to be – but of that which connects up; that is, the place, or position of – that which facilitates – this *connecting-up*. As the authors state in *A Thousand Plateaus*:

> We have been criticized for overquoting literary authors. But when one writes, the only question is which other machine the literary machine can be plugged into, must be plugged into in order to work. Kleist and a war machine, Kafka and a most extraordinary bureaucratic machine . . . (What if one became animal or plant *through* literature, which certainly does not mean literarily? Is it not first through the voice that one becomes animal?) Literature is an assemblage.[30]

Literature as assemblage seems indeed be to what *Finnegans Wake* as literature represents; that is to say, the question for Joyce in the *Wake* is not so much into which other machine, or machines, must the work be plugged, but how can the

Wake act as a *plug*; that is, as a connecting device: an endlessly connecting device that can inaugurate all sorts of *becomings*, alike to the *sinthome* (Lacan's question of the *Wake*, however, may well be the reverse side of this, as we will come to explore). In light of this question we will here introduce a diagram that combines those in chapters 3 and 4, and which we will provisionally call, for the purposes of referencing, and following Lacan, 'the full graph':

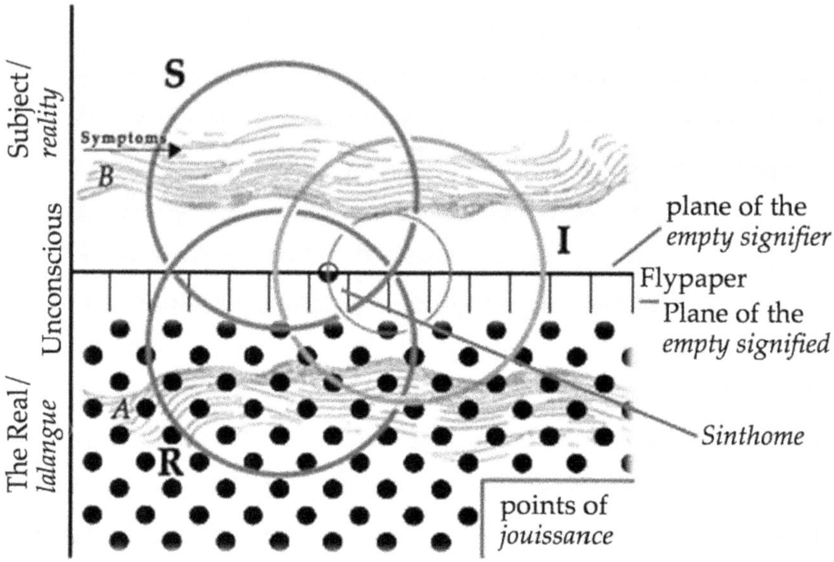

Figure 5.1 The 'full graph'

The full graph reads as such:

1 In the centre is the *sinthome*, represented in three ways; as the *sutural ring*, re-tying the Joycean knot of Real, Symbolic, and Imaginary; as the *empty signified* – that is, as the slot in the inverted 'comb schema' into which *a sinthome* (or *point of jouissance*) enters; and as *that sinthome* itself, which thus acts as the *plug* which connects *the planes of the empty signified and empty signifier*. Thus, this representation of the *sinthome* in these multiple ways allows its multifarious topology to connect up the multiplicity of its effects. In its third representation we see it as (having been) a *point of jouissance* which has perforated the 'flypaper' sheet from the side of the *empty signified* and thus become on its other side (that of the plane of the *empty signifier*) a symptom. Its *full* perforation is unable to occur because of the unificatory/separatory antagonistic forces of suppression (topographically from below)

and repression (from above) acting on both sides of the sheet. We should also see this point of *sinthomic*/symptomal perforation as that of the *hole-making* of the letter – of writing – to which we will return.

2 Below the horizontal axis (that of the flypaper sheet) we see the undifferentiated mass of *points of jouissance* (although they here are differentiated into multiple *points* for the purposes of illustration, yet *points* which do not differ one from another), as well as Saussure's 'wave' ('*A*') representing the signified (in its Lacanian position, below the bar). Above the axis is the realm of '*reality*', and the 'wave' ('*B*') representing the signifier, in which flows *symptoms*, or *particular signifiers* – as demarcated by the arrow – which are to be picked out and cathected into the perforating *sinthome*, via the dual process of signification/subjectivation. Thus, the non-shaded half of the *sinthome* on the graph becomes the *symptom* (or the *symptomal side*), which remains underwritten by its *lining*, its *other side*; that is, the *sinthome* itself (or the *sinthomic side*), represented by the shaded half. For further elucidation of this demonstration we could perhaps here give back to the *sinthome* the name of Joyce-the-Symptom; in this, the non-shaded *symptomal* side of the centrally cathected point on the full graph would thus become position 1, and the shaded *sinthomic* side position 2, to Joyce-the-Symptom in position A (as in Figure 3.3).

3 Over the top of this are the three rings of the Real ('R'), the Symbolic ('S'), and the Imaginary ('I'), in the Joycean knotting, sutured by the fourth ring of the *sinthome*, which doubles as the *empty signified* and the *point of jouissance*, in appearing to 'thread through' these positions on the graph. The Joycean knot is positioned so on the graph to demonstrate that each of the Orders have a share in the planes of the *empty signifier* and *empty signified*, though not an equal share: the Real is submerged deeper in the latter (whilst a little bit of it spills over into the former), whereas the Symbolic is more strongly established in the former (although not entirely). The rings of the Imaginary and the *sinthome*(*-Ego*) are divided equally over the planes, the reason for which being that it is the Imaginary which unifies/separates the two planes, and the two other Orders, unless it is deficient and runs the risk of coming away – such as in Joyce's knot – in which case the ring of the *sinthome*(*-Ego*) suppletes the Imaginary, and reties the Symbolic and Real (as is shown).

4 Along the vertical axis are the designations 'The Real/*lalangue*', 'Unconscious', and 'Subject/*reality*'. The first of these – which is level with the area underneath the horizontal axis – defines the realm in which the *undifferentiated* (the 'something of a One' to which we give the various names of – or designate little bits of as – *points of jouissance, lalangue*, etc.) resides; this is the realm of the babbling, nonsensical *jouissance* that is awaiting its first transformation into *jouis-sens*, which will inaugurate the 'senseless adventure of 'sense'', as Nancy puts it. The second designation, that is level with the dividing line of the horizontal axis, is the unconscious, in which typically the

> three Orders are continuous and consistent. It is in the unconscious, however, that the unificatory/separatory processes involved in the tying of the three Orders, or this tying's suppletion via the fourth ring of the *sinthome* – as well as the *significatory* processes involved in the *sinthome* – do their work, whilst *remaining unconscious to the subject*, but whilst also nevertheless producing subjective unconscious effects (e.g., elements of symptomal manifestation and of *sinthomic* singularity). The third designation denotes the realm of the subject (as if Figure 3.4 was turned clockwise on its side) and of language, which constitutes *symptoms*, in giving them their *sense*. This realm, above the horizontal axis, is that known to the subject, and is taken as their everyday situation: it is '*reality*' in precisely the Lacanian sense of being the opposite of the Real; that is, *reality* as the *symptom* (which at its most irreducible is the *sinthome*), without which there would be the lack of subjectivity, or utter and irresolvable subjective destitution.[31]

We will return to the graph, and the ways in which it can be read, throughout the rest of this work. Initially, however, we can now see how the *sinthome* can act as this form of *plug*, a connector that can link orders, senses, lines, planes, discourses, and even literatures, through its *writing*, or its *indelible sigla*. Deleuze and Guattari suggest that 'a book itself is a little machine', and ask: 'What is the relation (also measurable) of this literary machine to a war machine, love machine, revolutionary machine, etc. – and an *abstract machine* that sweeps them along?'[32] It could be argued that *Finnegans Wake* is thus an instance in literature that manages to get close to becoming a form of this *abstract machine* itself; that is, in its acting as a *discourse* machine (*discourse* in the Lacanian sense, which we will come to look at momentarily); even as a machine operating a *discourse without speech*. (Shortly after the aforementioned remarks, Deleuze and Guattari state that 'Joyce's words, accurately described as having "multiple roots," shatter the linear unity of the word, even of language, only to posit a cyclic unity of the sentence, text, or knowledge'.[33] We argue that Joyce in fact goes further than this, creating a *discoursing* and thus *riverlike* – as opposed to a rooted, or even rhizomatic – text that 'sweeps along' in the manner in which they describe an abstract machine doing earlier. Like a river, however, this text also has currents and swells. It is thus, as Joyce describes it, a 'writing [. . .] with lines of litters slittering up and louds of letters slettering down'.[34] Lines of flight appear everywhere in the text, through the slithery and slippery written markings and traces of its letters; their multiplicitous orthographic and contextual possibilities – in the letters' orderings within words, and words' orderings within sentences (orderings which Joyce leaves open to what may come of readings of the *Wake*) – their multi-possibilitous pronunciations (the loads of 'louds'); and, finally, even their disposability as 'litters'. As Harari suggests; with the *sinthome*, Joyce here – in a borrowing from Wyndham Lewis's art movement Vorticism (which Pound named) – creates his work in 'the context of the vortex; it is far removed from any dialectic of equilibrium. [. . .] There is invention, there is oneness, and not only various "elective" series', but ineluctable series too, and series which seemingly elect themselves.)[35]

Of discourse Lacan proffers a succinct definition through a line of questioning concerning 'reality' in Seminar XX:

> How is one to return, if not on the basis of a peculiar *(spécial)* discourse, to a prediscursive reality? That is the dream – the dream behind every conception *(idée)* of knowledge. But it is also what must be considered mythical. There's no such thing as a prediscursive reality. Every reality is founded and defined by a discourse.[36]

Here we are able to determine precisely the operation of discourse, as that which circumscribes reality – as a discursive *praxis* – itself. The idea of a *prediscursive reality*, however, is a mythical construction, and can only be dreamt; it is that realm within which the archetypes of Jungian analytical psychology are posited, and also that from which the underlying myths in *Finnegans Wake* which Lacan disparages in Seminar XXIII – such as that which inheres in the system of Viconian cyclicity – come, although it must here be remembered that the *Wake is* (at least in part intended to be) *itself a dream*.

In *The Archaeology of Knowledge* (1969), Foucault – whom Lacan draws much from, especially in the years 1968–1973 – comes to define discourses as 'practices that systematically form the objects of which they speak'.[37] This properly structuralist view takes us away from the realm of the Real (of *lalangue*, and of unmediated *jouissance*) and into that of signification and *sense*; that is, of *reality*, in which the object – always already lost – is posited, and sought after. Thus, we see discourse here acting as a structuring *support*; a word Lacan also uses in relation to both speech and writing, and which must be seen to encompass a certain *mutuality* that implies an integral interlinking between elements that are themselves *supports*. Thus, as a certain *support* in this conceptualisation, discourse is that on which *depends* what it is that it supports; it determines and facilitates that which it supports, inclusive of the subject, and thus arises out of the signifiers from one to another of which the subject is represented. Lacan definitionally delineates this in stressing that 'all determination of the subject, and therefore of thought, depends on discourse'.[38] Foucault further elucidates the manner in which discourse does this: 'Discourse finds a way of limiting its domain, of defining what it is talking about, of giving it the status of an object – and therefore of making it manifest, nameable, and describable'; circumscribing it, in the widest sense (that is, in the mode of 'inventing *in the sense of* discovery', as Lacan puts it in relation to Freud's discourse on the unconscious).[39]

Thus, there is of course not *one* discourse, but various types of discourse, which differ qualitatively, and which are locatable at different points in the psychoanalytic schema. Lacan comes to define a particular and primary type at the beginning of Seminar XVI, when he writes on the blackboard as a 'frontispiece' to the year's study: '*The essence of psychoanalytic theory is a discourse without speech* [*L'essence de la théorie psychanalytique est un discours sans parole*]'.[40] Gallagher's translation of the last part of this phrase is as 'discourse without words', but we here follow Grigg in his translation of it in Seminar XVII, in which Lacan reintroduces the concept at the beginning and gives an explanation of it that in fact encompasses both of these transliterations into English:

> Last year I managed, with much perseverance, to ascertain what discourse is about, as a necessary structure that goes well beyond speech, which is always more or less occasional. What I prefer, I said, and I even wrote it up on the board one day, is a *discourse without speech.*
>
> The fact is that, in truth, discourse can clearly subsist without words. It subsists in certain fundamental relations which would literally not be able to be maintained without language. Through the instrument of language a number of stable relations are established, inside which something that is much larger and goes much further than actual utterances [*énonciations*] can, of course, be inscribed.[41]

Whilst discourse exceeds language; as Lacan puts it, it would *literally* not be able to subsist without it. Discourse is – to play on the title of Lacan's 1953 essay – the *function and field* of speech and language. In its relation specifically to language, Lacan commented in a lecture given at Louvain in 1972:

> I call discourse that 'something' which *within* language fixes, crystallises, and uses the resources *of* language – of course, in a wider sense, there are many other resources – and it uses this so that the social bond between speaking beings functions.[42]

Through facilitating the social bond, discourse is shown here to provide the structurality of relation; a linguistic structurality. However; the emphasis on *literality* in *discourse without speech* brings us back to the unconscious, and to the very instance, and *insistence*, of *the letter* within it; that is, within the unconscious as 'the scene of writing', to put it in Derrida's phrasing. In Seminar XVI Lacan describes 'a discourse without speech, which means nothing other than this discourse that writing supports'.[43] Writing – which is not transcription, in relation to the voice (and thus to *speech*), but that which receives what is 'cut up' in that support – is shown here in itself to be the support of a *discourse without speech*; that is, as that which supports – or underwrites – discourse (including this particular kind of discourse that is the essence of psychoanalytic theory) through a further form of 'cutting up'; that of *hole-making*, a process similar to the opening up of *textual blanks* through *spacing* that is inherent in Derrida's concept of archē-writing. However, contrary to Derrida, in Lacan it is the letter itself (the signifier) – and its insistence and agency in the unconscious – that inaugurates the making of the hole. Indeed, as he analogously clarifies in Seminar III: one cannot make macaroni by taking a hole and surrounding it with flour.[44]

Thus, after this *initial* rupture – the rupture inaugurated by an *initial*, by a *letter* – discourse is set off, by this instance of writing, to circulate the environs of the hole; or, to put it in *Wake*an language: *the Hole (as quasi-Cause), and its Environs*.[45] Writing is the support of this recirculation of discourses that it launches. Thus, *discourse without speech* is that space – the clinic, perhaps, before the psychoanalytic session; the textual blank of the page before its printed words – of archē-writing; and thus it is a *discursive* space: a form of *writing* – precisely *sinthomic* writing – that provides the elementary matrix for words, for speech, to come into. This – initially (and although filled by words) – is the *writing* of the *Wake*. In its operation of a discourse without speech the *Wake*'s words advert the reader – at least, the non-expert reader (and no reader can be an *absolute* expert)[46] – back to their very formation, to the processes of their decoding and decipherment in reading, to their soundings in the mouth, to the discursive processes of reading, and pronunciation from written text; that is, back to their *writing* itself. Subsequently, its words, its sigla, become more familiar; however, they always retain a sense of foreignness because of their amalgam formation: the combination of a plethora of world languages; the utilisation of inverted letters, diagrams, algebraic sigla, and even doodles; the coining and neologising of words, and the conjoining and separating of letters in ways unrecognisable to usual grammatical construction, for the purposes of pun and portmanteau. All this in the attempt to create a great language of *Witz*, a language – to invert Lacan's famous phrase – structured like the unconscious.[47]

Discourse without speech, however, is an extension of that maxim that proclaims that *the unconscious is structured like a language*, in that it emphasises this statement's structure as simile. That the unconscious is a discourse that is structured *like* a language implies that it is not language, nor *a* language, itself, but that its structurality bears resemblance to the structurality of a language. Like a language it adverts its reader-listener to *it* when it is not understood; we see this in both the analytic session, when a symptom manifests itself and inaugurates its interpretation, and in *Finnegans Wake*, when its *sinthomic* writing inaugurates the decodings – and recodings – involved in interpretative practice itself. In a statement on discourse in Seminar XXIV Lacan alerts us to precisely these operations, in a formulation transposable to a position as commentary on the *Wake* itself:

> What discourse is useful for from the outset, it serves to order, I mean to convey the commandment that I allow myself to call the intention of the discourse, because there remains something of the imperative in every intention. Every discourse has an effect of suggestion. It is hypnotic. The contamination of discourse by sleep is worth highlighting, before being highlighted by what one can call intentional experience, in other words taken as a commandment imposed on facts. A discourse is always soporific, except when one does not understand it. Then it wakes you up.[48]

Like a dream, *Finnegans Wake* amnesiacally resists remaining in one's mind, in the manner in which Freud describes in this précis from the postscript to 'Little Hans', in which he suggests that

> any one who is familiar with psycho-analysis may occasionally experience something similar in sleep. He will be woken up by a dream, and will decide to analyse it then and there; he will then go to sleep again feeling quite satisfied with the result of his efforts; and next morning dream and analysis will alike be forgotten.[49]

Thus, despite the *Wake* being a '*hypermnesic* machine' – in Derrida's words – it enacts this 'overtaking by *amnesia*' that Freud describes taking place in the aftermath of both psychoanalysis and sleep.[50] The *Wake*, then, operates as both this soporific discourse – as a repetitive and hypnotic book of the night, of dream – and as this discourse which *wakes up* – by forcing *ununderstanding*; as a stuttering, spluttering, stertorous text of conjunctions, juxtapositions, and defamiliarisations – and it operates as these *at once*, as will be further discussed in relation to the waking of its read to follow (that is, in postulating it as an instance of 'ob-literature').

First, however, we can trace Joyce's move from a focus on the *imperative* of discourse – which itself derives from the signifier, as Lacan claims in suggesting in Seminar XX that 'the signifier is, first and foremost, imperative' – as that which serves to order, in *Ulysses*, to the contamination of discourse by sleep, and how this can be subverted to effect awakening, in *Finnegans Wake*.[51] Indeed, during the making of *Ulysses* Joyce was asked by his friend Frank Budgen about how the process of its composition was coming along. As Budgen recounts in his *James Joyce and the Making of 'Ulysses'*:

> "I have been working hard on it all day," said Joyce.
> "Does that mean you have written a great deal?" I said.
> "Two sentences," said Joyce.
> I looked sideways but Joyce was not smiling. I thought of Flaubert.
> "You have been seeking the *mot juste*?" I said.
> "No," said Joyce. "I have the words already. What I am seeking is the perfect order of words in the sentence. There is an order in every way appropriate. I think I have it."[52]

Whilst such order may radically have shifted in the *Wake* – having opened out much more onto the Real; that is, into the aleatory possibilities of both writing and reading (with the imperative given to the reader to take the words in any order desired, for example) – Joyce is nonetheless dealing with a discourse, in the above anecdote, without speech; that is, one in which order – discourse itself – *precedes* words; systematically forms them, and their meaning, as Foucault puts it; structures their connections, their chimings with one another and their chordal tonalities: an order, a discourse, that is, which *writes* them. Thus, the *Wake* stages this *writing* itself, and seeks therefore to demonstrate – to put it punningly, and yet precisely – that the pen is in fact *mightier than the words*.

About to write a letter: a

Jack B. Yeats's *About to Write a Letter* (1935) is a painting that depicts a man standing forlornly yet imperially over a table, on which lays his writing apparatus, with which he is about to write a letter. When not seen in greyscale, the painting's use of a vibrant contrast of colours makes it shimmer to look at – almost as if it is shaking, or vibrating – despite its actual stasis. Whilst the writer in the foreground, and the portrait of the woman in white behind him, are distinct, the rest of the scene is as if it is moving: blurring through kinesis. Its colours stand out in their brightness, but also literally; in the Braille-like dimensionality of the ridges and contours of the dried oils that convey them. There is a Picasso-esque pile to the writer's side in the bottom left of the picture and billowing blood-red curtains that meld together in their middle to the right-hand side of it. The writer is inscribed in this imaginary-symbolic 'reality', about to inscribe its 'chaosmos' in a siglum of the Real: about to write *a letter*.[53] The letter the man is about to write, however, can of course not be known to us, but is rather more likely to be an epistle than a single instance of an alphabetic character (although it will no doubt be composed

Figure 5.2 Jack B. Yeats, *About to Write a Letter* (1935)

Jack B. Yeats, Irish, 1871–1957: *About to Write a Letter*, 1935. Oil on canvas, 61 × 91 cm.

of a collocation of these). We will look at both of these kinds of letter in the remainder of this chapter, taking first the siglum – as designating the letter as mark or notation beyond a purely alphabetic/numeric/etc. sense; even as that 'which is fundamentally *outside of sense*', as Laurent puts it – and in particular the letter '*a*', in this section, and secondly the 'hen's letter' in *Finnegans Wake* in the next.[54]

In the *Wake* Joyce introduces his own picto-typographic sigla, the majority of which he collects together about halfway through the book under the name of 'the Doodles family, ᗰ, Δ, ⊣, X, □, Λ, ⊏'.[55] These signs (as Joyce himself called them, rather than using the term – as we do, and as has become standard in Joycean reference – *sigla*) are used to *denote* characters in the text – HCE, ALP, Shem, Shaun and Issy, for example – as well as *as* characters in the text; that is, in retaining an autonomy of their own, *as letters*, before – or away from – their narratological significations.[56] In this respect they bear a relation to Lacan's *mathemes*: a form of *letters*, marks, or notation – such as those used in the Lacanian formula for fantasy, for example: '$\$ \lozenge a$' (barred subject, lozenge, *objet petit a*)[57] – that function *as* the terms that they denote; that is, that function mathematically, as opposed to literarily.

As Lacan states in Seminar X:

> Algebraic notation has precisely the purpose of giving us a pure identity marker, we having stated already that marking out something with a word is only ever metaphorical, that is to say, that it can only leave the function of the signifier itself outside of any signification that is induced by introducing it.[58]

He then qualifies this with the demonstration that 'the word *good*, if it gives rise to the signification of good, isn't good in and of itself, far from it, because by the same token it gives rise to the bad'.[59] With the word 'read', however – if the letters of the word that spell 'red' are coloured red – we begin to see the inverse of this through the word's lettering, with the coloured letters themselves wrenching away the *metaphoricity* of the word (because of their being *directly* red). It is thus in this that the letter must be seen as being in itself *material*, or as *a bit of Real*. Therefore, with the introduction of the letter at this point, we can now visualise our formulations so far against two axes, as follows:

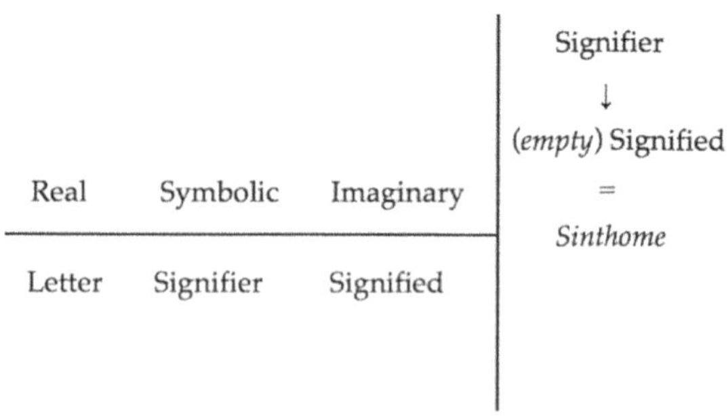

Figure 5.3 Multiaxial graph of signifier and signified

Along the horizontal axis we have the correspondence between the Orders and components of signification, and along the vertical the formation of, and the formulation for, the *sinthome*. Thus it is that on the horizontal axis the letter, *qua* material, is presented as an element of the Real; the signifier, as the basis of the Symbolic order; and the signified – if it is to be seen as the 'fixed' destination for a signifier; as the 'completion' of a concept that comes from the signifier – as locatable on the plane of the Imaginary. However, we can here see how the signified can come to be viewed differently when presented along the vertical axis in its role as the initiatory *empty signified*; that is, as the beginning of the *sinthome*. Thus, to apply these multiaxial reflections to the subject of our study we can see that in Joyce, in his writing, the *sinthome*, the *empty signified*, becomes increasingly apparent, but that throughout the trajectory of his corpus signifieds themselves begin to dwindle; that is, by the time of the *Wake* there are almost none of those imaginary 'fixed' signifieds retained in its language, and in this we can see to what extent the imaginary order has come away in Joyce's composition by this time. Here, the signified has given way to its material underpinning, the letter.

As Thelma Sowley puts it, Lacan thus postulates that the letter is

> the very material of the signifying chain. It is the materiality of letters and phones that brings Lacan to say that the letter is the matter of the signifier, and that it belongs to the Real and not to the order of the Symbolic, while the signifier itself is a symbolic production, extracted from the Real, which, in a second step, is submitted to the Imaginary.[60]

The extraction process that we have already discussed – that of the extraction of the signifier from *lalangue* to make language – is now seen to be given its material underpinning; that of (the Real of) its under- or *Ur*-writing (which thereafter enters into submission to the Imaginary; that is, cathexis in the fixed, or fixated, signified). However, in terms of the letter itself, Lacan describes one of its pure forms, the *matheme* – specifically in relation to the algorithm for fantasy featured earlier – as that which 'breaks the phonemic element constituted by the signifying unit right down to its literal atom'.[61] (As in the distinction between mathematicality and literarity made earlier, 'literal' here must be taken to oppose '*literary*', and as an instance of mathematicality/materiality.) As he precisely puts it; the algorithm, and its analogues, 'are not transcendent signifiers; they are indices of an absolute signification', or what we have called previously *full sense*, which encompasses all sense *and* nonsense in the Real.[62] Nonetheless, the algorithm – or *matheme* – is yet 'designed to allow for a hundred and one different readings, a multiplicity that is acceptable as long as what is said about it remains grounded in its algebra'.[63] Returning to this in Seminar X, Lacan defines

> an algebraic equation [a]s something very straightforward that's designed to make something very complicated manageable, to make it pass into a mechanical state, without you having to understand it. [. . .] As has been seen in mathematics from the start, the equation just has to be correctly put together.[64]

It is this operation of the letter that not only Lacan, but Derrida too, sees occurring in the work of Joyce, particularly in the *Wake*. Alike to Lacan's statement that 'what gets read passes through the writing whilst surviving there intact', Derrida suggests in 'Two Words for Joyce' that in the *Wake*

> despite the need to "phonetize," despite the book's appeal for reading out loud, for song and for timbre, something essential in it passes the understanding, as well as the hearing[;] hear in that a graphic or literal dimension, literally literal, a muteness that one should never pass over in silence.[65]

Thus, the 'literally literal', 'manageable', 'mechanical', and 'mute' state of the letter is something that the understanding need not actually subtend. The letter, *as it is*, operates without the understanding – as an element of the Real, *before* the Symbolic Order – with what gets *read* in it, *by* the subject, *passing through* it, *to* the subject (as analyst, 'transferential addressee'; *reader*, in the most general sense), as Lacan confirms, whilst – in the sense of '*it* reads' – the letter also bypasses this very process, *passing the understanding*, as Derrida suggests, thus confirming Lacan's thesis; that is, that *the read* – in both the senses of *what gets read* (*by the reader*) and '*it* reads' – *survives there*, in the letter, intact.

We can thus now (re)turn to a certain letter, to the letter *par excellence* in algebra, which occupies a privileged place in Lacan's, Derrida's, and Joyce's works; that is, the letter '*a*'. The *Oxford English Dictionary* tells us that *the word* 'a' derives originally from being a variant of the word 'one', and that in place of this letter/word 'in Older Scots the form *o* is occasionally found, as an irregular Anglicized form (by analogy with variation between *a* and *o* in other words)'.[66] This vacillation between the two seems to have been known to Joyce, and is apparent in *Finnegans Wake* in the lingering question:

> What was it?
> A. . . . .!
> ?. . . . . .O![67]

Thus, not only does this interchangeability between 'a' and 'o' here offer us the impossible translation of the word Lacan's French '*a*' in part stands for ('*autre*') into English – as '*o*' ('other') – but the derivation of the word 'a' from the singular determiner 'one' also suggests the inherent – necessitous – ambiguity that enshrouds the claim that 'there is (something of) *a* One' (as 'a' and 'one' in fact derive from the same root); *necessitous*, as it is this (something of a) One that ultimately does not cease to write itself.[68]

On the impossibility of *a*'s translation, however, Miller hints that it occurs because of the distinction that has to be made between the signifier and the letter (here in the form of the 'proper name'), in his talk 'A and a in Clinical Structures', in which he claims that Lacan wrote the *objet petit a*, or 'Lacanian object'

> with a small (a), and wanted it to be kept like that, in all the different languages, as a proper name. Many of you were struck this morning to hear that proper names are not translated into languages, and Lacan insisted very much that the letters of these mathemes not be translated. For instance, the capital "A," the small "a" which are taken in French from the word *l'autre*, which means "other," are not to be translated as capital "O" or small "o."[69]

As Lacan points out in Seminar X, the reason for this is that this '*a* is precisely what resists any assimilation to the function of a signifier and this is indeed why it symbolizes that which, in the sphere of the signifier, always presents itself as lost, as what gets lost in signifierization'.[70] Utilising Lacan's mathematical lettering, we can now visualise this in a depiction of the formula for fantasy, which includes the resistant *a* – as deriving from the process of a signifier representing a subject for another signifier – in which subjective 'existence', as Zupančič puts it, must be seen as 'something cast off by the signifier, the 'spittle' of the signifier'; that is, seen in its state of hanging subscripted between two signifiers:[71]

$$S_{\$}S$$

$$\downarrow$$

$$\$ \diamond a$$

Figure 5.4 Derivation of the fantasy formula from the subject's representation between signifiers

What the arrow points or 'zooms in' to is the fundamental subjective experience or existence encountered because of the subject's representation between signifiers: the desirous fantasy in which the *a cuts into* the subject. As Lacan puts it: '$\$$ is the term of this operation in the form of division, since *a* is irreducible, it is a remainder, and there is no way of operating with it.'[72] *a* is thus the *indivisible remainder* that cuts into $\$$ 'in the form of division' (causing its barring: the bar – / – thus can be viewed as splitting the subject – S – in half). In this we could 'rephrase' the graphic formulation in terms of the unificatory/separatory principle and show *a* in position A, the desiring subject ($\$$) in position 1 and the enigmatic relation ($\diamond$) in position 2, as it is from the *a*, as the waste product of 'signifierisation' – the representation of the subject from one signifier to another – that the subject-*qua-desiring* and its relation to the *a* derives. As Lacan indeed puts it: 'It is precisely this waste product, this scrap, which resists signifierization, that comes to find itself constituting the desiring subject as such.'[73] Thus, we see here that the *topology* of the *letter*, or *matheme*, is always subject to what we could call its *phrasing*; that is, how it is articulated and perceived in variegated angularity and dimensionality. Similarly, we have earlier seen how we can deploy differing demonstration axially, in Figure 5.3.

Thus, we will again briefly return to the *sinthome* here, in relation to the *a*. We can postulate that the *sinthome* is *as* – but extends further than – an *objet a*; that is, that it is located, in our earlier graph (Figure 5.1) – with the *a* – in the hole in the intersection of the three Borromean rings. This indeed is where Lacan places the *a* in his drawings of the rings in Seminar XXII, for example. The *sinthome*, however, is only *as* an *a* in that whilst its unanalysability and indissolubility are indeed as pertinent as those of the *objet petit a* itself, it yet extends beyond the *a* topologically; that is, whilst its ring *threads through* the place of impossibility that is the hole in the centre of the three rings, it also ties itself onto the real and symbolic rings, and sutures the imaginary to them in the process. This can all be seen in the following demonstration, which is a 'close-up' extraction of an element from the 'full graph':

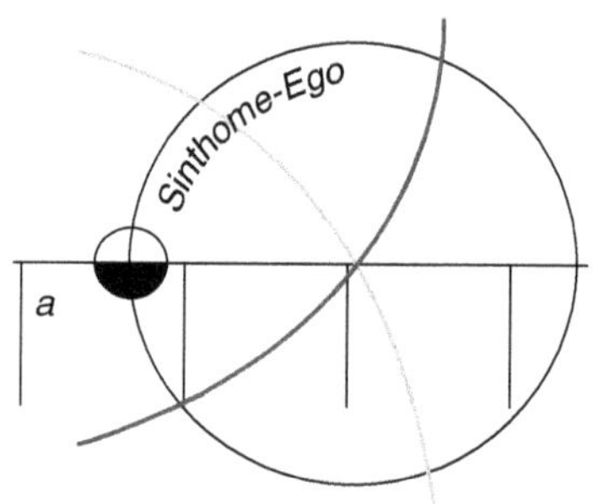

Figure 5.5 Element of the 'full graph', showing the *objet petit a*

Thus, whilst its representation as the sutural ring in the Borromean knotting can account for its extension beyond the *a* topologically, the *sinthome* has yet to have been given a siglum that can reify its ownmost multitudinous operationality. In Lacanian formulae the *symptom* has been variously depicted using '*s* (A)', 'f(*x*)', and 'Σ' (the Greek letter sigma). When 'the place of the symptom is to be found at *s* (A)' – as Miller puts it – it here represents the 'signified of the Other' (with this capital 'A' indeed standing for the big Other (*Autre*)).[74] This Real-bearing signified, demarcated by '*s*', we have discussed in chapter 1 in relation to Lacan's use of it at points to signify the subject – and thus we see in this formula that the symptom is to be found in the subject's position as residual signified of the Other; indeed, a further confirmation that the symptom is 'reality', as Lacan has it in 'Joyce le Symptôme I' – and have alluded to it implicitly in relation to the *empty signified* of the *sinthome* throughout chapter 3. Herbert Wachsberger extends this siglum, in relation specifically to psychosis, with the formula 's_o', which he describes as the

> absence [that] initiates an intransitive "it means/it wants to say" [*ça veut dire*], an unaccomplished signification – enigmatic emptiness, s_0, degree zero of signification – soon to be doubled by an 'it means/it wants to say something' [*ça veut dire quelque chose*] – signification of signification, $s(s_0)$ – where the certainty of the subject that is implicated in its being through this phenomenon is anchored.[75]

Thus, this inaugural *meaning/wanting to say*, apparent in psychosis – which nonetheless remains initially *empty* of *said meaning* – already brings us remarkably close to the *sinthome* as *empty signified.*

Second, with 'f(x)' Lacan clarifies the function of the symptom in Seminar XXII. 'What is this x?' he rhetorically asks; and answers: 'This is what can be expressed of the unconscious by a letter.'[76] He later explains that this letter – which expresses, for example, the *jouissance* of the unconscious – is 'a variable [. . .] that can be brought into f(x), namely, into a function of x'.[77] As Marie-Hélène Brousse puts it: 'Lacan says that it is a letter – (x) in f(x) – that condenses *jouissance* for a given subject.'[78] Thus it is that here 'x' marks the symptomal spot of the derivation of *jouissance* from the unconscious in each subject.

The last of these sigla – the 'Σ', or sigma (which roughly stands in for the 'S' of 'symptom') – was used by Lacan in his 'Conférences et entretiens dans des universités nord-américaines'; that is, during lectures given in America in 1975, in denoting the symptom as the sutural ring in the Borromean knot, and for this reason it is naturally the closest siglum to that which will be chosen for the *sinthome.*[79]

For this siglum itself a candidate may be found in Joyce. As a letter, as a *matheme* – that is, in its siglic notation, as opposed to its topological demonstration – Joyce's variable siglum 'E' (which also crops up throughout *Wake*an sigla as ш, ꟽ, and ∃; and of course bears more than a passing resemblance to Lacan's symptomal siglum 'Σ') is perhaps the best choice to use to demarcate the *sinthome*. With this siglum we thus encounter the 'e' of the *empty signified* (and by representation by the opposite that of the *empty signifier*) and 'E' of the '*Ego*', as well as in ꟽ the *sinthome* as that which entraps a *point of jouissance* (that is, as an extracted element of the rotated 'comb schema'), and in its inverted state, ш, that which takes into it, or gives rise to, the signifier.

To return to the *a*, though, Laurent writes it in relation to the hole as:

$$\frac{\text{Hole}}{(a)}$$[80]

Thus, in seeking the lost object in the hole we will only ever come to find that it is bottomless (as is the hole constituted by Freud's *navel*; an equivalent of the *a*, as a denoter of lack itself); that is, that it is completely burned-through by the letter. Thus, we as subjects, and the discourses in which we subsist, are set off to encircle this hole inaugurated by the ever-resistant – toxic, even – 'waste product of signifierisation', the letter. The letter thus also becomes the primary marker of waste, in its materiality (as a material that *wastes away* or *wastes through*; creative of holes). Joyce himself equates these two concepts in the exclamation 'The letter! The litter!', and even stresses the primordiality of the latter later in the *Wake* in deriving the 'letter *from* litter'.[81] As Fritz Senn identifies, this 'A' (as aleph or alpha) is even the 'first letter' of *Finnegans Wake*, in that its 'riverrun' flows out of Samuel Taylor Coleridge's 'Kubla Kahn'; that is, from 'where Alph, the sacred river, ran'.[82] Indeed, these terms of primordiality extend also into Freud's studies, in which the '*a*' is seen to be the first descriptor for human excrement, and – between 'o' and 'a' – as that of loss. According to Freud in *The Psychopathology of Everyday Life* focus on excrement arises in childhood in

> the vulgar joke of repeating the syllables 'a' and 'po' when they occu[r] at the beginnings of words, a form of amusement which quite commonly leads to stammering in children ['*A–a*' and '*Popo*' are the German nursery words for 'faeces' and 'buttocks']

and the tropes of stammering and stuttering are of course prevalent throughout the language of *Finnegans Wake*.[83] Further, in terms of loss, Freud discusses that which is *lost purposefully* – in order to be regained – in the '*fort/da* scene' of *Beyond the Pleasure Principle*, in which instead of '*fort – da*' Freud's grandson Ernst was actually articulating 'oooo – aaa', as Alan Bass recalls it in his definition of the word 'a' in a French context in his glossary to Derrida's *Post Card*, which we will now turn to to further draw out this letter/word's connotations and consequences:[84]

> *a* (*à*) (*a–*): as the heading indicates, *a* [in French] has three major uses, all of them switching each other on and off. *A* as a verb is the third person singular of *avoir*, to have. The preposition *à* means "to" or "in." [In *The Post Card* there is] the alternation between *a* ("the lack *has* its place") and *à* ("the lack *in* its place"). One of the letters dated 9 September 1977 tells us that *The Post Card* is "dedicated to 'to,' devoted to the dative." [. . .] *A–* in French and English is also the prefix of negation; thus Derrida's neologisms *adestination* for the structural lack of a certain destination in any postal system, and *athesis* for the lack of a definable thesis in *Beyond the Pleasure Principle*, a book that always takes another step forward no matter what point it reaches. [*A* is also] one of the sounds of the *fort/da* scene: according to Freud, Ernst actually said "oooo – aaa." [. . .] *The Post Card* is dedicated also to drawling o and long a[.] Nor will you have forgotten that *a* is the "letter" of *différance*.[85]

Thus, whilst the different types of 'a' in French are used by Derrida in *The Post Card* to inaugurate all sorts of relays, connections, *intrajouissances*, pluggings-in, and *postalities*, it is in the 'a' of the originary Derridean neographism *différance* that we can see how the word comes to *enact* itself. This 'a' in *différance* operates in a remarkably similar yet oppositional way to the Babelian 'a' of our word 'read' earlier; an integral 'a' – for without it we could have 'red' or 'reed' – which disturbs the word's univocal pronunciation (i.e., it can only be said or heard one way or the other at any one time, whilst it can be read both ways). As Derrida puts it in an exact precursory formula to that used in 'Two Words for Joyce'; in '*différance*'

> this graphic difference (*a* instead of *e*), this marked difference between two apparently vocal notations, between two vowels, remains purely graphic: it is read, or it is written, but it cannot be heard. It cannot be apprehended in speech.[86]

Like its interchangeability with the 'o', the vowel 'a' here can be exchanged for *difference*'s original 'e' without this being 'apprehendable' to the ear, via speech. In both instances, then – of the 'a' of *différance* and of the 'a' of the 'Babelian confusion' in 'read' – there is something in the letter which can be written and which can be read, but which cannot make it into univocal speech, and yet it is this *lettering* that underwrites speech (indeed, there can be discourse without speech, as supported by *writing*, but there cannot be speech without discourse). Thus, speech is – to use and to play on a word important to Lacan in his essay 'Lituraterre' – *littoral*; that is, speech – the *oral* – is cut up into writing and attaches to the letter – the *literal* – in a relation of *support* (as Lacan has it in Seminar XVI).[87] Further, the letter – as the materiality of the signifier or signifying chain; that is, as its *earthly* element (the 'terre' of 'lituraterre' being 'earth' in French) – also gives rise to the littoral itself, the coast- or shoreline of the *hole* that the letter constitutes. The littoral is thus the inverse, or *envers*, of the hole (made by the letter), in precisely those terms of the *logic of inversion* outlined in chapter 3 earlier.

Thus it is that the letter 'a', in the case of *différance*, creates the very hole around which the processes and discourses of differing and deferring that *différance* encompasses are set going. 'A' acts similarly as a hole-maker throughout *Finnegans Wake*, and we will here investigate two instances (which can be loosely described as one female, one male). In the first instance the 'A' which is the scarlet letter in Nathaniel Hawthorne's 1850 novel of that name infiltrates the *Wake* and condenses this letter's allegorical significance into the singularity of its appearance in the text, whilst putting its multiform meanings into play through its very positioning; that is, through its instance and insistence. The letter 'A' in *The Scarlet Letter* – which has to be worn at all times by the protagonist Hester Prynne, emblazoned on her dress above her chest, in her banishment – is seen predominantly to stand throughout the book for 'adultery' or 'adulteress', or 'affair', as well as for 'angel', in a redemptive scene in the latter stages of the work. Thus, this splitting of the figure of Hester Prynne between 'sacred and profane' chimes with 'the tendency to debasement in the sphere of love' that Freud identified in the essay of that name of 1912, and this distinction is brought out explicitly by Joyce in his treatment of Hester Prynne's *dirty laundry* in the *Wake*:[88]

> Here is her nubilee letters too. Ellis on quay in scarlet thread. Linked for the world on a flushcaloured field. Annan exe after to show they're not Laura Keown's. O, may the diabolo twisk your seifety pin! You child of Mammon,

> Kinsella's Lilith! Now who has been tearing the leg of her drawars on her? Which leg is it? The one with the bells on it. Rinse them out and aston along with you! Where did I stop? Never stop! Continuarration! You're not there yet. I amstel waiting. Garonne, garrone![89]

The laundry itself is being cleaned as it's being talked about by the washerwomen on the banks of the river in this scene in the *Wake*; hence the names of rivers – of which there are hundreds of instances in this episode – permeating the text (Ñuble, Annan, Exe, Amstel, Garonne, not to mention Dublin's Ellis and Aston Quays). It must be remembered that Hester Prynne is not here a 'full' character, but fills certain significations in the morphological female correspondence that is at stake and being talked about in this passage. Nonetheless, the clues in the text certainly reveal that it is her that is being alluded to. As James Atherton puts it in *The Books at the Wake*, 'the 'Scarlet letter' was sewn on Hester's dress but she felt as if it had been branded on the flesh', hence Joyce's use of the word 'flushcaloured', in which is rendered the very heat ('calor' in Latin) that *flushes* the *flesh*.[90] In this word the 'a' has come to replace the first 'o' of 'colour', confirming that Joyce's allusion is to the red-hot scarlet letter itself. Indeed, *The Scarlet Letter*'s last words are signalled in the full phrase 'a flushcaloured field' (as is the infiltrating 'a' itself, in the doubled reference: 'a ← flushc*a*loured field'); those words are, 'ON A FIELD, SABLE, THE LETTER A. GULES' (that is, *against a black backdrop, the letter A 'reds'*), which of course represents the exact inverse of the non-coloured 'a' amidst the field of the red letters 'r', 'e', and 'd', if the word 'read' is presented as such.[91]

This passage is thus laced with Hester Prynne's sexual (mis)deeds: the 'nubile' letter 'A' safety-pinned to her dress; the torn leg of her knickers; the signification of 'Lilith' – who was Adam's first wife – in the sense of Hester's being *first* wife to Roger Chillingworth, before committing adultery and becoming pregnant with the cleric Arthur Dimmesdale; and the 'child of Mammon', possibly alluding to the inheritance her child Pearl receives from her husband Chillingworth, who is of course not Pearl's father. Whilst these allusions subsist they are covered over by a language that conceals at the same time as revealing them. Indeed, we pick up on these multiple senses in the word 'drawars', which Joyce uses; in women's clothing, drawers being that covering garment, often *laced*, which conceals and can reveal the sexual organs (and for this item of clothing Joyce would reverentially always only the use the term 'drawers' – as Ellmann tells us – as 'he never accepted the word 'panties'').[92] However, it is again the 'a' that infiltrates this word and expands (whereas normal spellings *expend*) its semantic possibilities. 'Drawars' – with the single changed letter being 'a' – thus implies 'drawn wars', a fitting summation for the dual and duelling processes of suppression and resistance operative in so many of the *Wake*'s words, puns, and portmanteaus (such as in the drawn war – or rumble – in the jungle between Jung and the young girl discussed in the chapter 1, in the word 'jungerl').

Now, in the second instance of '*a*' taken from the *Wake*, we will explore exactly its lack, which is of course what the *objet petit a* designates. When in the *Wake* '*a*' *lacks* in 'the spell of hesitency' we are alerted precisely to what Hélène Cixous terms 'the (r)use of writing' in Joyce.[93] This 'spell' or spelling of 'hesitancy' as 'hesitency' – with a misplaced 'e' coming to fill the place of the lacking 'a' – was that which came to exonerate the founder and leader of the Irish Parliamentary Party Charles Stewart Parnell when he met with charges of collaborationism. As James Fairhall summates in *James Joyce and the Question of History*:

> Forgery, always carrying overtones of Parnell, is one of the *Wake*'s great themes. Along with other themes, it reverberates with echoes of the sinister event in Phoenix Park [the vague vagary that HCE is charged with, which doubles here with the Phoenix Park murders of 1882]. Parnell had been accused in 1887, in a series of articles run by *The Times* on Parnellism and crime, of having condoned the [Irish National] Invincibles' crime [the group responsible for the murders]. His prolonged trial before a special commission ended in 1889 with the unmasking of Richard Piggott [*sic*] as the forger of incriminating letters ascribed to Parnell; Piggott [*sic*] gave himself away in the witness-box by repeating a misspelling – "hesitency" for "hesitancy" – that appeared in one of the letters.[94]

This misspelling of 'hesitancy' as 'hesitency' that was present in the letter sent to *The Times* – falsely in Parnell's name – reappeared when Pigott was asked to write the word in court, in which writing it gave itself – and thus Pigott – away. It was therefore only in the *use* of writing that Pigott's *ruse* of writing could itself come clean. Indeed, the cross-examiner Sir Charles Russell had insisted on Pigott's *writing* 'hesitancy' – over spelling it out loud – so as to have been able to misdirect the emphasis of the inquiry onto the writing of the word, and more specifically, onto the writing of the word's first letter. The events in court transpired thus:

> "*Russell*. 'Will you write your own name? Will you write the word "proselytism," and finally (I think I will not trouble you at present with any more) "Patrick Egan" and "P. Egan"?'
>
> "He uttered these last words with emphasis, as if they imported something of great importance. Then, when Pigott had written, he added carelessly, 'There is one word I had forgotten. Lower down, please, leaving spaces, write the word "hesitancy."' Then, as Pigott was about to write, he added, as if this were the vital point, 'with a small "h."' Pigott wrote and looked relieved.
>
> "*Russell*. 'Will you kindly give me the sheet?'[95]

Having made out that all rested on the 'h' being lowercase – an instance solely realisable in writing – Pigott's attention was directed away from the actual letter in which the fault would lay; thus, where the 'a' was the 'e' would come to lie, and in so lying would expose the forgery's truth. We can thus see here how – as Lacan says – 'in short, half-saying is the internal law of every species of enunciation of the truth'.[96] In effect, this instance of 'hesitency' could only ever have been half-*said* – that is, *out loud* – as the difference between the 'a' and the 'e', like that in *différance*, would not have been able to have been heard. Its truth comes out by halves too in its writing, in having to have been *either* 'hesitancy' *or* 'hesitency' when produced. Truth (A) is thus unificatory/separatorily split here between positions 1 (hesitancy) and 2 (hesitency). Thus it is that in Pigott's writing of the word, 'hesitancy' has been infected by its symptom; the *it* [*ça*] of the unconscious had *spoken* itself through its misspelling, confessing itself with an 'e' where the 'a' lacked. Thus it is seen in this trial that the truth is in fact not *whole and nothing but*, but that it comes out through *half-saying*, and that this 'hesitency' (with the incriminating 'e' inserted where the 'a' should be) is that which precisely *betrays*; in the double sense of its initial betrayal of Parnell in the forged letter, and then of its *betraying itself* in court by the recurrence of its false spelling.

Hesitancy thus becomes one of the master tropes in *Finnegans Wake*, appearing in countless reiterations of the word – across a gamut of spellings and splicings – and in the work's very form itself, in which hesitant stuttering and stammering is rife. The *Wake*'s stilted lilt, or its 'tautautology', is thus founded on the very 'breaks-flows' – to use Deleuze and Guattari's terminology – of hesitancy itself.[97] In one recursive passage towards the end of the work we are given an instance which encompasses all these multiform facets of hesitancy at once; that is, an emphasis on the misspelling – and the letter that is the cause of the misspelling – as 'hesitency'; an emphasis on division, specifically *halving*, which gives rise to the slicing and splicing of the word; and – through this – an emphasis on the very form that renders the stammer in the word/sentence's articulation. The passage is this: 'Every letter is a hard but yours sure is the hardest crux ever. Hack an axe, hook an oxe, hath an an, heth hith ences. But once done, dealt and delivered, tattat, you're on the map.'[98]

In this segment of the *Wake*'s *ricorso* (the replaying of all the book's events in its last stages, before the recirculation of them, through its readerly Möbian topology) we find the difficult letter for Pigott repeating in the 'e's in 'every letter' (as it was indeed that he had found '*a* hard') and we see this event contaminating the male correspondence, HCE, who is located in the 'hardest crux ever' – and, as Shaun had insinuated earlier, in 'HeCitEncy' itself – as well as of course seeing 'hesitency' here in 'heth hith ences'.[99] The excerpt also subtly refers back to the female correspondence of our previous passage (ALP), in the recurrence of the river Annan in 'an an', and also hints at the hen's letter (it does so more explicitly a few lines before, in: 'Scratching it and patching at [. . .] what scrips of nutsnolleges I pecked up me myself').[100] In the 'an an', which is hacked at by an axe ('axe' and 'oxe' here – while hinting at the river Exe – both also contain the maleficent 'e' of 'hesitency'), demonstrates the very *indivisibility of the literal atom* that Lacan identifies earlier, in that 'an' – which is what 'a' has to be when preceding a word beginning with a vowel, or, in older usage, an 'h', the letter with which this sentence is suffuse – cannot be halved (or 'hathed'): it only repeats again as 'an'. Thus we see again through this 'e' in the place of 'a' that it is insofar as it hooks onto language that the symptom subsists, as Lacan formulated it in

Seminar XXIII; and that in the repeated homonymy with 'half' – in 'hath', 'heth', 'hith', or more loosely in the twice-repeated 'hard', and in 'hack' and 'hook' – the prevalence of *half-saying* makes itself palpable.

At the end of all this, all becomes 'done, dealt and delivered'. In its being *done* it has been *dealt with*, and thus in finally being *delivered* – as Lacan has it – the letter has arrived at its destination, as it always does.[101] However, the letter is not here 'signed, sealed and delivered', and in the words chosen in their stead elements of doubt, chance and division still persist, particularly in 'dealt', which can imply the chance involved in being dealt a hand of cards, and the division of a deck in their shuffling and dealing. The ironic 'tattat, you're on the map' that closes the passage goes to reinforce this with the implication of the trickery and sleight of hand that culminates in the card-proffering magician's 'tadaa' ('tattat'), and the false assurance that there can be an end, or destination, to (the *Wake*'s) exegesis.

In his essay 'La facteur de la vérité' (1975) – featured in *The Post Card* – Derrida argues this point about the letter's destiny, claiming that:

> A letter does *not always* arrive at its destination, and from the moment that this possibility belongs to its structure one can say that it never truly arrives, that when it does arrive its capacity not to arrive torments it with an internal drifting.[102]

Here the 'a' rejoins again in its negatory function, yielding Derrida's *adestination*. In elucidating throughout 'La facteur de la vérité' that a letter can always *not* arrive at its destination – that it can get lost or stuck in the post; that it can end up in the Dead Letter Office; or that it can drift off from its desired effect, for example – Derrida is putting stress on the possibilities of division, drifting, and *souffrance* (although this is precisely what guarantees a letter's arrival for Lacan) inherent in the network of the postal system itself. His term for this circuitous systematicity of the post is 'postality'.[103]

However, it would seem that in the *Wake* postality itself is its letters' very destination; that is, that – as Jean-Michel Rabaté puts it – 'both ends of the letter's trajectory are thus [always] open'.[104] Thus, the letter in *Finnegans Wake* – whether siglum or epistle, enveloped or unsealed – is always in play, always open, discoursing and circuiting around the littoral of the very hole it creates, and this postality itself is the very *destiny* of Joyce's letters.[105] The sigla of the *Wake* is thus indelible in that it is that which sets off all manner of discourses and postalities in the environs of the hole that it itself has created.

Waking the read: reading

In a letter of 27 January 1963 Foucault wrote to Derrida: 'Probably the first act of philosophy for us – and for a long time to come – is *reading*.'[106] In psychoanalysis too *reading* is primary, as it is *what gets read* that psychoanalysis speaks about, since its very speech – as Lacan puts it – 'is devoted to the unconscious, namely, what gets read above all else.'[107] But the act of reading – that of *waking the read* – itself is difficult to pin down precisely. It is as Deleuze in *The Logic of Sense* describes 'the infinitely divisible event'; that is, as 'eternally that which has just happened and that which is about to happen, but never that which is happening'.[108] We are therefore only ever *before* or *after* reading; the process – *reading* – itself seems to occupy that place of antagonism (position A) in the principle of *enverity*, to an extent; it is ineffable, unpin-downable as a singularity in itself; that is, in its *verbal* state (as a verb). Subsequently – subsequent to reading – a *reading* (as a noun), or *readings*, can be construed as singularities, as Attridge always assures us, but in the very process of reading itself something similar to the 'madness of writing' that Derrida describes in 'Two Words for Joyce' takes place: 'In this madness of writing' – he claims in the essay – 'whoever writes effaces himself, leaving, only to abandon it, the archive of his own effacement.'[109] To reconfigure this to reading we could conclude in effect that whoever reads effaces the writing, leaving in its wake only their *reading*.

This formulation should not seem new to us; we have seen it materialise throughout this work, particularly in relation to dreams, and to interpretation. As Freud put it in '*Gradiva*', any attempt at interpretation of a dream is an attempt to 'replac[e] it by the latent thoughts from whose distortion it must have arisen'; (a) reading, like (an) interpretation, is thus – to paraphrase Joyce – only what comes after, 'what is left over afterward, in the memory'.[110] There is here however perhaps a scale of proximity involved, as – as we have suggested – being in the position of having just read, especially of having just read *Finnegans Wake*, is like being in that of having just awoken to interpret the dream that Freud describes at the end of 'Little Hans', which, when we are close to that dream – or to that reading that has just taken place – we analyse and find so much within, but the dream and reading themselves disappear, along with their interpretations, when we reawaken after a subsequent sleep. But of course even an initial analysis or reflection on the dream or reading is not that dream or reading itself. Analogously, in the terms of the formulation for trauma put forward in chapter 1, we might here position reading as an encounter with the real the first symbolic impressions of which we imaginarily connect to and subsequently interpret, and thus subjectively work from. Reading construed in this way offers us a demonstration of the written *empty signified* – that is, the *sinthome* – coming to signify through a signifier plugging into it.

Whilst this microscopic and unconscious *sinthomic* process that is reading might take place in this way, what we know and see of it, as subjects – that is, what we can only experience *after* it – is the replacement of the writing with *the read*, and it is in this replacement (which has taken place through this *sinthomic plugging-in*) that subjectivity itself arises, as Maniglier reminds us:

> Subjectivity can only escape in the form of slips of the tongue, symptoms and dreams: because it is precisely nothing other than these slippages, qua slippages. The truth about the subject is not so much in the meaning of the dream as in the endless process of associations, that is, in the substitutions of signs which constitute the interpretation.[111]

Thus, to put reading in the place of speech in Lacan's words of Seminar I: the subject 'finds himself, afterwards [after reading], other than he was before'.[112] *Finnegans Wake* of course aims at the other side of this; that is, to be the dream itself – not what is left over afterwards – in effect, to be reading itself (and it achieves this in its *reading itself*; in the '*it* reads' that Lacan identifies is always going on within and throughout the *Wake*; indeed, as Joyce puts it: 'It will remember itself from every sides.'[113] It achieves this, finally, *as writing*, in the Nancian sense; that is, as a verb, as that which does not cease to write itself, as 'continuarration' in the senseless adventure of 'sense'). As Simon Critchley and Tom McCarthy thus put it: 'As such, *Finnegans Wake* is literature in reverse.'[114] The *Wake*, that is, is the *envers* of literature; its obverse. It is – as we will shortly come to term it – *ob-literature*.

To come to this, however, we will first look at the second type of letter we are investigating in *Finnegans Wake*; the 'epiepistle', hidden in the midden, that the hen, Biddy Doran, comes to uncover.[115] The midden is a heap of litter, a dunghill '(dump for short)' in which the hen is scratching and uncovering bits and fragments of a scrambled letter vindicating HCE, which because of its discomposition leads to the question: 'Where in the waste is the wisdom?'[116] Although intimated beforehand, this uncovering of the letter – and its contents (albeit completely jumbled) – comes about in chapter 5 of the *Wake*. The letter is inferably ALP's – the section begins with praise of her to the tune of the Lord's Prayer: 'In the name of Annah the Allmaziful, the Everliving, the Bringer of Plurabilities, haloed be her eve, her signtime sung, her rill be run, unhemmed as it is uneven!' – and the 'many names' by which 'her untitled mamafesta' (as the letter is called) has been known 'at disjointed times' are given (a list covering four pages).[117] Whilst composed by ALP, in the last words of the chapter we learn that the letter had been written by 'that odious and still today insufficiently malestimated notesnatcher [. . .] Shem the Penman'.[118]

At the end of the section we see the letter referred to as 'th[e] new book of Morses', giving us the indications that it concerns HCE (as *Moses*; the venerable Father of the Law to the Children of Israel); that it is, however, only in scraps, only made up of *morsels*; and, as so, that it needs to be decoded – indeed, like *Morse code*, which is made up of dots and dashes (plenty of which are found in the diacritics littering the letter), and which, when combined with the perforated tape of the Murray code (derived from the Baudot code) yields the 'numerous stabs and foliated gashes made by a pronged instrument' that Joyce points to here.[119] Indeed, the letter at this point is littered with such marks and sigla, and seems to be talking about itself, but in so doing it is in fact describing the incident in the park:

> These paper wounds, four in type, were gradually and correctly understood to mean stop, please stop, do please stop, and O do please stop respectively, and following up their one true clue, the circumflexuous wall of a single-minded men's asylum, accentuated by bi tso fb rok engl a ssan dspl itch ina, – Yard inquiries pointed out ' that they ad bîn "provoked" ay Λ fork of a grave Brofèsor; àth é's break – fast – table; ; acùtely profèššionally *piquéd*, to = introdùce a notion of time [ùpon à plane (?) sù' 'fàc'e'] by pùnct! ingh oles (sic) in iSpace?![120]

These sigla, their diacritics, and their encoding are self-referential: the passage circumflexes – to use this word as a verb – in its indicated contraction and variation; circumflex, grave and acute accents pop up everywhere and are mentioned by name ('circumflexuous', 'grave', 'acùtely'; 'accentuated'); 'these paper wounds' are the perforations ('pùnct! [ured] oles') in the coding tape; their meaning being full stops on full stops (those of telegrams). But these stops are also obviously pleas; 'O please do stop' being their highest pitched. We here come to realise that the scene in the park is being investigated: the 'one true clue' is being followed up; 'inquiries' are being made by '[Scotland] Yard'. We know we are in the Phoenix Park in Dublin because the pointed 'fork', 'Λ', which towers over the other letters in the line – and thus is not the '∧' of Shaun or the '∆' of ALP – must represent the Wellington Monument, and indubitably the phallus, and the 'circumflexuous wall' is most likely the Magazine Wall; the original scene of the original sin. So originary is this scene of sin in fact that it possibly refers further back than the incident in the park to masturbation in youth. Indeed, as Sheldon Brivic puts it: 'Though the Magazine Wall is a place in Phoenix Park, this sin may have corrupted reality by involving sex with a magazine. It is original in the sense that many modern adolescents have their first sex with "maggies." '[121]

This delving deeper into subjective history and uncovering of unconscious repressed memory is evidently the procedure of psychoanalysis, which is echoed in the hen digging around and unearthing the instance of the letter in the midden heap (an apt metaphor for the unconscious). It is indeed in this episode concerning this instance of the letter hidden in the midden that Joyce engages most directly, or at least most concentratedly, with the practice of psychoanalysis, and its theory, in the whole of the *Wake*, characterising psychoanalysts, in reference to Lucia of course – along with himself, as her father, in the use of the word 'our' – as 'grisly old Sykos who have done our unsmiling bit on 'alices, when they were yung and easily freudened'.[122]

Indeed, the figure and name of the father haunt the chapter, with the presiding question lingering over it: 'Be who, farther potential?'[123] For Joyce, of course, this question loomed – as Lacan alerts us to in Seminar XXIII – and it is one that he took up directly in *Ulysses*, in claiming that 'paternity may be a legal fiction. Who is the father of any son that any son should love him or he any son?'[124] Derrida in 'The Night Watch' stretches Joyce's question and its resonances to encompass not only paternity, but maternity also.[125] The mother here, however, is only (m)uttered after the long disquisition (occupying fourteen lines) on the position of the father following the earlier question from the *Wake*, in the next two-word sentence: 'And Mm.'[126] Joyce's critique of psychoanalysis here thus seems to imply that on mum the practice *keeps mum*. Thus it is that at this juncture we will limit ourselves to the psychoanalytic aspects surrounding the hen's letter – and particularly to the concatenation of the figures of the father (and the son) and the horse – for the sake of brevity and so as to be in keeping with the direction of the treatment of the *Wake* in this work.

If this is the letter of a little hen's it is also that of Little Hans, whose phobia was horses. Like Johnny in Patti Smith's 'Land', in this chapter we suddenly get the feeling we're surrounded by horses, horses, horses, horses, coming in, in all directions. First we get a reference to 'Elberfeld's Calculating Horses'; a group of horses who could supposedly solve arithmetical problems, the premier of whom was in fact called Clever Hans.[127] Thus we see Little Hans here, in the reference to the most famous of Elberfeld's horses, and this is further bolstered by the fact that 'Elberfeld's Calculating Horses' of course implies HCE (ECH = HCE), father to the writer of the letter, Shem. In a 1911 psychological study by Oskar Pfungst it was determined that the 'calculating' horse Clever Hans was in fact only responding to inadvertent bodily movements in his questioner, instead of actually doing sums himself; this phenomenon came to be known as the 'Clever Hans Effect' (CHE), which is thus another indicator of the roles of Little Hans and HCE in Joyce's text.[128]

We next receive the photographer's 'tip' – *tips* run throughout the *Wake*; connoting those given in horseracing, monetary tokens and rewards, and, of course, rubbish dumps – 'that if a negative of a horse happens to melt enough while drying, well, what you do get is, well, a positively grotesquely distorted macromass of all sorts of horsehappy values and masses of meltwhile horse.'[129] In the darkroom of the memory here horses melt and meld together as the morphological characters of the *Wake* do, but also as Little Hans's father and the horses he's scared of do in his unconscious. This analogy between psychoanalysis and photography is furthered in the description of the process of developing photographs with 'chemicots'; that is, developing film with chemicals, but also the chemical development of the brain, and of the unconscious, which can never escape the initial stages of its infantile development (the 'cots' it's caught up in).[130]

In returning – through superimpositions of *photographic memory* – to these early stages in the psychoanalytic session, or, indeed, in silently eliding them, Joyce critically claims that in psychoanalysis we 'sell our feebought silence *in camera*'; that is (in Joyce's critique), that psychoanalysis puts under a lens certain aspects of the unconscious – or injects into its silences certain standards in the psychoanalytic repertoire; predominantly, *the father* – magnifying and repeating them over the course of purchased sessions, until they become veritable hobbyhorses of their own for the patient, before any attempt is made at their unknotting.[131] Indeed, so much as this is intimated in Joyce's parenthesis concerning the father: '(often held up to our contumacy)'.[132] Here we see that the symptom of the father is stopped on in psychoanalysis, and examined – 'held up' to the light so that its image becomes clear, but also 'held up', in the sense of retarded, so as to redouble its financial reward (if the practice is seen cynically, as Joyce of course sees it) – and put in quarantine (as the phrase 'to hold the contumacy' means), but in so being, it is repeated through so many associations (precisely non-*free*; as they are paid for, or 'feebought'). In this, 'contumacy' itself reveals the weightiest and most damning of charges in literature of paternal punishment that James Harlowe, Sr made loom over his albeit duteous and filial daughter Clarissa in Samuel Richardson's 1747–1748 epistolary novel that bore the name of the latter as its title.[133] Thus, here – through representation by the opposite – John Joyce, who was held up to the contumacy of his son James, is revealed as *the other side* of James Harlowe; that is, as the obscene father to this unyielding Father of the Law.

Qua horse the father multiplies in this chapter as we glimpse the four horsemen of the apocalypse ('the four shortened ampersands under which we can glypse at').[134] Thereafter, we are made twice to directly return to horses in the text: 'And so back to our horses, for we also know [. . .] that Father Michael about this red time of the white terror equals the old regime', and, in 'to volt [implying both the *bolting* horse and the *vaulted* pommel horse] back to our desultory horses'.[135] Thus, as Joyce indeed puts it, the '*father* in such virgated contexts' (Bloom's father was called Virag in *Ulysses*: 'The father's name that poisoned himself') 'is not always that undemonstrative relative', but is rather that poisoned signifier 'of the old regime' in the unconscious that receives its indiminishable varity through whatever potential horseplay with words it can hook onto, unless of course this process can be reversed, and the words, the writing, can be provided supplementarily to the lacking father; that is, be put in the place of it as symptom, as signifier, by incarnating itself as *sinthome*.[136]

Thus it is through the symptom here – underwritten, for Joyce, by the *sinthome*; as that which supports his writing (and, like the unificatory/separatory transparent sheet, allows him to resist its symptomal traps) – that the contents of the letter become established (as well as disestablished and re-established), through their symptomal multi-meaning and variegated signification, which often revolves around the same knots and staples. We thus 'notice [here] how something that spreads throughout language like wildfire is readable, that is to say, how it hooks on, creates a discourse', as Lacan puts it – apropos the symptom – in Seminar XVII.[137] We find that these symptoms are thus in circulation between all the family members implied in this episode of the letter: HCE, whom the letter concerns; ALP, its composer; and the brothers (or perhaps we should call them *scriblings*) Shem the 'Penman' (meaning 'copywriter'), and Shaun the 'Post' (or postman), to whom it will fall to send the letter.[138] Through this, we here see that these family members are as close to undifferentiable *points of jouissance* as literary characters can be, and that their uncovering in the text comes about because of the (something of *a*) *One* that positivises them; that is, precisely because of the 'hen', which is the animal responsible for revealing them, and which is the Greek word for 'one'. Thus, the distribution of these symptoms indistinguishably amongst the members of this family unit hints at the archetypal incestuousness – in Jungian terminology – that plagues it, and thus brings HCE and ALP's daughter Isabel back to it, as an object, in his dream, of HCE's desire (particularly piqued – and thus incestuously redoubled – because of her resemblance to his own mother) the guilt-inducing incident of which gets construed anagrammatically as: 'Insects appalling, low hum clang sin!'[139]

The letter itself is written *palimpsestually* by Shem; that is, on his own body, in his own faeces. This process is described onomatopoeically at the end of the chapter: 'kak, pfooi, bosh and fiety'.[140] We here see that the text (*corpus*) is condemned to its own body, to use Lacan's phrase: it writes itself on itself with that which it produces; with its own waste product. The text of the hen's letter is thus *ob-literated*: it is in smithereens throughout the chapter; it conceals its contents through the obliviousness, even oblivion, of its language, whilst also revealing them through the obviousness of its innuendo; it is written by Shem from 'the basis of oblativity' – as Lacan construes it in his introduction to the 'Names-of-the-Father' Seminar, the rest of which never took place – in which 'an infant releasing its feces surrenders them to what appears for the first time as dominating the Other's demand, namely the Other's desire' (or the mother's, ALP's, desire; in fact, the whole family's desire); and, as *ob-literature*, it is, finally, the obverse of literature: an obscene, bodily, earthly *lituraterre*.[141] As such, the letter's *lalangue* hovers somewhere between language (the Symbolic) and the Real, the impropriety of both of which is manifested because of, and in, this very limbo state. As Lacan summarises in Seminar XXIV:

> It is rather annoying that the Real can only be conceived of as being improper. It is not quite the same as language. Language is only improper for saying anything whatsoever. The Real is only improper by being realised; according to the usage of the word *to realise* [in English] that means nothing other than *to imagine as sense*. There is one thing which is in any case certain, if indeed a thing can be so, it is that the very idea of the real involves the exclusion of all sense. It is only insofar as the Real is emptied of sense, that we can grasp it a little.[142]

The letter in the midden, the wisdom in the waste, is only ever grasped a little – that is, in *little bits* – here, because of the *lalangue* that it subsists in being precisely 'an obscenity' (in its exclusion of all sense), as Lacan defines the word in the same Seminar.[143] It is such due to the difficulty of its parts' (or non-parts') (non)differentiality and (in)distinguishability, and, as such – as Lacan says – 'it is what Freud designates as [. . .] *l'obrescène*' (that is, the obscene 'other scene'); 'what he calls *the other stage*, the one that language occupies because of what is called its structure, [its] elementary structure which is summarised in that of kinship'; an elementary structure which we have seen in the *Wake* is a kind of kinship that is too close for comfort.[144]

Nevertheless – or, as is to be expected – there is in this *lalangue* of the letter and language of the *Wake* a certain *jouissance*, but not one that can be read singly, or univocally, precisely because of its very (Joycean) *singularity*; that is, that singularly enigmatic mode of signification which gives rise to all of the letter's readerly *rejouissances* throughout *Finnegans Wake* – echoes of the original and unrecoverable *jouissance* in the park which rise like phoenixes from ashes in all the construals and misconstruals of the readings of the letter, from which so much surplus enjoyment is derived – and which also gives rise to the very Joycéance of reading the *Wake*, and waking the read, itself.[145] Involved in this Joycéance are thus the strategies of bringing to bear on the continuarration of *Finnegans Wake* all of the details known to scholars about Joyce's life and work, references and influences, and of making connections from our own knowledges and idiocultures that ring with and resonate in its words and sentences. Thus, while we always notice the *symptom* hooking on and spreading through the *Wake*'s language like wildfire – as Lacan puts it – we are also made acutely aware of the other side of this, operative always at the same time; that is, the *sinthomicity* of the *Wake*'s discourse (without speech), in its being unhooked – and unhookable – onto language. Its discourse is not fastened fast to singular meaning, but the glassy surface of its words, sigla, and symbols is refractive and reflective; resistant to any sinking of hooks into it, shooting them off in so many other directions, and hailing so many other semantic possibilities, fed by our, and its, *jouissances* and *rejouissances*: as Derrida states in *Glas*, in its language 'the element of contagion, the infinite circulation of general equivalence relates each sentence, each stump of writing [. . .] to each other' ('stumps around which thinking embroiders', to put this into Lacan's words, relating to the Real).[146] In this way – as Jim LeBlanc puts it – '*Finnegans Wake* is like a Rorschach test: our glosses of words, phrases, and passages often reveal more about ourselves than about the latent narrative content of Joyce's text.'[147]

Indeed, Lacan confirms this in Seminar XXIII in claiming that it was Joyce's desire 'to be an artist who would occupy everyone, or anyway as many people as possible' – and this through the very *sinthomic* varity of his text – but he also warns us to be wary of this very process in stressing the necessity of guarding against the *sinthome*; that is, through stressing that – as we have previously mentioned – the only weapon we have against the *sinthome* is equivocation; the object *meaning*, which in analysis, in interpretation, we attempt to raise to the dignity of the Thing.[148]

In this chapter of the present study, instead of going from A to Z, we have moved only from 'a' to *read* in *Finnegans Wake*, and in doing so have expended tremendous exegetical exertion, whilst really covering relatively little ground. This of course is how to have lots of fun at *Finnegans Wake*; indeed, it is the source of its 'funferall' and the guarantor of its longevity.[149] Such fun as this should in no way be disparaged in reading (it should of course be encouraged!), but to extend beyond this we must come to see reading in the light that Deleuze does, for example, for whom a text

> is simply a small cog in an extra-textual practice. It's not about commenting on the text by a method of deconstruction, or a method of textual practice, or other methods, it's about seeing what use it is in the extra-textual practice that extends the text.[150]

Indeed, if we want the *Wake*, as a literary machine, as opposed to a purely abstract machine, to *extend* in this way, to plug directly into other machines – political, social, psychoanalytical, for example (*after* – or rather contemporaneously with – the fun of reading that is the motor of the educational machine) – it will be by approaching it from an *other side*, as Lacan does in Seminar XXIII, that this can be most fruitfully achieved. We must thus always be devoted to the

Wake – as Lacan was – but also always aware of its possible snares. Perhaps, then, his teaching on the *Wake* boils down to the insistence that we can find more (if not as much) in it, and get more (if not as much) out of it, by reading it in the other direction; that is, by penetrating further into how it reads us, and into how, precisely, *it* reads.

Indeed, to an extent, it is the *Wake*'s (own, as well as our) ceaseless exegetical work, with all its supposed decipherment (which is in fact only so many recipherments); that is, precisely the *reading* of *Finnegans Wake*, that is its *trap*, its 'captivating myth', as Lacan calls it. This is precisely analogous to the trap of the unconscious – *in itself* – as it ties itself in so many knots and becomes entangled in so many symptomal repetitions. The very unconscious itself Joyce was able to render in his work without becoming entrapped by it, because of being unsubscribed from it, and because of his deployment of (and resubscription to) the *sinthome*, as *empty signified*, or indeed, that which subverts the imaginarily 'fixed' signified. Thus, here in Joyce we see – as Miller puts it in 'Interpretation in Reverse' – that

> the unconscious is wholly situated in the space [*décalage*] that is repeatedly produced between what I want to say and what I do say – *as if* the signifier deflected the programmed trajectory of the signified, which provides the material of interpretation

– that is, 'that interpretation is nothing other than the unconscious, that interpretation is the unconscious itself'.[151]

The *sinthome*, which Joyce employs in his composition, can thus be doubly seen as the way out of 'the age of interpretation', out of this very entrapment of unconscious-interpretative repetition compulsion – that is, in its identificatory moment; that which Joyce achieved through unsubscription, or which may come about at the end of analysis – and yet also it must be seen as the inaugural way in – that is, in its being the symptom's subsistual other side, its lining; the facilitator of the initial and instantiating moment of signification/subjectivation itself. It is thus that which in the 'museyroom' of the unconscious insists: 'Mind your boots going out' and 'mind your hats goan in!'[152] To be post-Joycean means knowing this.

C'est la vie, ça se lit.

Notes

1 On music and botany in relation to *Finnegans Wake*, see Philip McShane, *Plants and Pianos: Two Essays in Advanced Methodology* (Dublin: Milltown Institute of Theology and Philosophy, 1971), a study which – similarly to the processes involved in the first part of this chapter – aims 'to call attention not so much to the object of investigation as to the subject investigating, to the reader or the listener' (p.13).

2 Jacques Derrida, 'Two Words for Joyce' [1982], trans by Geoff Bennington, in *James Joyce: A Collection of Critical Essays*, ed. by Mary T. Reynolds (Upper Saddle River: Prentice-Hall, 1993) pp.217–218. For a more up-to-date translation by Bennington,

which differs substantially at this passage, see Jacques Derrida, 'Two Words for Joyce', trans. by Geoffrey Bennington, in *Derrida and Joyce: Texts and Contexts*, ed. by Andrew J. Mitchell and Sam Slote (Albany: State University of New York Press, 2013) p.36.

3 James Joyce, *Finnegans Wake* [1939], ed. by Robbert-Jan Henkes and others (Oxford: Oxford World's Classics, 2012) p.18, 18–19.

4 See Roland McHugh, *Annotations to Finnegans Wake* (Baltimore: The John Hopkins University Press, 1980) p.18. Further, as Saussure clarifies, '*rede* almost corresponds to "speaking" but adds the special connotation of "discourse"', which has especial relevance to the Lacanian formulae for writing that we will propose within this chapter. See Ferdinand de Saussure, *Course in General Linguistics* [1906–1911], ed. by Charles Bally and others, trans. by Wade Baskin (Glasgow: Fontana/Collins, 1974) rev. ed., p.14.

5 Edgar Allan Poe, 'The Man of the Crowd' [1840], in *The Complete Tales and Poems of Edgar Allan Poe* (London: Penguin Books, 1982) p.475. With regard to that which is *unreadable*, see Jean-Jacques Lecercle's concept of '*délire*' – possibly translatable as '*un-*' or '*dereading*' – as delineated in his *Philosophy Through the Looking-Glass: Language, Nonsense, Desire* (London: Hutchinson, 1985). See also Joyce's recorded reading of a segment of the 'Anna Livia Plurabelle' section of the *Wake*, made in 1929, available on *James Joyce: The Complete Recordings* (Brussels: Sub Rosa, 2003, SR 060).

6 It is this type of 'Babelian' homophony that is exemplified by Miguel de Cervantes in an instance of wordplay in *Don Quixote* in which Sancho Panza responds irreverently to Don Quixote's mentions of Julius and Augustus, not caring for 'Julys or Augusts'. As Edith Grossman explains: 'In Spanish *julio* is the month of July, while *Julio* is the equivalent of Julius; *agosto* is the month of August, while *Agosto* is the equivalent of Augustus.' Thus, only the reader is privy to this slip made by Sancho, as Don Quixote cannot read the absence of capital letters in Sancho's speech and therefore misses the opportunity to correct Sancho, which otherwise he would not fail to seize upon. See Miguel de Cervantes, *Don Quixote* [1605/1615], trans. by Edith Grossman (London: Vintage Books, 2005) p.507, note 3.

7 Jacques Lacan, *The Seminar of Jacques Lacan, Book III: The Psychoses, 1955–1956*, ed. by Jacques-Alain Miller, trans. by Russell Grigg (New York: W. W. Norton, 1993) p.34 [my emphasis].

8 Derrida, 'Two Words for Joyce', in *Derrida and Joyce*, p.32.

9 Jacques-Alain Miller, 'The Other Without Other' [2013], trans. by Philip Dravers, *Hurly-Burly*, 10 (2013) 15–29 (p.19).

10 Jacques Lacan, *The Seminar of Jacques Lacan, Book XX: Encore: On Feminine Sexuality, the Limits of Love and Knowledge, 1972–1973*, ed. by Jacques-Alain Miller, trans. by Bruce Fink (New York: W. W. Norton, 1998) p.142 [trans. modified]. Fink's translation of *lalangue* into English is 'llanguage', but for clarity's sake, and in keeping with other translators, I retain '*lalangue*' when quoting from his translations.

11 Jacques Lacan, *The Seminar of Jacques Lacan, Book XXIV: L'insu que sait de l'une-bévue s'aile à mourre, 1976–1977*, trans. by Cormac Gallagher (London: Karnac, unofficial translation, n.d.) session 8, p.99.

12 Saussure, *Course in General Linguistics*, trans. by Baskin, p.120.

13 Jacques Lacan, *The Seminar of Jacques Lacan, Book XVII: The Other Side of Psychoanalysis* [1969–1970], ed. by Jacques-Alain Miller, trans. by Russell Grigg (New York: W. W. Norton, 2007) p.89.

14 See Jacques Lacan, 'The Function and Field of Speech and Language in Psychoanalysis' [1953], in *Écrits: The First Complete Edition in English* [1966], orig. ed. by François Wahl, trans. by Bruce Fink, in collaboration with Héloïse Fink and Russell Grigg (New York: W. W. Norton, 2006) p.246, for example.

15 Jacques Lacan, *The Seminar of Jacques Lacan, Book II: The Ego in Freud's Theory and in the Technique of Psychoanalysis, 1954–1955*, ed. by Jacques-Alain Miller, trans. by Sylvana Tomaselli (New York: W. W. Norton, 1991) p.47.
16 Lacan, *Seminar III: The Psychoses*, pp.115–116.
17 Richard Ellmann, *James Joyce: New and Revised Edition* (Oxford: Oxford University Press, 1983) p.649.
18 See Joyce, *Finnegans Wake*, p.223, 11, and Hugh B. Staples, 'Beckett in the "Wake" ', *James Joyce Quarterly*, 8th ser., 4 (1971) 421–424 (p.422).
19 Lacan, *Seminar XXIV: L'insu que sait de l'une-bévue s'aile à mourre*, session 8, p.98.
20 Comte de Lautréamont [Isadore Ducasse], *Les Chants de Maldoror* [1869], trans. by Guy Wernham (New York, New Directions, 1966) p.263.
21 Jacques Lacan, *The Seminar of Jacques Lacan, Book XVI: From an Other to the other, 1968–1969*, trans. by Cormac Gallagher (London: Karnac, unofficial translation, n.d.) session XX, p.10.
22 William S. Burroughs, 'Origin and Theory of Tape Cut-Ups' [1976], recorded lecture on *Break Through in the Grey Room* (Brussels: Sub Rosa, 1986; SUB 33005–8).
23 Jacques Derrida, *Of Grammatology* [1967], trans. by Gayatri Chakravorty Spivak (Baltimore: John Hopkins University Press, 1997) p.51.
24 We here use '*Ur*-writing' as a term homologous to 'archē-writing' in accordance with a postscript Derrida makes to the text of section V of 'Ulysses Gramophone' in 1987, in which he uses the three homologies: 'A "word-origin," an archi-word (*Urwort*).' See Jacques Derrida, 'Ulysses Gramophone: Hear Say Yes in Joyce' [1984], trans. by François Raffoul, in *Derrida and Joyce*, p.32.
25 Derrida, *Of Grammatology*, p.70.
26 Jacques Lacan, 'Postface to the French Edition of *Seminar XI*' [1973], trans. by Adrian Price, *Hurly-Burly*, 7 (2012) 17–21 (p.17).
27 Jean-Luc Nancy, 'Blank Opening', trans. by Ian Maclachlan, in *Reading Derrida's Of Grammatology*, ed. by Sean Gaston and Ian Maclachlan (London: Continuum, 2011) p.107.
28 Patricia Gherovici, 'The Transsexual Body Written: Writing as *Sinthome*', in *The Literary Lacan: From Literature to Lituraterre and Beyond*, ed. by Santanu Biswas (Calcutta: Seagull Books, 2012) p.295.
29 Gilles Deleuze and Félix Guattari, *Anti-Oedipus: Capitalism and Schizophrenia, Vol. 1* [1972], trans. by Robert Hurley, Mark Seem and Helen R. Lane (London: Continuum, 2004) p.123.
30 Gilles Deleuze and Félix Guattari, *A Thousand Plateaus: Capitalism and Schizophrenia, Vol. 2* [1980], trans. by Brian Massumi (London: Continuum, 2004) pp.4–5. Although an overquoting of *theoretical* authors might be levelled at this work, full(er) studies of passages in Joyce are still to follow in this chapter; however, the quoting of literary authors, and the use of the pronoun 'we' – 'since each of us [is] several' (p.3) – are procedures used by the authors that are taken seriously, and thus have been followed, within this work.
31 Although this recapitulation in the form of the full graph represents a concised version of the contents of chapters 3 and 4, it could not have been arrived at without the work of those chapters having taken place heuristically. Indeed, for those chapters, as Žižek puts it (in relation to Wagner's operas): '[their] long narrative [was] the true site of [their] dramatic shift'. See Slavoj Žižek, *Event* (London: Penguin, 2014) p.151.
32 Deleuze and Guattari, *A Thousand Plateaus*, p.4.
33 Ibid. p.6.
34 Joyce, *Finnegans Wake*, p.114, 17–18.

35 Roberto Harari, 'The *sinthome*: Turbulence and Dissipation', trans. by Luke Thurston, in *Re-inventing the Symptom: Essays on the Final Lacan*, ed. by Luke Thurston (New York: Other Press, 2002) p.54.
36 Lacan, *Seminar XX: Encore*, p.32.
37 Michel Foucault, *The Archaeology of Knowledge* [1969], trans. by A.M. Sheridan Smith (Abingdon: Routledge Classics, 2002) p.54.
38 Lacan, *Seminar XVII: The Other Side of Psychoanalysis*, p.152.
39 Foucault, *The Archaeology of Knowledge*, p.46.
40 Lacan, *Seminar XVI: From an Other to the other*, session I, p.1 [trans. modified]. He describes the phrase as a 'frontispiece' in session IV, p.9.
41 Lacan, *Seminar XVII: The Other Side of Psychoanalysis*, pp.12–13.
42 Jacques Lacan, 'Conférence de Louvain suivie d'un entretien avec Françoise Wolff' [1972], trans. unknown, in *Jacques Lacan parle*, video [Online] Available from: www.youtube.com/watch?v=31iQQTPY-kA [accessed 29 April 2014; my emphases].
43 Lacan, *Seminar XVI: From an Other to the other*, session X, p.6.
44 See Lacan, *Seminar III: The Psychoses*, p.317.
45 See ibid. pp.245ff., for the use of the term 'the environs of the hole'.
46 Miller's thesis, more than Lacan's (shared, but also questioned by Derrida in 'Ulysses Gramophone'), is that the devoted reader of Joyce (the *Joycean*) is an *expert*, or is *made into* an expert – is *expertised*, in the sense of 'hystericised' – by Joyce's writing. Contrary to this, however, the *Wake* rather seems to go to expose that the *reader-supposed-to-know* that it postulates does, in fact, *not* – and *cannot* – *know* (or, at least, not know *all*, and is therefore *non-all*), much in the way that a psychoanalysis goes to deconstruct the postulation of the analyst by the analysand as the *subject-supposed-to-know*; that is, through moving from an Other (*Autre*) to the other (*autre*). The *Wake*, similarly, moves from an Absolute to 'the absolute absence of the Absolute', as Beckett puts it. See Beckett, 'Dante . . . Bruno. Vico . . . Joyce', in *Our Exagmination*, p.22.
47 In this respect the *Wake* is like the unconscious in its *wild* state. As Miller describes this position that it fulfilled for Lacan:

> Lacan resorts to *Finnegans Wake*, namely, to a text that unceasingly plays on the relations between speech and writing, sound and sense, a text full of condensations, equivocations, homophonies, but nevertheless has nothing to do with the old unconscious. In *Finnegans Wake*, every quilting point is made obsolete. This is why, despite heroic efforts, this text can neither be interpreted nor translated. That's because it is not itself an interpretation, and it wonderfully brings the subject of reading back to perplexity as the elementary phenomenon of the subject in *lalangue*.

See Jacques-Alain Miller, 'Interpretation in Reverse', in *The Later Lacan: An Introduction*, ed. by Véronique Voruz and Bogdan Wolf, trans. by Heather Chamberlain and others (Albany: State University of New York Press, 2007) p.8.
48 Lacan, *Seminar XXIV: L'insu que sait de l'une-bévue s'aile à mourre*, session 10, p.114.
49 Sigmund Freud, '"Postscript (1922)" to "Analysis of a Phobia in a Five-Year-Old Boy"' [1909], trans. by Alix and James Strachey, in *SE*, X, p.149.
50 Ibid. [my emphasis]. On *Ulysses* as a 'hypermnesic machine' ('to say nothing of *Finnegans Wake*'), see Derrida, 'Ulysses Gramophone', in *Derrida and Joyce*, p.60, and for a further extension of this thesis to the *Wake* itself, see Peter Mahon, *Imagining Joyce and Derrida: Between Finnegans Wake and* Glas (Toronto: University of Toronto Press, 2007) p.65.
51 Lacan, *Seminar XX: Encore*, p.32.
52 Frank Budgen, *James Joyce and the Making of 'Ulysses'* [1934], in *James Joyce and the Making of 'Ulysses' and Other Writings* (Oxford: Oxford University Press, 1972) p.20.

53 Joyce, *Finnegans Wake*, p.118, 21.

54 Eric Laurent, 'Three Enigmas: Meaning, Signification, Jouissance', in *The Later Lacan*, p.122 [my emphasis]. Atherton stresses the importance of the letter, giving it a privileged place in his 'axioms of the *Wake*': 'As each atom has its own individual life (according to Bruno) so each letter in *Finnegans Wake* has its own individuality.' See James S. Atherton, *The Books at the Wake: A Study of Literary Allusions in James Joyce's* Finnegans Wake [1959] (Illinois: Southern Illinois University Press, 2009) p.53.

55 Joyce, *Finnegans Wake*, p.299, footnote 4. Jonathan McCreedy conjectures that 'in *Finnegans Wake*, [Joyce] refers to his collected character system' as 'the Doodles family' as this designation 'perhaps indicates the method of their composition.' Perhaps they were "doodled' on scraps of paper, or restaurant napkins, and not in a notebook at all', as was Joyce's usual method of preparatory composition during working on the *Wake*. See Jonathan McCreedy, '"Everyword for oneself but Code for us all!": The Shapes of Sigla in *Finnegans Wake*', *Genetic Joyce Studies* [electronic journal], 10 (2010) Available from: <www.antwerpjamesjoycecenter.com/GJS10/GJS10_Jonathan McCreedy.htm#_edn31> [accessed 15 May 2014].

56 When talking of them in correspondence Joyce indeed calls these 'signs', but he does in fact use the word 'sigla' at *Finnegans Wake*, p.119, 19, in relation to 'Δ'. In *Ulysses* we see also the autonomy of the letter in it becoming a *title* in Stephen's recounting of his youthful daydreams in the third person, concerning his writerly ambition: 'Have you read his F? O yes, but I prefer Q. Yes, but W is wonderful. O yes, W.' See James Joyce, *Ulysses* [1922], ed. by Hans Walter Gabler and others (New York: Vintage Books, 1986) 3.139–140, p.34; James Joyce, *Ulysses: The 1922 Text*, ed. by Jeri Johnson (Oxford: Oxford World's Classics, 1998) pp.40–41. 'O' is of course seen to be the prevalent letter here, *outside of this titular sense*. Further, in precisely this relation, see Jean-Luc Nancy and Philippe Lacoue-Labarthe, *The Title of the Letter: A Reading of Lacan* [1973], trans. by François Raffoul and David Pettigrew (Albany: State University of New York Press, 1992): 'The *title* [has] the sense that it signifies that document which establishes a right, attests an ownership or capacity – and it is indeed this *title* of the Lacanian letter that it will be necessary to produce, decipher, and authenticate' (p.2).

57 Adrian Johnston offers a remarkably lucid description of this *matheme* in his essay on Lacan's 'Science and Truth', which provides all the requisite tools for its decoding:

> Generally speaking, in Lacanian theory, the barred subject and object *a* co-implicate each other in the form of fantasies as fundamental formations of the unconscious. The co-implication between the subject and object of fantasy invariably entails one or more schematizing incarnations of conjunction (∧), disjunction (∨), and relative positions of being greater than (>) or less than (<), with the 'lozenge' of the '*poinçon*' (◇) designating all of these possible permutations fleshed out by various fantasies of union or fusion, rejection or abandonment, domination or mastery, submission or slavery, and so on.

See Adrian Johnston, 'Turning the Sciences Inside Out: Revisiting Lacan's 'Science and Truth'', in *Concept and Form: Volume 2, Interviews and Essays on the* Cahiers pour l'Analyse, ed. by Peter Hallward and Knox Peden, 2 vols (London: Verso, 2012) p.112.

58 Jacques Lacan, *The Seminar of Jacques Lacan, Book X: Anxiety* [1962–1963], ed. by Jacques-Alain Miller, trans. by A. R. Price (Cambridge: Polity, 2014) p.86.

59 Ibid.

60 Thelma Sowley, 'Crossing Boundaries', in *Phantom Sentences: Essays in Linguistics and Literature Presented to Ann Banfield*, ed. by Robert S. Kawashima, Gilles Philippe and Thelma Sowley (Bern: Peter Lang, 2008) pp.364–365.

61 Lacan, 'The Subversion of the Subject and the Dialectic of Desire ', in *Écrits*, p.691.

62 Ibid.
63 Ibid.
64 Lacan, *Seminar X: Anxiety*, p.65.
65 Derrida, 'Two Words for Joyce', in *Derrida and Joyce*, p.36.
66 'a, *adj.*', in *Oxford English Dictionary*.
67 Joyce, *Finnegans Wake*, p.94, 20–22.
68 Contrary to the official translators of Lacan's works, Gallagher renders the *objet petit a* as 'the little 'o' object' – despite Lacan's suggestion that it is untranslatable – claiming that 'the reader can see the frequent anomalies that come from not adopting object-o rather than holding to the French object a'; whilst this may hold for the letter's designating the *other*, it does not for *the letter* itself. See Cormac Gallagher, 'Re-Englishing *Encore*', *The Letter: Irish Journal for Lacanian Psychoanalysis*, 33 (Spring 2005) 15.
69 Jacques-Alain Miller, 'A and A in Clinical Structures' [1988], *The Symptom* [electronic journal], 6 (Spring 2005) Available from: <www.lacan.com/symptom6_articles/miller.html> [accessed 23 May 2014].
70 Lacan, *Seminar X: Anxiety*, p.174.
71 Alenka Zupančič, *Ethics of the Real: Kant and Lacan* (London: Verso, 2000) pp.178–179.
72 Lacan, *Seminar X: Anxiety*, p.174.
73 Ibid.
74 Miller, 'The Sinthome, a Mixture of Symptom and Fantasy', in *The Later Lacan*, p.68.
75 Herbert Wachsberger, 'From the Elementary Phenomenon to the Enigmatic Experience', in ibid. p.111.
76 Jacques Lacan, *The Seminar of Jacques Lacan, Book XXII: R.S.I., 1974–1975*, trans. by Cormac Gallagher (London: Karnac, unofficial translation, n.d.) session IV, p.59.
77 Ibid. session V, p.78.
78 Brousse, 'Hysteria and Sinthome', in *The Later Lacan*, p.86.
79 See Jacques Lacan, 'Conférences et entretiens dans des universités nord-américaines', *Scilicet* n°6/7 (1975) 38–41. For reference to the Borromean knot that Lacan constructed – which utilises the symptom as 'Σ' to tie the symbolic back to the imaginary – see A. Leupin, 'Subject, Topology of', in *Dictionary of Continental Philosophy*, ed. by John Protevi (New Haven: Yale University Press, 2006) pp.564–566.
80 Laurent, 'The Purloined Letter and the Tao of the Psychoanalyst', in *The Later Lacan*, p.38.
81 Joyce, *Finnegans Wake*, p.93, 24; p.615, 1 [my emphasis].
82 See Fritz Senn, 'First Words and No End', *A Wake Newslitter*, new ser., 2.3 (June 1965) 17–20 (p.17), and Samuel Taylor Coleridge, 'Kubla Kahn' [1798], in *The Major Works*, ed. by H. J. Jackson (Oxford: Oxford World's Classics, 2000) p.103.
83 Sigmund Freud, *The Psychopathology of Everyday Life* [1905], trans. by Alan Tyson, in *SE*, VI, p.82, footnote 5 [added in 1924]. The note in parentheses on these syllables is Tyson's.
84 Alan Bass, 'Glossary', in *The Post Card: From Socrates to Freud and Beyond* [1980], ed. by Jacques Derrida, trans. by Alan Bass (Chicago: Chicago University Press, 1987) p.xiv. See Sigmund Freud, *Beyond the Pleasure Principle* [1920], trans. by James Strachey, in Freud, *SE*, XVIII, p.15:

> What [Ernst] did was to hold the reel by the string and very skilfully throw it over the edge of his curtained cot, so that it disappeared into it, at the same time uttering his expressive 'o-o-o-o'. He then pulled the reel out of the cot again by the string and hailed its reappearance with a joyful '*da*' ['there']. This, then, was the complete game – disappearance and return.

Although Freud doesn't give the syllable 'aaa', as Bass does, it is easily inferable from empirical knowledge of infantile speech patterns.
85 Bass, 'Glossary', in *The Post Card*, pp.xiii–xiv.

86 Jacques Derrida, 'Différance' [1968], in *Margins of Philosophy* [1972], trans. by Alan Bass (Chicago: University of Chicago Press, 1982) p.3.
87 See Jacques Lacan, 'Lituraterre' [1971], trans. by Beatrice Khiara-Foxton and Adrian Price, *Hurly-Burly*, 9 (2013) 29–38. Like the language of the *Wake*, in this essay Lacan's concept of 'lituraterre' puts literature *under erasure*. The French phrase for this process that Derrida uses in *Of Grammatology* is of course '*sous rature*'; thus, whilst it puts literature *under* erasure 'lituraterre' also *draws out* (and erases) that very erasure *in* liter*ature* itself.
88 See Sigmund Freud, 'On the Universal Tendency to Debasement in the Sphere of Love (Contributions to the Psychology of Love II)' [1912], trans. by Alan Tyson, in *SE*, XI, p.183. In something of a tendency to debasement in itself, this propensity in some men has become referred to as the 'Madonna-whore complex' in certain subsequent psychological literature.
89 Joyce, *Finnegans Wake*, p.205, 7–15. For the exegesis of this passage that follows McHugh's *Annotations* has been consulted.
90 Atherton, *The Books at the Wake*, p.254. Atherton mistakenly here gives the spelling 'flushcoloured'.
91 Nathaniel Hawthorne, *The Scarlet Letter* [1850], ed. by Nina Baym (London: Penguin Classics, 2003) p.228.
92 Ellmann, *James Joyce*, p.438.
93 See Joyce, *Finnegans Wake*, p.97, 25; and Hélène Cixous, 'Joyce: The (r)use of writing' [1970], trans. by Judith Still, in *Post-Structuralist Joyce: Essays from the French*, ed. by Derek Attridge and Daniel Ferrer (Cambridge: Cambridge University Press, 1984) pp.15–30.
94 James Fairhall, *James Joyce and the Question of History* (Cambridge: Cambridge University Press, 1993) p.216 (the instances of the forger's name are here ironically misspelled with two 'g's instead of one). From the fact that the Phoenix Park murders took place in 1882 we might be able to autobiographically infer that this is a contributing reason for them constituting such an integral facet of the central 'incident in the park'. Despite having occurred a few months after Joyce's birth the coincidence of dates is close enough for the returns to the Phoenix Park, encircling this date (and others closely clustered with it), to represent something of the fantasy of the 'primal scene', which has been described by Lecercle as 'the most archaic scene, the scene of [one']s own conception. Fantasy is this impossible gaze'; that is, it is the navel which constitutes the gaze of *Finnegans Wake*, of the dream, and even of one's own life. See Jean-Jacques Lecercle, *Frankenstein: Mythe et Philosophie* (Paris: Presses Universitaires de France, 1988) pp.98–99, quoted in (and trans. by) Slavoj Žižek, *Looking Awry: An Introduction to Jacques Lacan Through Popular Culture* (Cambridge, MA: The MIT Press, 1992) p.172, note 6.
95 Richard Barry O'Brien, quoted in Francis L. Wellman, *The Art of Cross-Examination, with the Cross-Examinations of Important Witnesses in Some Celebrated Cases* [1903] (New York: Touchstone, 1997) 4 edn, p.377. O'Brien was Russell's biographer.
96 Lacan, *Seminar XVII: The Other Side of Psychoanalysis*, p.110.
97 Joyce, *Finnegans Wake*, p.6, 30. Joyce uses the word 'tautautologically' here.
98 Ibid. p.623, 33–35.
99 Ibid. p.421, 23.
100 Ibid. p.623, 31–32.
101 See Jacques Lacan, 'Seminar on "The Purloined Letter"' [1956], in *Écrits*, p.30. Lacan prefaced his *Écrits* with this text – which was thus the only one to have appeared out of chronological order – when it was published in French in 1966. When the shorter *Écrits* – translated by Sheridan and overseen by Lacan – came out in English in 1977, this text was omitted from it, thus adding an interesting nuance to the notion that 'a letter always arrives at its destination'. We of course have now the full *Écrits* in English in Fink's translation.

102 Derrida, *The Post Card*, p.489.
103 Ibid. p.65.
104 Jean-Michel Rabaté, 'Psychoanalysis Applicable and Inapplicable: The Case of Literature', in *The Literary Lacan*, p.64. This essay puts Lacan and Derrida's disagreement on this point into conversation with Žižek's reflections on the letter's destination in *Enjoy Your Symptom!*
105 Derrida makes (rather too) much of the fact that Lacan – as Antony Easthope puts it – '(typically, nonchalantly) misquotes (and more than once) the lines from Crébillon's *Atrée* in Poe's story, substituting *dessein* ('design') for *destin* ('destiny')' in the 'Seminar on "The Purloined Letter" '. See Antony Easthope, *Privileging Difference*, ed. by Catherine Belsey (Basingstoke: Palgrave, 2002) p.143. However, this mistake rather confirms Derrida's theses on the divisibility of the letter in that the destination at which Crébillon's arrives (in an inverted form, to be Lacanian about it) is *divided* from its original destiny.
106 Michel Foucault, 'Letter to Jacques Derrida, 27 January 1963', quoted in Benoît Peeters, *Derrida: A Biography*, trans. by Andrew Brown (Cambridge: Polity Press, 2012) pp.129–130.
107 Lacan, 'Postface to the French Edition of Seminar XI', *Hurly-Burly*, 7, p.17.
108 Gilles Deleuze, *The Logic of Sense* [1969], ed. by Constantin V. Boundas, trans. by Mark Lester, with Charles Stivale (London: Continuum, 2001) p.10. Indeed, Derrida draws this out too in 'Force and Signification' in asking:

> Is not the experience of *secondarity* tied to the strange redoubling by means of which constituted – written – meaning presents itself as prerequisitely and simultaneously *read*: and does not meaning present itself as such at the point at which the other is found, the other who maintains both the vigil and the back-and-forth motion, the work, that comes between writing and reading, making this work irreducible?

See Derrida, 'Force and Signification', in *Writing and Difference*, p.12.
109 See Derek Attridge, 'Signature/Countersignature: Derrida's Response to *Ulysses*, in *Derrida and Joyce*, pp.265–280, and of course Attridge, *The Singularity of Literature*; Derrida, 'Two Words for Joyce', in *Derrida and Joyce*, p.23.
110 See note 19 in chapter 2; these words of Joyce precede this note in the chapter also.
111 Patrice Maniglier, 'Acting Out the Structure', in *Concept and Form, Vol. 2*, p.28. (See again the abovementioned note.)
112 Lacan, *Seminar I: Freud's Papers on Technique*, p.107. See note 55 in chapter 1.
113 Joyce, *Finnegans Wake*, p.614, 20.
114 Simon Critchley and Tom McCarthy, 'Of Chrematology: Joyce and Money', in *Derrida and Joyce*, p.250.
115 Joyce, *Finnegans Wake*, p.108, 24.
116 Ibid. p.110, 26 and p.114, 20.
117 See ibid. p.104, 1–5, and pp.104–107. 'Disjointed times' of course here evokes the time 'out of joint' in *Hamlet*.
118 Ibid. p.125, 21–23.
119 Ibid. p.123, 35 and p.124, 2–3. It is perhaps also to HCE as Moses that Beckett is referring in *Watt* when he describes that 'Knott was also addicted to solitary dactylic ejaculations of extraordinary vigour, accompanied by spasms of the members. The chief of these were: Exelmans! Cavendish! Habbakuk! Ecchymose!' (that is, the pattern: ECH—ECCH—Mose[s]). See Samuel Beckett, *Watt* [1953], in *The Selected Works of Samuel Beckett*, ed. by Paul Auster, 4 vols (New York: Grove Press, 2010) I, pp.339–340, and the reflections on Joyce and Freud embodying a Moses narrative in chapter 4.
120 Joyce, *Finnegans Wake*, p.124, 3–12.

121 Sheldon Brivic, *Joyce's Waking Women: An Introduction to Finnegans Wake* (Madison: University of Wisconsin Press, 1995) p.86.
122 Joyce, *Finnegans Wake*, p.115, 21–23.
123 Ibid. p.115, 20–21.
124 Joyce, *Ulysses*, 9.844–845, p.170; Joyce, *Ulysses: 1922*, p.199.
125 See Jacques Derrida, 'The Night Watch (over "the book of himself")' [2001], trans. by Pascale-Anne Brault and Michael Naas, in *Derrida and Joyce*, pp.187–203.
126 Joyce, *Finnegans Wake*, p.115, 35.
127 Ibid. p.108, 15–16. For this correspondence, see Adaline Glasheen, *Third Census of Finnegans Wake: An Index of Characters and Their Roles* (Oakland: University of California Press, 1977) p.118.
128 See Oskar Pfungst, *Clever Hans (The Horse of Mr. von Osten): A Contribution to Experimental Animal and Human Psychology*, trans. by Carl L. Rahn (New York: Henry Holt and Company, 1911).
129 Joyce, *Finnegans Wake*, p.111, 27–30.
130 Ibid. p.111, 26.
131 Ibid. p.115, 25. Psychoanalysis as a *private*, or *privatised*, business is also implied here, as it is that '*in camera*' means 'private, in the room' in Latin; however, the implication is also that this is where our most private intimacies now get aired; that is, broadcasted *on camera*. For this Latin allusion, see McHugh, *Annotations to Finnegans Wake*, p.115.
132 Joyce, *Finnegans Wake*, p.115, 27–28.
133 In the novel it is in Clarissa's mother's words that her father's charge of contumacy is transmitted, and Clarissa recounts this in letter 17 to her best friend Anna Howe. Thus, despite these relays and substitutions, the father's decree has survived its transmission intact, which shows its force as the key signifier of the unconscious. Clarissa writes to Howe that her mother had told her that her father warned, 'if I were to be contumacious, I might thank myself for all that would follow.' See Samuel Richardson, *Clarissa, or, The History of a Young Lady* [1747–1748], ed. by Angus Ross (London: Penguin Classics, 1985) p.98.
134 Joyce, *Finnegans Wake*, pp.121, 36-p.122, 1.
135 Ibid. p.116, 4–8; and p.118, 6.
136 Ibid. p.115, 26–27. See Joyce, *Ulysses*, 12.1639–1640 p.276; Joyce, *Ulysses: 1922*, p.323. Bloom's father changed his name by deed poll; he later committed suicide.
137 Lacan, *Seminar XVII: The Other Side of Psychoanalysis*, p.189.
138 Concerning the brothers Shem and Shaun, Joyce – in a unificatory/separatory verse – renders their tripartite connection: '*Three in one, one and three./Shem and Shaun and the shame that sunders em./Wisdom's son, folly's brother.*' See Joyce, *Finnegans Wake*, p.526, 13–15.
139 Ibid. p.339, 22. We could also read this *insectuousness* literally, through schizoanalysis, putting HCE in the position that Deleuze and Guattari assign to Gregor in Franz Kafka's *Metamorphosis*. 'In becoming-insect', they imply, Gregor, or HCE, does not try to 'flee his father but rather to find an escape where his father didn't know to find one', that is, by escaping incestuousness into insectuousness, by becoming *literally* insect. See Gilles Deleuze and Félix Guattari, *Kafka: Toward a Minor Literature* [1975], trans. by Dana Polan (Minneapolis: University of Minnesota Press, 1986) p.13. However, with Kafka's work Joyce was 'unacquainted'. See Ellmann, *James Joyce*, p.853, p.702.
140 Joyce, *Finnegans Wake*, p.125, 22.
141 Jacques Lacan, 'Introduction to the Names-of-the-Father' [1963], in *On the Names-of-the-Father* [2005], trans. by Bruce Fink (Cambridge: Polity, 2013) p.66.
142 Lacan, *Seminar XXIV: L'insu que sait de l'une-bévue s'aile à mourre*, session 8, p.99.
143 Ibid. session 10, p.110.

144 Ibid.

145 This process Žižek sees as that which has always been at work in reading involved in philosophy: he claims that 'all great "dialogues" in the history of philosophy were so many cases of misunderstanding; [all] grounded in a productive misreading'. See Slavoj Žižek, *Organs Without Bodies: On Deleuze and Consequences* [2004] (Abingdon: Routledge Classics, 2012) p.xix. Or, indeed, as Bataille puts it: 'The apparent unchangingness of books is deceptive: each book is also the sum of the misunderstandings it occasions.' See Georges Bataille, *On Nietzsche* [1945], trans. by Bruce Boone (London: Continuum, 2004) p.173. The Joycéance of waking the read in reading the *Wake* is facilitated by Shaun the Post. The hen's, or Shem's, letter is disseminated (or indeed 'discheminated', to use Derrida's word from *The Post Card*, which he derives from '*shem*' being the Hebrew word for 'name') by Shaun, who is – as Andrew J. Mitchell puts it – 'a mediator[,] a postman charged with delivering a letter, a medium at a séance channeling the voice of HCE, Christ bearing God's message and "in reality . . . only" a barrel rolling down the Liffey.' See Andrew J. Mitchell, 'Meaning Postponed: *The Post Card* and *Finnegans Wake*', in *Derrida and Joyce*, p.149, and Derrida, *The Post Card*, p.165. Joyce wrote of Shaun as a barrel rolling down the Liffey in a letter to Harriet Shaw Weaver of 24 May 1924. See Mitchell, 'Meaning Postponed', p.160, note 8.

146 Jacques Derrida, *Glas* [1974], trans. by John P. Leavey, Jr. and Richard Rand (Lincoln: University of Nebraska Press, 1986) p.1, column 2.

147 Jim LeBlanc, 'The Ass Dreams of Shaun's Bottomless Heart', in *Renascent Joyce*, ed. by Daniel Ferrer, Sam Slote and André Topia (Gainesville: University Press of Florida, 2013) p.88.

148 Lacan, *Le seminaire XXIII: Le Sinthome*, p.88; Lacan, 'Le Sinthome', p.40.

149 Joyce, *Finnegans Wake*, p.111, 15. 'Lots of fun at Finnegan's Wake' is a lyric from the chorus of the original song on which the book is in part based.

150 Gilles Deleuze, 'Comment Made at the Cerisy Colloquium on Nietzsche, 1972', *Nietzsche aujourd'hui*, 1 (1973) 186–187 (p.186). Quoted, and translated by Peeters, in *Derrida: A Biography*, p.242. See also Daniel W. Smith, 'Introduction: "A Life of Pure Immanence": Deleuze's "Critique et Clinique" Project', in Gilles Deleuze, *Essays Critical and Clinical* [1993], trans. by Daniel W. Smith and Judy A. Greco (Minneapolis: University of Minnesota Press, 1997) pp.xv–xvi.

151 Miller, 'Interpretation in Reverse', in *The Later Lacan*, pp.3–4.

152 Joyce, *Finnegans Wake*, p.10, 22–23, p.8, 9.

Chapter 6

The object meaning raised to the dignity of the Thing

I'm not a man, not a poet, not a leaf,
Only a wounded pulse that circles the things of the other side.
– Federico García Lorca, 'Double Poem of Lake Eden'

That's how it was
and the awakened earth cast off trembling rivers of moths.
– Federico García Lorca, 'Crucifixion'

Post-Joycean psychoanalysis

In beginning this final chapter we might perceive the import to Leopold Bloom of *concluding*, which – in the catechistic penultimate episode of *Ulysses*, Ithaca – is intimated in the precautionary proviso: 'To conclude lest he should not conclude'.[1] This risk of not concluding is of course that which we court when discussing Joyce's work – most particularly *Finnegans Wake* – but it also proves true that it is nigh on impossible to find *the moment to conclude* with either Joyce or Lacan (and thus this work will come to its end in the extensions into other thinkers' works and theories that these two creative forces pave ways for). Exegeses, as we have seen, can expand exponentially with Joyce, and whilst his texts necessitate these, they are not the primary concern of this work; however, we may draw recourse once again to Figure 3.1, which we modify here, to demonstrate this very varity involved in the *sinthomic* side of Joyce's writing in the *Wake*; that is, its *unhookability*, which ensures that as soon as we hit upon something in the *Wake*, we simultaneously fall away from it, that these are in fact the same Möbian processes:

Position A

Joyce's writing

(Fall) / \ *(Fall)*

Position 1 Position 2

Upon *From*

Figure 6.1 Unificatory/separatory principle (A: *Joyce's Writing* < 1: *Upon*, 2: *From*)

Whilst this is the case in relation to the *sinthomic* side of Joyce's writing, when we bring it in relation to the symptomal side, we of course see the fixities and fixations of its language's repetitions. It is between these positions of *enverity* that we might now broach a psychoanalytic examination of neurosis and psychosis in relation to Lacan's ruminations on Joyce's work, and on the *sinthome*, made in Seminar XXIII. In this respect, Véronique Voruz and Bogdan Wolf claim in their introduction to *The Later Lacan* that

> the analytic process is different according to the structure of the patient. [. . .] While the neurotic subject needs to be disalienated *from* the signifier, the psychotic subject must find ways to treat his *jouissance with* the signifier. In short, the differential direction of the treatment is as follows: from the symbolic to the real of the symptom in neurosis, and from the real to the symbolic in psychosis.[2]

In this work we have treated variously the subjects of the symptom and the *sinthome*; the three Lacanian orders: the Real, the Symbolic, and the Imaginary; the psychical state of psychosis (primarily); meaning and signification; and the work of art – and these all in relation to reading, writing, and psychoanalysis, and the literature of James Joyce, mainly *Finnegans Wake*. To discuss these in relation to the stratagems outlined earlier in Voruz and Wolf's statement, we see initially that we are here returned to the other side of the phenomenon of psychosis, neurosis. Neurosis, particularly hysterical neurosis, was what Freud's studies into symptoms and thus into the unconscious set out from in the late 1880s and 1890s; studies which were to inaugurate the practice of psychoanalysis. By the end of Lacan's psychoanalytical work we come to a formulation for the treatment of psychosis, which is of course the phenomenon that he set out from in his own studies, beginning with his 1932 thesis in psychiatry.

As Voruz and Wolf state, in today's clinic, 'following the later Lacan, the analyst takes his or her bearings from the fantasy rather than from the meaning of the symptoms complained about by the analysand'.[3] For the neurotic – as the aforementioned authors point out – subscription to the signifier, or overidentification with the symbolic, needs to be tempered in the fundamental fantasy, and thus the *sinthome* needs bringing to the fore. In psychosis, however, there may be too close a subjective connection with the *sinthome*, precisely as *empty signified*, in that the analyst as *subject supposed to know* might become to the psychotic subject the figure of the *subject who knows too much*, thus 'produc[ing] a paranoid effect: "the analyst knows everything about me"' ("though I know nothing about myself", as we might add).[4] The analyst – as a (possibly) paranoia-inducing *knowing* productive signifier in the psychotic's ideation – might thus even be seen by this subject to be inserting their knowledge *into* the *empty signified* that the psychotic represents for them, and this mode of analysis therefore courts the risks of 'transferential modalities' that 'take the form of an imaginary identification, erotomania, persecution, and so on'; forms which are overladen with, and overdetermined by, *jouissance*, and that therefore push in the direction of the real.[5]

Thus, we might here expand Voruz and Wolf's statement on the differential direction of treatment slightly, to further draw out its resonances in relation to the aforementioned, and to the work done in the preceding chapters. Thus we see that in neurosis the treatment moves from the symbolic to the *sinthome* (which is, of course, *the real of the symptom*); and in psychosis it moves from the real to the symptom (where *jouissance* begins to become *jouis-sens*, via the symbolic). To put it more poetically: in the treatment of psychosis the subject emerges from the state of being that wounded pulse of the other side, described in Lorca's 'Eden'; and in that of neurosis the subject – through the *reading* of symptoms in analysis – can be awakened and may begin to cast off that trembling river of moths in which he or she believes that they are drowning, as Lorca has it in the 'Crucifixion'.[6]

The unmentioned third in these descriptions of the direction of the treatment is of course the imaginary, on which so much rests, in being the structuring principle of the fundamental fantasy. In its relation, we thus see its fundamentality as the basis not only of the constitutive fantasy, but also as integral to the *sinthome* itself, as that which sustains – that is, unites and separates at once – the conception of its *bodily* aspect. Thus, through the imaginary, the materiality of the *sinthome* is demonstrated to be precisely of the order of *abstract materialism*, which – as Žižek defines it – here locates the *sinthome* in an 'abstract (mathematical) space endlessly divided between the I and the non-I'; that of the unificatory/separatory principle.[7]

However, we also here become aware of the risk of imaginary identification plugging into and exacerbating the psychotic subject's paranoia; its role as that which underpins and fortifies the Other for the neurotic, which initially demands a response to its question '*Che vuoi?*' ('what do you want?'), which in turn becomes the question that the subject demands of the Other – especially the Other in the guise of psychoanalyst, *qua subject supposed to know* – that is, of the Other's *imaginary knowledge*; and we also see the imaginary as detachable in Joyce, whose especial relation to it enabled an epiphanic access to the real and to the symbolic during its dehiscence and supplementation by the *sinthome*, which allowed Joyce to refuse psychoanalysis whilst nonetheless drawing on its refuse for his work.[8] This is indeed what allowed Joyce to realise the inexistence of the Other; that is, to have become disinvested from the Other, to have divested himself of it. It is this very inexistence that we can perceive in the final reading of Lacan's statement that 'there is no Other of the Other' that we will offer here; that is, that 'there is no Other of the Other' can also imply that there is no Other at all, a proposition we can algebraically demonstrate if we translate this maxim into the formula: there is no X of X.[9]

But what of readers of Joyce's work, particularly of *Finnegans Wake*? The direction of their treatment by its reading is of course multi-directional; it reads 'thithaways end to end and turning, turning and end to end hithaways' it reads.[10]

Post-Joycean reading

Moderately, as Rabaté has it, 'Joyce [can be] called upon as much as the author of interconnected puns that make *Finnegans Wake* a perfect pastime for retired linguists as the launcher of an "Odyssean repetition"', in the words Derrida uses to describe the Joycean project in his introduction to Edmund Husserl's *Origin of Geometry*.[11] In the extremes, it – the *Wake*'s reading, its treatment, of its readers – may hystericise, by overcharging a subject's signifiers; or push towards a decathection from language, because of its overwhelming *sense qua non*; or inaugurate a hallucinatory response, because of the possibility of falling through or into the holes its letters have created and because of the dancing of its sigla's shapes; or it of course may create that obsessional who will attempt to dedicate to the book the three hundred unsleeping years that Joyce demanded, despite the inherent impossibility of this.

Indeed, in 'The Function and Field of Speech and Language', Lacan characterises the obsessional paradoxically as always 'in the anticipated moment of the master's death, at which time he will begin to live; but in the meantime he identifies with the master as dead and is thus already dead himself'.[12] The Joycean obsessional will therefore always remain the Joycean obsessional, as Joyce's work will of course never die. Thus, instead of into the lots of fun of *Finnegans Wake* (it's being the 'perfect pastime'), the obsessional rather plugs, or plunges, into its *jouissance* and into its death drive.

The protagonist of Sylvia Plath's *The Bell Jar*, Esther Greenwood, is a reader of the *Wake* who displays a number of these response formations: she is initially hystericised by the suggestion by her English professor that she write a thesis on the role of twins in *Finnegans Wake* (in effect, a demand from the Other), and thus turns to the text only to find hallucinations fizzing on its first page, the confusion of which pushes her towards withdrawal and silence. When she encounters the thundred-letter word in the third paragraph she begins to think there is something in this and tentatively explores it critically. She tries to pronounce the word aloud, but the page becomes distorted in front of her eyes. Not long after, she decides to 'junk' her thesis.

This response – which is something of a push towards psychosis, in its flight from the text's *Symbolic* – would thus constitute the opposite of that locatable in the obsessional neurosis that the *Wake* might be capable of instantiating. These readerly responses we could thus categorise with reference to two words that Lacan makes much of in 'Joyce the Symptom I' and Seminar XXIII respectively; that is, '*interdit*', which can be translated as 'dumbfound', and '*soufflé*', which can be rendered 'flabbergast'.[13] Between these we can erect a readerly, or analytic, sliding scale:

Dumbfound -- Flabbergast

(*interdit*) (*soufflé*)

Figure 6.2 Sliding scale between dumbfound (*interdit*) and flabbergast (*soufflé*)

Indeed, as these are two resultant possibilities of reading the *Wake*, so are they two drastic ends of analysis. Both of these words of course have the meaning of 'to confound', but they do so in slightly different ways, which can be stretched out to these binary lengths. 'Dumbfound' of course means 'to strike dumb'; that is, 'to render speechless' or 'to *interdict* speech' (to give '*interdit*' its direct translation, in the original French of which is nonetheless hidden the separated-out '*inter-dit*' – 'inter-said' – that is, that which *cuts* speech (cuts it off, or divides it), but also which disseminates it, makes it *inter-said*; a resonance Lacan himself highlights in 'Subversion of the Subject').[14] To become flabbergasted, however, is not to have one's speech interdicted, but to become momentarily lost for words, quite possibly through having *exhausted* one's words, as the extensions of 'flabbergast' indicate. As a noun, the *OED* gives to 'flabbergast' the meaning of 'bombast', with its sense possibly deriving dialectically from 'gasconade', meaning 'extravagant boasting or exaggeration; boastful or bombastic language'.[15] As a verb, 'the formation is unknown; it is plausibly conjectured that the word is an arbitrary invention suggested by flabby *adj.* or flap *n.* and aghast *adj.*'.[16] Although this invented conjunction means 'to put (a person) in such confusion that he does not for the moment know what to do or say', this confused state itself seems to derive from an *overtalking*; that is, a varity that takes into itself all the bombastic, overwrought and *flabby* verbiage – in the *flapping* of tongues, *conflab* or confabulation, *gassing* or having a gas with the gift of the gab – and blabbering and jabbering that the word 'flabbergast' thus contains and implies.[17] The French word from which 'flabbergast' is translated, '*soufflé*', means 'a murmuring or breathing sound': that in which speech tries to find its words; the bubbling and babbling *lalangue*, before it is made into speech; the '*the*' of the 'ruah' before the *fiat*; the originary discourse without speech; a discourse, even, of *différance*.[18]

Flabbergastation is thus that aghast silence after the exhaustion of *empty, blabbering* speech, in which nothing was in fact said; in which words had not found their meaning, a meaning which would thus remain as unresolved and irresolute as it was before speech; that is, as *flabbergasted* as it was before it, when speech itself was in that state of being lost for words, in which there is only *the spectre of speech*, as Joyce has it in his own rendering: 'Flabberghosted'.[19] As an end to analysis, and to reading, such a terminus is unsatisfactory in that no new dimension – or '*dit-mension*', as Lacan has it in Seminar XX – will have arisen out of its work.[20] This double-pronged confoundedness is precisely that which Lacan experienced in being confronted in Noam Chomsky's work by the assertion that language is 'determined by a genetic fact', or 'in other words, [that it] is an organ', as Lacan puts it.[21] In Seminar XXIII he states in a response to a question about this statement he made in its second session:

> I was flabbergasted to be sure. Yes. [. . .] I might have hoped to see a glimmer of apprehension of what I am showing about the Symbolic[; however,] th[e] assimilation in Chomsky of something, which, to my eyes, is of the order of the symptom, namely, that confuses the symptom and the Real, is very precisely what flabbergasted me.[22]

In Joyce, however, this confusion of symptom and Real is not apparent, precisely because he discovers the real of the symptom in its other side, the *sinthome*, and takes this 'to the power of language'. This is what dumbfounds Lacan. As he states in 'Joyce the Symptom I':

> The symptom is purely what conditions *lalangue*, but in a certain way, Joyce gives it all the power of language without, for all that, any of it being analyzable, which is what strikes the reader and leaves one literally dumbfounded – in the sense that one is struck dumb. I remain dumbfounded.
>
> That we use "to prohibit" (*interdire*) to say "to dumbfound" (*stupéfaire*) in French is significant. This is what gives substance to Joyce's contribution, and this is why literature after him can never be what it was before.[23]

By Joyce the analyst has become dumbfounded, and thus his work on the writer that will occupy the course of the year's Seminar is inaugurated, in the attempt to lift or alleviate – or at least to investigate – this interdiction; that is, to open out its inter-diction. But should the analysand, or the reader, become dumbfounded – as in the case of Esther Greenwood, or in that of the 'feebought silence' in psychoanalysis that Joyce predicted – the process of analysis will again have proven *terminal*. Thus, it is on this sliding scale between these two states that the direction and duration of analysis should attain to remain – heading from *soufflé* towards *interdit* in neurotic treatment, until a safe proximity to the *sinthome* (to allow of its identification) is arrived at; and from *interdit* towards *soufflé* in psychosis, until the signifier comes into focus and the symptom can be reckoned (that is, identified) with – whilst other work, in analytic theory and in art, might venture forth to open up and extend these parameters bookended by the Real. This *in-between* is thus that of an animating antagonism that subsists between dumbfoundedness and flabbergastation.

What we have here called this *sliding scale* of animating antagonism – on which the dignity of the subject therefore rests – is, then, that of a certain kind of sublimation. Following André Breton, Lacan states in *The Ethics of Psychoanalysis* that

> the most general formula that I can give you of sublimation is the following: it raises an object – and I don't mind the suggestion of a play on words in the term I use – to the dignity of the Thing.[24]

('The Thing' here translates Freud's '*das Ding*'; that 'extimate' and ultimately uncanny element of the Real which Lacan describes as 'in and of itself [. . .] what is closest to [the subject,] while escaping [the]m more than anything else'.)[25] The play on words that Lacan suggests here arises in sublimation's being the recathexis of libido; that is – as Freud originally put it – the 'capacity to exchange its originally sexual aim for another one, which is no longer sexual but which is psychically related to the first aim'.[26] Of course metaphorically the 'undignified' (or 'uncivilised') sexual rise to the state of phallus in male erection is yet implied in this raising of an object in the formula for sublimation – that is, a formula that inescapably remains *sexualised* – the paradox of which is rendered best in writing by Joyce in *Finnegans Wake* in the command: 'Phall if you but will, rise you must'.[27]

Thus, in analysis – on its sliding scale between the bookends of Real, *interdit* and *soufflé* – as in the reading-analysis of Joyce's texts, it is the object *meaning* (a phenomenon that is indeed as *objectal* as the *a*; and that is in fact an *objet petit a* in and of itself) that can be elected to be raised to the dignity of the Thing. This promotion itself might be achieved through the bringing in of meaning in analysis of psychosis; and in the bringing of it to the *Wake*, so as to subsist in its reading, rather than becoming lost at sea to its 'oceanic feeling'; that is, it might be achieved by the putting of meaning in the place of *das Ding*.[28] Thus, in psychosis meaning itself must be imbued as an object with that dignity that the Thing – which is precisely *beyond sense* – has. In analysis of neurosis, it may come about in the attempt to show meaning's *Thinghood*; its position as *sinthomic* thingamajig, or 'theogamyjig', as Joyce has it in the *Wake* (another word demonstrating the plurability of signifiers that can indeed come into the *sinthome*'s *empty signified*).[29] This is thus an attempt that can extend to that *dialect of neurosis* that expresses itself in the obsessional; an attempt which might temper the urge for, and surge towards, more and more meaning – in the *Wake*'s endless exegesis, for example – via the (precisely Joycean) decathexis of the imaginary, and its supplementation by the *sinthome*. So much as this is to reveal in the object meaning – as its *envers* or its *endroit* – the *dignified* place of the Thing; i.e., – in terms of the unificatory/separatory principle – this can find its demonstration diagrammatically, as:

das Ding

/ \

envers *endroit*

(Meaning) (Meaning)

Figure 6.3 Unificatory/separatory principle (A: *das Ding* < 1: *envers*, 2: *endroit*)

If meaning on the side of the *endroit* is sense and that on the side of the *envers* nonsense, it is nonetheless the Real – as the *full* (or *beyond of*) *sense* of *das Ding* – that is being headed towards in this direction (that is, the direction of the treatment; here, the treatment of the neurotic), unattainable though the Real of course is. As Alain Badiou – who has Lacan as a master, and whose work opens up the possibilities of Lacanianism in philosophical thought – puts it, this direction thus represents the

> ethic of the Real, if it is true that – as Lacan suggests – all access to the Real is of the order of an encounter. And consistency, which is the content of the ethical maxim 'Keep going!' [*Continuer!*], keeps going only by following the thread of this Real;

the thread of the Real that thus in analysis – as in Beckett – guides and tugs at the stilted lilt of the subject's speech, and that is rendered best in the formula from the end of *The Unnameable*: 'I can't go on, I'll go on.'[30]

As we have seen in our discussion of the *de-scission*, and fidelity to it, in chapter 2, types of event for Badiou fall into the quadrivium of love, politics, science, and art. Thus here the (meaning of) the *sinthome* is an *event* – that is, a *de-scissive* event – for the neurotic (an event which it will be up to their subjective organisation to categorise into one of the four abovementioned types) – just as *meaning itself* is such an event for the psychotic – fidelity to the truth of which, in both, may thus be seen as an appropriate *end of analysis*.

Post-Joycean writing

In the event of the *sinthome* Joyce, in the *Wake* – that is, *the* artistic event of literature – worked directly with the *objets a* of language to get at the *lalangue* of (his own) *jouissance* and of the Real (or, to put it in Badiou's phrasing; because of his fidelity to the *sinthomic* event, Joyce's *jouissant* writing in the *Wake* was the resulting truth he was able to produce). In this penetration into these bits of Real (*lalangue* and *jouissance*, which he, only by a thread – by a *transparent sheet* – remained separated from) – that is, through the puncturing of his letters' holes and the encircling of the environs of their littorals – he was able to demonstrate that in these very processes, as Lacan puts it in Seminar XVI,

> the *objet petit a* plays this [*jouissant*] role with respect to the vacuole. In other words it is what tickles *das Ding* from the inside. There you are. This is what constitutes the essential merit of everything that is called a work of art.[31]

Whereas it is negotiation on the sliding scale of an animating antagonism between the bookends of Real that is the sublimation involved in analysis, this ticklish object that gets raised to the dignity of the Thing is the sublimation involved in art. The work of art – or, indeed, *objet d'art* – thus provides an access from an other side (its *inside*) to *das Ding*, unobtainable from any other angle. As Marcel Proust puts it in *In Search of Lost Time* in relation to the artist Bergotte and his singular *sinthomic* production: 'Every fresh beauty in his work was the little drop of Bergotte buried at the heart of a thing and which he had distilled from it.'[32] This Lacanian position is confirmed in Freud, who in the short 1908 essay 'Creative Writers and Day-Dreaming' can only speculate on

> from what sources that strange being, the creative writer, draws his material, and how he manages to make such an impression on us with it and arouse in us emotions of which, perhaps, we had not even thought ourselves capable.[33]

As Badiou puts it in *The Communist Hypothesis*: 'An event is the occurrence of the real as its own future possibility.'[34] This *incapable* of Freud – the *impossible* of the Real – Joyce thus realised through the very event of his *sinthomic* writing.

Indeed, as Lacan argues, Joyce conducted 'the other work' that we identified earlier – work done *on the other side psychoanalysis* – with the *sinthome*; work which may, as Lacan puts it in Seminar XXIV, indeed inaugurate 'a new signifier, one that would have no kind of sense, that would perhaps be what would open us up to what, in my lumpish way, I call the Real'.[35]

For Joyce's part, this opening up towards the real was an *individual* act *par excellence*, as it was with the *sinthome* – most particularly and most spectacularly in *Finnegans Wake* – that he achieved it; that is, with that 'which is what there is singularly in each individual' – as Lacan puts it in the Joyce Seminar – and which allowed Joyce, 'as it is written somewhere, [to] identif[y] with the *individual*'.[36] But this brings us to the question that we have perhaps been evading as much as courting throughout this work; that is, does this emphasised singularity entail that we must come to view the *sinthome* as a purely individualist category – a category of 'autosotorisation', as Joyce has it in the *Wake*, which can translate as 'self-saving' – with all that this might politically entail?[37] We will let Lacan lead us towards addressing this question. As he warns in Seminar XVI:

> Try not to lose the thread about what you are as effect of knowledge. You are split apart in the phantasy ($\$ \lozenge a$). You are, however strange this may appear, the cause of yourself. Only there is no self. Rather there is a divided self [thus – as *divider* – the *lozenge*, ◊, occupies position A of the principle of *enverity*, and $\$$ and *a* 1 and 2, here]. Entering onto this path is where the only true political revolution may flow from. Knowledge serves the master. I am coming back today to underline that knowledge is born from the slave.[38]

This knowledge is the imaginary knowledge of the Other. It is that knowledge in which the obsessional reader of *Finnegans Wake* sets up the figure of the dead master; that is, of *Joyce supposed to know*, Joyce as the all-knowing Other up to whose expectations our exegesis must – but can never – live. This is the very knowledge that Joyce managed to unsubscribe himself from, through the deployment of the *sinthome* in his composition of *Finnegans Wake* and in the concentration on – and of – his own *jouissance* in that composition; and it is this that perhaps constitutes the truly political *event* of the *Wake*.

In this period of his life, Joyce famously claimed to be – and claimed that the *Wake* was – *apolitical*, to the extent that in conversation with Beckett he suggested that World War II 'was distracting the world from reading *Finnegans Wake*, in which the unimportance of wars in the total cycle of human activity was made perfectly clear', as Ellmann puts it.[39] However valid this response to the war was, it was in Joyce's act of brandishing a new signifier that can open us up to the Real; in the raising of a dimension of meaning – that isn't the fascistic *meaning of the Other* – to the dignity of the Thing; in tickling its insides – as he splits our sides – from *an other side* (which he was willing to explore with only the safeguarding of a transparent sheet); and in the inscription of *something of a sexual relation* in the *Wake* (that is, in the attempt to put this in the place of a purely religio-political history, on the myths of which he nonetheless drew) – that Philippe Sollers's assertion that '*Finnegans Wake* is the most formidably anti-fascist book produced between the two wars' finds its bearing.[40]

In this, we see that it is thus through the *sinthome* – as that which is most singular and most individual in each of us; and as that which never ceases to write itself, and is thus constantly opening up new dimensions and possibilities – that the scourge of a conformity, in thrall to the Other, that seeks to eradicate alterity, and the desire that desires its own repression, that is the motor of all microfascism – as Deleuze and Guattari have it – can be combatted; and through this also that a communality celebratory of its multiplicity – that is, *a grand funferall* – can be attained to. The *sinthome* is that hinge that unites and separates us at once to and from the impossible of the Real; to and from meaning in the Symbolic; and to and from the fantasy in the Imaginary; and it is thus that which keeps us animated on the sliding scale of this antagonistic toing and froing. It is thus what ensures that not only literature, but *subjectivity* itself – and reading, writing, and psychoanalysis – will never be as it was before, *post-Joyce*.[41] To add a psychoanalytic qualifier to Marx and Engels's statement in *The Communist Manifesto*; it is thus with the *savoir-faire* (or *know-how*) with the *sinthome* – that Joyce opened the way to, and left in his wake – that we should aim at a *free* '*association*, in which the free development of each is the condition for the free development of all', and in which we might wake the rewards of what we read.[42]

Singularly,
Ǝ m E ш
Indanified Brigstoll[43]
Chippenham–Nottingham–Worcester, 2011–2014

Notes

1 James Joyce, *Ulysses* [1922], ed. by Hans Walter Gabler and others (New York: Vintage Books, 1986) 17.2059–2060, p.599; Joyce, *Ulysses: 1922: The 1922 Text*, ed. by Jeri Johnson (Oxford: Oxford World's Classics, 1998) p.681.
2 Véronique Voruz and Bogdan Wolf, 'Preface', in *The Later Lacan: An Introduction*, ed. by Véronique Voruz and Bogdan Wolf, trans. by Heather Chamberlain and others (Albany: State University of New York Press, 2007) pp.xiv–xv.
3 Ibid. p.xiv.
4 Ibid. p.xv.
5 Ibid.
6 See Federico García Lorca, 'Double Poem of Lake Eden', in *Poet in New York* [1940], trans. by Greg Simon and Steven F. White, ed. by Christopher Maurer (London: Penguin Classics, 2002) p.83, and Lorca, 'Crucifixion', in ibid. p.145.
7 Slavoj Žižek, *Less Than Nothing: Hegel and the Shadow of Dialectical Materialism* (London: Verso, 2012) p.157.
8 On *Che vuoi?*' see Jacques Lacan, 'The Subversion of the Subject and the Dialectic of Desire', in *Écrits: The First Complete Edition in English* [1966], orig. ed. by François Wahl, trans. by Bruce Fink, in collaboration with Hélöise Fink and Russell Grigg (New York: W. W. Norton, 2006) p.690.

9 As Lacan explains in Seminar XXIV:

> So that no one would speculate about it, I wrote this something which is the signifier, the signifier of the fact that the Other does not exist, which I wrote like that: (Ø). But the Other, the Other in question, must indeed be called by its name Other, it is the sense, it is Other than the Real.

As non-existent; that is, as underpinned by the Imaginary, the Other is precisely non-Real. See Jacques Lacan, *The Seminar of Jacques Lacan, Book XXIV: L'insu que sait de l'une-bévue s'aile à mourre, 1976–1977*, trans. by Cormac Gallagher (London: Karnac, unofficial translation, n.d.) session 8, p.97. In Lacan's original, of course, it is the 'A' that is barred to represent the inexistence of the Other.

10 See James Joyce, *Finnegans Wake* [1939], ed. by Robbert-Jan Henkes and others (Oxford: Oxford World's Classics, 2012) p.114, 16–17, as quoted in the first chapter.

11 Jean-Michel Rabaté, 'Two Joyces for Derrida', in *Derrida and Joyce: Texts and Contexts*, ed. by Andrew J. Mitchell and Sam Slote (Albany: State University of New York Press, 2013) p.290. Rabaté is here quoting Jacques Derrida, *Edmund Husserl's "Origin of Geometry": An Introduction* [1962], trans. by John P. Leavey Jr. (Lincoln: University of Nebraska Press, 1978) p.103.

12 Lacan, 'The Function and Field of Speech and Language in Psychoanalysis', in *Écrits*, p.259.

13 See Jacques Lacan, 'Joyce le Symptôme', in *Le seminaire XXIII: Le sinthome* [1975–1976], texte établi par Jacques-Alain Miller (Paris: Éditions du Seuil, 2005) p.167 (this translation is shared by Benanav and Collins); and Lacan, *Le seminaire XXIII: Le sinthome*, p.39; Jacques Lacan, *Seminar XXIII: Joyce and the Sinthome, 1975–1976*, trans. by Cormac Gallagher (London: Karnac, unofficial translation, n.d.) session II, p.13 (the same translation of the word is also used by Thurston).

14 See Lacan, 'The Subversion of the Subject and the Dialectic of Desire ', in *Écrits*, pp.677–678.

15 'flabbergast, *n.*' and 'gasconade, *n.* and *adj.*', in *Oxford English Dictionary*.

16 'flabbergast, *v.*' in ibid.

17 Ibid. For 'gas' in the sense of 'enjoyment, amusement, fun', the *OED* in fact gives *Dubliners* as its first quoted source: 'He told me he had brought it [*sc.* a catapult] to have some gas with the birds. Mahoney used slang freely.' See 'gas, *n.1* and *adj.*' in ibid., and Joyce, 'An Encounter', in *Dubliners* [1914] (London: Penguin Modern Classics, 1973) p.20.

18 See Jacques Derrida, "La parole soufflée', in *Writing and Difference* [1967], trans. by Alan Bass (London: Routledge Classics, 2001) pp.212–245, for consideration of this word in relation to Antonin Artaud and his relationship with language.

19 James Joyce, *Finnegans Wake* [1939], ed. by Robbert-Jan Henkes and others (Oxford: Oxford World's Classics, 2012) p.494, 3.

20 Jacques Lacan, *The Seminar of Jacques Lacan, Book XX: Encore: On Feminine Sexuality, the Limits of Love and Knowledge, 1972–1973*, ed. by Jacques-Alain Miller, trans. by Bruce Fink (New York: W. W. Norton, 1998) p.21.

21 Lacan, *Le seminaire XXIII: Le sinthome*, p.31; Lacan, *Seminar XXIII: Joyce and the Sinthome*, session II, p.5.

22 Lacan, *Le seminaire XXIII: Le sinthome*, p.39; Lacan, *Seminar XXIII: Joyce and the Sinthome*, session II, p.13.

23 Lacan, 'Joyce le Symptôme', in *Le seminaire XXIII: Le sinthome*, p.167 (trans. by Collins).

24 Jacques Lacan, *The Seminar of Jacques Lacan, Book VII: The Ethics of Psychoanalysis, 1959–1960*, ed. by Jacques-Alain Miller, trans. by Dennis Porter (London: Routledge Classics, 2008) p.138. Breton defined Surrealist readymades as 'manufactured objects promoted to the dignity of works of art through the choice of artist'. See André

Breton, 'Lighthouse of the Bride' [1934], in *Surrealism and Painting*, trans. by Simon Watson Taylor (Boston: MFA Publications, 2002) p.88. If we bring the symptom and *sinthome* into relation with this formula for sublimation we could take Lacan's formulation from Seminar XVIII, that 'when [a symptom] has something to say, well then, it says it', as the other side of what he says of Joyce in 'Joyce the Symptom II': that he 'wanted nothing but to climb the ladder [*l'escabeau*] to magisterial saying'. That is, if the symptom desires to say *it* well – to raise its nagging, disruptive thing to the plane of meaning, in order to give it vent, or even to raze or erase it – the *sinthome* desires to *say* well, to establish what it says *as itself*, irreducibly. Thus we might claim that the ladder that *Finnegans Wake* climbs is that which raises whatever is on the work's hod to the dignity of the Thing. See Jacques Lacan, *The Seminar of Jacques Lacan, Book XVIII: On a Discourse That Might Not Be a Semblance, 1971*, trans. by Cormac Gallagher (London: Karnac, unofficial translation, n.d.) session V, p.15, and 'Joyce le symptôme II', in *Joyce avec Lacan*, p.33 [my translation].

25 Jacques Lacan, 'Remarks on Daniel Lagache's Presentation: "Psychoanalysis and Personality Structure"' [1960], in *Écrits*, p.550.

26 Sigmund Freud, '"Civilized" Sexual Morality and Modern Nervous Illness' [1908], trans. by E. B. Herford and E. C. Mayne, in *SE*, IX, p.187.

27 Joyce, *Finnegans Wake*, p.4, 15–16.

28 The 'oceanic feeling' is that which Romain Rolland communicated to Freud and that the latter comments on as a religious feeling of connection, 'a feeling of indissoluble bond, of being one with the external world as a whole', in *Civilization and its Discontents* (p.65). To be lost at sea in this *oceanic feeling*, then, would be the 'psychoticising' effect of the *Wake*; a too-strong affect of alienation *and* connection *beyond the unificatory/separatory principle*. See Sigmund Freud, *Civilization and Its Discontents* [1930], trans. by James Strachey, in *SE*, XXI, pp.64–66.

29 Joyce, *Finnegans Wake*, p.332, 24.

30 Alain Badiou, *Ethics: An Essay on the Understanding of Evil* [1993], trans. by Peter Hallward (London: Verso Radical Thinkers, 2012) p.52. See Samuel Beckett, *The Unnamable* [1953], in *The Selected Works of Samuel Beckett*, ed. by Paul Auster, 4 vols (New York: Grove Press, 2010) II, p.407.

31 Jacques Lacan, *The Seminar of Jacques Lacan, Book XVI: From an Other to the other, 1968–1969*, trans. by Cormac Gallagher (London: Karnac, unofficial translation, n.d.) session XIV, p.18 [trans. modified].

32 Marcel Proust, *Remembrance of Things Past* [1913–1927], trans. by C. K. Scott Moncrieff and Terence Kilmartin, 3 vols (Harmondsworth: Penguin, 1983) I, p.593. The translation of the novel's title as *In Search of Lost Time* has generally come to replace Moncrieff's Shakespearean choice of English moniker.

33 Sigmund Freud, 'Creative Writers and Day-Dreaming' [1908], trans. by I. F. Grant Duff, in *SE*, IX, p.143.

34 Alain Badiou, *The Communist Hypothesis* [2008], trans. by David Macey and Steve Corcoran (London: Verso, 2010) p.243.

35 Lacan, *Seminar XXIV: L'insu que sait de l'une-bévue s'aile à mourre*, session 12, p.127.

36 Lacan, 'Joyce le Symptôme', in *Le seminaire XXIII: Le sinthome*, p.168 (trans. by Benanav) [Lacan's emphasis in the original].

37 Joyce, *Finnegans Wake*, p.352, 18. McHugh gives the Greek 'autosôtêr', meaning 'self-saver', at this point in the *Annotations*. To bring this question to bear too on the concept of the *sinthome* as *empty signified* we might here have recourse to Žižek, who describes such *emptiness* as that which the *sinthome* initially consists of as *revolutionary* (potential): 'The exceptional 'empty' element [. . .] is also at first an empty place to be filled up with some positive content through revolutionary turmoil.' This means

that there isn't an a priori *essence* – the same in every case – to this empty element, waiting to be realised, or actuated, but rather that the contingent content that comes into it activates, or individuates, it, constituting a revolutionary 'break with the Past' (even if that content arises out of the Past, as it in fact must. In this, the *sinthome* is its *sublation*). It is perhaps then a property of the *sinthome* also – as this empty element – to retain the 'will to break with the Past', which Žižek here describes. As Joyce's work seems to prove, one can break even with their own Past, *resinthomising* themselves. See Slavoj Žižek, 'Class Struggle or Postmodernism? Yes Please!', in *Contingency, Hegemony, Universality: Contemporary Dialogues on the Left*, ed. by Judith Butler, Ernesto Laclau, and Slavoj Žižek (London: Verso, 2000) p.131, note 23.

38 Lacan, *Seminar XVI: From an Other to the other*, session XXV, p.1 [trans. modified].

39 Richard Ellmann, *James Joyce: New and Revised Edition* (Oxford: Oxford University Press, 1983) p.728.

40 Philippe Sollers, 'Joyce & Co.', in *In the Wake of the Wake*, ed. by David Hayman and Elliott Anderson (Madison: University of Wisconsin Press, 1978) p.109. On this last point, Sollers states that

> Joyce represents the same ambition as Freud: to analyze two thousand years of manwomankind, and not ten hundred years of politics. What is monotheism? What is Christianity? What is reason? *Finnegans Wake* teems with "answers," but these answers are not of a scientific order; they come from a knowledge that will never present itself as systematic, any more than as definitively centred or serious. This is why it is a matter of the most forceful act ever accomplished against political paranoia and the overhanging weight of deadening discourse, outside all humor.
> (ibid. pp.108–109)

41 This is not only the response of Lacan, but of Derrida too. As Rabaté indeed puts it: 'Going further than the main modernist writers who all dreamed of creating a new audience by a new mode of writing, Derrida postulates the birth of a new subject in the wake of Joyce's works.' See Rabaté, 'Two Joyces for Derrida', in *Derrida and Joyce*, p.294.

42 Karl Marx and Frederick Engels, *Manifesto of the Communist Party* [1848], trans. by Samuel Moore, in Karl Marx, *Political Writings: Volume 1, The Revolutions of 1848*, ed. by David Fernbach, 3 vols (London: Verso, 2010) I, p.87 [my emphasis].

43 Joyce, *Finnegans Wake*, p.133, 28/29; see also the first of the names – that is, 'Bristow' – in the list of English deaths that the citizen reads out from the supposedly '*Irish for all Ireland Independent*' newspaper in Joyce, *Ulysses*, 12.222 and 230, p.245; Joyce, *Ulysses: 1922*, p.285 and p.286. Thus, whilst it is with the most singular of written marks that this work is signed it is yet with a *countersignature*. As Derrida puts it, in relation to Joyce, the paradox of the *sinthome* – as *signthome* (that most singular mark or letter in us all) – is that

> on the one hand, one must write, one must sign, one must make new events with untranslatable marks happen – and this is the desperate call, the distress of a signature that demands a *yes* from the other; but on the other hand, the singular novelty of any other *yes*, of any other signature, already finds itself programophoned in the Joycean corpus.

The Joycean *sinthome* thus reflects that within his work – if we look for it – anything can be found

> narrated in advance in its dated singularity [. . .] by this hypermnesic machine capable of storing in a giant epic work, with the memory of the West and virtually all the languages of the world, *the very traces of the future*. Yes, everything has already happened to us with *Ulysses*, and in advance signed by Joyce.

See Derrida, 'Ulysses Gramophone', in *Derrida and Joyce*, p.61 and p.60. 'Yes' is of course the last word of *Ulysses*; thus, with all its resonances, the *envers* of Joyce's last words – which, according to his sister Eva, were in fact 'does nobody understand?' – is: 'The yes stead dead', which is precisely the reason why we must always remain in the process of *waking the read.* (For Joyce's purported last words, see Bernard Benstock, *Joyce-Again's Wake: An Analysis of Finnegans Wake* (Seattle: University of Washington Press, 1965) p.122.)

Index

For Product Safety Concerns and Information please contact our EU
representative GPSR@taylorandfrancis.com
Taylor & Francis Verlag GmbH, Kaufingerstraße 24, 80331 München, Germany

www.ingramcontent.com/pod-product-compliance
Ingram Content Group UK Ltd.
Pitfield, Milton Keynes, MK11 3LW, UK
UKHW022126190926
475702UK00013B/1672
* 9 7 8 1 1 3 8 5 8 7 2 2 9 *